P9-CFP-279

A
Cup of
Comfort
Cookbook

Favorite Comfort Foods to
Warm Your Heart and Lift Your Spirit

Jay Weinstein, Chef de Cuisine

Colleen Sell, Editor

Adams Media Corporation
Avon, Massachusetts

Copyright ©2002 by Adams Media Corporation.
All rights reserved. This book, or parts thereof, may not be reproduced in any form without permission from the publisher; exceptions are made for brief excerpts used in published reviews.

A Cup of Comfort is a trademark of Adams Media Corporation.

Published by
Adams Media Corporation
57 Littlefield Street, Avon, MA 02322. U.S.A.
www.adamsmedia.com
www.cupofcomfort.com

ISBN: 1-58062-788-9

Printed in Canada.

J I H G F E D C B A

Library of Congress Cataloging-in-Publication Data
Weinstein, Jay
A cup of comfort cookbook : favorite comfort foods to warm your
heart and lift your spirit / Jay Weinstein, chef de cuisine;
Colleen Sell, editor.
p.   cm.
ISBN 1-58062-788-9
I. Sell, Colleen. II. Title.
TX714 .W332 2002
641.5—dc21
2002009982

This publication is designed to provide accurate and authoritative information with regard to the subject matter covered. It is sold with the understanding that the publisher is not engaged in rendering legal, accounting, or other professional advice. If legal advice or other expert assistance is required, the services of a competent professional person should be sought.
—From a *Declaration of Principles* jointly adopted by a Committee of the American Bar Association and a Committee of Publishers and Associations

Cover illustration by Eulala Conner.

Special thanks to Colleen Cunningham for her interior design
and Kate McBride for her editorial direction.

This book is available at quantity discounts for bulk purchases.
For information, call 1-800-872-5627.

Table of Contents

Chef's Preface . . . v

Introduction . . . vii

Chef's Preface

Comfort food is slow food—food that gives the cook time to enjoy the process, to smell the rising aromas, and to immerse himself in the making of food. Gathering and mixing ingredients is part of the joy. Though I'm eager to taste the result when making a four- or six-hour stew, I find that the regular trips to the stove to stir and to sip are therapeutic. It breaks up my normal routine with a different, soothing rhythm.

So, enjoy the time you have with these foods. These are take-an-afternoon-with-your-old-friend-the-wooden-spoon kind of recipes. When I'm sick and forced to give myself the day off, I don't just open a can of chicken soup; I make it. When friends ask, "Do you need anything?" I tell them to pick up a chicken and some onions and some carrots for me. I put them in a huge cauldron of water and cook until the house is a vaporous mess and all the windows are fogged. By the time I'm sitting down to a bowl, I'm halfway healed.

Slow cooking does magical things for flavors, drawing them out of the ingredients that house them, mingling them to create complexity and new sensations. Certainly, a batch of chili is edible and even tasty after a half hour on the stove, but three hours later, it's a whole different dish, deeper and more profound—sublime.

Within these pages, you will find some of my most comforting recipes, both to create and to eat. You'll also find a wide range of family recipes from home cooks throughout the United States, Canada, and even Europe, all of which have been tested for their ultimate comfort quotient—simple, tasty, and memorable. Each of the contributed recipes cites the name and hometown of the person who has so graciously shared it with us. The others, marked with J.W., are my personal recipes or tips, which I gladly share with you.

I urge you to take your time when preparing these foods, not only to make them the best that they can be, but also to reap the personal rewards that slow cooking brings.

—Jay Weinstein

Introduction

Our three basic needs—for food and security and love—are so mixed and mingled and entwined that we cannot straightly think of one without the others.

—M. F. K. Fisher

As Mary Francis Kennedy Fisher, America's most revered food writer, so often claimed: Nothing says comfort more eloquently or universally than sharing lovingly prepared food in the security of a home and in the pleasant company of family and friends. For most of us, our fondest memories of the people and experiences we most cherish are interwoven with simple and grand feasts filled with favorite and flavorful foods and beverages. These are the origins, the essence, of comfort foods.

The *Cup of Comfort* book series is all about giving and receiving comfort, about serving and sharing and enjoying and spreading comfort all around, in all its myriad manifestations. It's a simple concept, really: Comfort begets comfort. In comforting others, we are comforted. And one of the most delicious ways to do that is through storytelling, in sharing with others the relationships, experiences, and simple blessings that give meaning and joy to our lives.

From the beginning of human existence on Earth, people of all cultures have found solace and communion in both food and storytelling.

And so, A *Cup of Comfort Cookbook* combines these two great sources of joy and comfort.

A *Cup of Comfort Cookbook* is filled to the brim with comfort-food recipes and memories: 200 simple and delicious favorite foods and beverages, from the classics to the creative! Uplifting stories of preparing and "breaking bread" with the folks we hold dear! Treasured photos of family and friends! Sprinkled with a charming collection of inspiring quotes and "old cook's" tips. All these make for a most enjoyable, practical, and comforting literary repast.

Bon appetit!

—Colleen Sell

chapter one

Coming in from the Cold
Soups and Chowders

First, You Eat

By Carol M. Hodgson, Gibsons, British Columbia, Canada

My Grandma Josephine ran a classic Polish kitchen: all tomato and dill and cabbage and caraway, with fragrant pots steaming from early morning until early evening. Just before supper was served, the pots and pans were finally emptied and cleaned for the next day. Supper was served late, at around 8:00 P.M., and usually consisted of cold cuts, sausage, homemade bread, dill pickles, beet relish, and perhaps reheated *holubtsi* (cabbage rolls).

The farmhouse sat near the railroad tracks, making it a natural stop for men down on their luck. No one but Grandma would hear the tentative, barely audible knock at the wooden screen door. She'd open the door to a gaunt and raggedy man, eyes too big for his pale grim face, his baggy clothes dusty from traveling in the boxcar or alongside the road. His hands might tremble as the aroma from the simmering pots wafted out to the porch where he stood. Politely, he'd ask whether there was some work he could do, anything at all, in exchange for a meal. Grandma's answer was always the same.

"First, you eat," she would say, and open the door wider so the man could enter.

Once inside, the man was handed a towel and shown the washroom. Cleaned up, he was invited to sit at the table.

My grandparents didn't have much: a handful of milk cows, a few chickens, hills of potatoes, rows of beets. My mother tells of living one entire winter on potatoes and beets with an occasional chicken thrown in. Whatever they had, they shared, and for the man at the door, there might be borscht, potato and dumpling soup, and pyrohy with potato filling—more food than he'd seen in a long time.

When he had eaten, the stranger would set about doing whatever tasks my grandmother needed done. As he worked, she'd pack him some bread and cold pyrohy to take with him on his journey. Hours later, Grandma would find the bundle gone—and, sure enough, the firewood split, the garden weeded, and the henhouse cleaned, just as she'd asked. Often, leaves would be raked and the front sidewalk swept, too, as though a meal and the unconditional compassion that went with it were worth far more than the original asking price.

Unlike my grandparents, I did not live through the famines of the Ukraine.

Josephine Zatylny
standing by her barn

I never spent a whole winter eating nothing but potatoes. I never had a hungry, down-on-his-luck man knock on my door, offering to mend a fence for a bit of food. But I can hear my grandma's voice, just as clearly as if I were sitting in her steamy, dill-scented kitchen, responding to the tap, tap, tapping at her door:

"First, you eat."

I am about the age now that my grandmother was then. As though driven by Zatylny genetics, without recipe books to guide me, I make traditional foods and think about her kitchen in that little white farmhouse.

A longing flutters in my stomach and rises to my throat . . .

I want to make soup and give it away, no questions asked.

Grandma Zatylny's Borscht

SUBMITTED BY CAROL M. HODGSON, GIBSONS, BRITISH COLUMBIA, CANADA

Throughout the fall and winter, a pot of this earthy soup often simmers in my kitchen. I make it large and enjoy sharing it with those in need.

Servings: 8

3 cups water
4 medium beets, peeled and diced
1 medium potato, peeled and chopped
2 medium carrots, peeled and chopped
1 large onion, chopped
1 cup shredded cabbage—white, red, or
   a combination
4 cups vegetable stock or water
¼ cup vinegar or lemon juice

1 cup chopped fresh tomatoes or 1 can
   (14.5 ounces) of diced tomatoes
2 Tbs. chopped fresh dill or 1 Tbs. dried
2 Tbs. fresh parsley
1 crushed garlic clove
2 tsp. salt
Pepper to taste
1 bay leaf

1. Combine 3 cups water, beets, potato, carrots, onion, and cabbage in a large saucepan, bring to a boil, and cover. Simmer about 20 minutes or until vegetables are cooked through.

2. Add 4 cups stock, vinegar, tomatoes, dill, parsley, garlic, salt, pepper, and bay leaf. Cover and simmer at least another 30 minutes.

3. In the Polish tradition, top with a dollop of sour cream and serve with pickled herring, rye bread, dill pickles, and slices of cheese.

Miso Soup

The delicious cloudy broth you've been served in Japanese restaurants, garnished with diced tofu and seaweed, is made with a fermented soybean and grain paste called miso.—J.W.

Servings: 4

5 cups vegetable or mushroom stock
1 piece kombu (kelp, a dried seaweed),
    about 5 inches square
1 tsp. soy sauce
3 Tbs. light (yellow) miso, such as shiro
    mugi miso
2 scallions, chopped
2 ounces firm tofu, diced into small cubes
4 tsp. wakame seaweed (instant)

1. Bring stock and kombu to a boil in a soup pot. Cover; remove from heat and let stand 5 minutes. Strain; stir in soy sauce.

2. In a mixing bowl, mix about ¼ cup of the warm stock into the miso paste with a wire whisk until the miso is dissolved. Pour this mixture back into the remaining stock.

3. Place scallions, diced tofu, and wakame into four bowls. Gently ladle soup into the bowls.

Taking Stock

Stock is a flavored broth made by simmering flavorful ingredients, such as roasted bones, herbs, and vegetables, until their flavor pervades the cooking liquid. Stock forms the foundation of most soups, sauces, and gravies, but sometimes water is better. In vegetable-based soups, such as minestrone and lentil, using a water base allows the vegetal taste, rather than the meaty stock taste, to suffuse the dish. Chowders are also fine with just water. I tend to make soups with stocks in the winter and with water in warmer weather.

Chicken Noodle Soup

Simplicity is elegance.—J.W.

Servings: 8

1 chicken (about 2½ pounds)
4 cups chicken stock or broth, plus 6 cups water
6–8 parsley stems
½ medium onion (keep the skin on)
1 bay leaf
1 cup uncooked thin egg noodles
2 tsp. salt or to taste

1. Wash the chicken well. Place it in a pot with the broth and enough water to completely cover. Bring to a boil and skim off any foam that rises to the surface. Reduce heat to a simmer.

2. Using cotton twine or string, tie together the parsley stems, the onion half, and the bay leaf. Add this bundle to the soup and simmer over low heat until the chicken is cooked, about 45 minutes.

3. Remove the chicken from the soup; set aside. Discard the onion bundle. Add the noodles to the soup and simmer until they are cooked. Meanwhile, dice about one-quarter of the chicken meat. Save the rest of the meat for another use, such as potpie.

4. Add diced chicken meat back to the soup. Season to taste.

How to Make Basic Soup Stock

Bones give stock the best flavor. Roast bones in the oven until lightly browned, or use the carcass from a roasted chicken. Put the bones (or a whole raw chicken), a halved onion, a chopped rib of celery, and a peeled carrot in a large pot. Bring to a boil. Add a dozen peppercorns and a bay leaf (or not), and simmer for 1½ hours. If any foam rises to the surface, spoon it off. When it's done, strain it.

Butternut Soup

SUBMITTED BY JANE LOOM, DURBAN NORTH, SOUTH AFRICA

My husband, Marc, who passed away at age thirty-three from a brain tumor, loved my Butternut Soup. He especially appreciated it after chemotherapy, when he could eat little. Today, my two children, ages two and four, and I continue to enjoy this mellow yellow family favorite that is steeped in so many loving memories.

Jane Loom and her children

Servings: 8

2 Tbs. butter

2 medium butternut squash, peeled
　　and cut into pieces

2 medium onions, sliced

1 quart chicken stock or bouillon

2 green apples, peeled and sliced

1 tsp. salt

Ground black pepper to taste

½ tsp. ginger powder

¼ tsp. nutmeg

¼ tsp. paprika

1 cup cream

Chopped parsley

½ cup cream, stiffly whipped (optional)

Garlic and rosemary or other seasoned
　　croutons (optional)

1. Melt the butter in a large saucepan and fry the butternut pieces and onions till golden brown. Add stock and apples and heat to boiling point.

2. Reduce heat, cover, and simmer for 30 minutes until soft. Remove from heat, and purée in a food processor (or mash in a sieve). Return to saucepan. Add salt and pepper, ginger, nutmeg, paprika, and cream, and heat until ready over a low heat.

3. Serve in mugs, sprinkled with parsley and a dollop of fresh whipped cream (optional) or garlic and rosemary croutons. This soup freezes very nicely.

Jewish Penicillin

By Hanna Geshelin, Worcester, Massachusetts

The wonders of Jewish chicken soup have been discovered by many non-Jews, including a man I worked with many years ago in Idaho. Jack, who had grown up in a small community in Pennsylvania, was a great raconteur who regaled us with tales during coffee breaks. One day, he told us about his childhood friend Abie Silverman. As a boy, Jack would hang around the Silverman home, hoping for an invitation to supper. What he remembered best was Mrs. Silverman's chicken soup: matzo balls floating in a clear golden broth with fat globules glistening on the top and shredded chicken on the bottom.

"Heaven!" Jack said, still lost in his culinary reverie. Suddenly he looked at me. "Did your grandmother make Jewish chicken soup?"

"Sure," I said. "So does my mother, and so do I."

"You do?" He sounded as though I'd just told him I had wings on my back.

"Do you want the recipe?" I asked.

"I'd love it," he said, as though I'd just offered him the Holy Grail.

On my lunch break, I jotted down the recipe and brought it to him. Raising his eyebrows, he asked, "Do you have a cookbook at your desk?"

"No," I said.

"You called your mother?"

"No, I know how to make it." It's one of those things a Jewish woman just learns, like tying shoes.

Jack studied the recipe. "This is all there is to it? It can't be this easy."

"Try it," I said with a smile.

Monday morning Jack came into my office as if he was floating six inches off the ground, a beatific smile on his face.

"Hanna," he said, "I made your chicken soup over the weekend." He sighed and shook his head. "It was just like Mrs. Silverman's."

Basic Chicken Soup

Chicken soup should be clear, fragrant, and about 60 percent broth. Start with a good stock or bouillon and then fortify it with flavor from fresh chicken.—J.W.

Servings: 8

1 whole stewing chicken (about
   2½ pounds), cut in quarters
4 cups chicken stock or broth, plus
   2 cups water
2 large onions, roughly chopped (about
   4 cups)
2 carrots, chopped (about 2 cups)

2 ribs celery, chopped (about 2 cups)
3 parsnips, peeled and sliced into
   1-inch pieces
1 bay leaf
3 sprigs flat-leaf (Italian) parsley
2 Tbs. chopped fresh dill, or 2 tsp. dried
Salt and pepper to taste

1. Rinse the chicken well, and place in a large soup pot with the stock and enough water to completely cover. Bring to a simmer over medium heat. Add the vegetables, bay leaf, and parsley.

2. Simmer gently over low heat until chicken is cooked, about 1 hour, occasionally skimming off the foam that rises to the surface. Take the chicken from the pot, remove the skin, and chop or shred one-third of the meat. Save the remaining meat for another use, such as chicken salad.

3. Add the chicken meat back to the soup, stir in the dill, remove the bay leaf, and season to taste.

Stock to a cook is voice to a singer.

Anonymous

Acorn Squash Soup with Anise and Carrots

When the weather turns chilly, acorn and other fall and winter squashes start showing up in the markets—just in time to make this smooth, soothing, velvety soup. For a crunchy soup garnish, remove the seeds from the squash, salt and toast them for twenty minutes in a medium oven.—J.W.

Servings: 6

1 slice bacon, chopped

2 medium onions, chopped

1 tsp. salt

1 medium acorn squash (about 2 pounds), peeled and cut into 1-inch chunks

2 carrots, peeled and cut into 1-inch chunks

1 tsp. anise seeds, toasted in a dry pan 2 minutes until fragrant

¼ cup cognac or brandy

1 pint chicken stock or broth

12 cups skim milk

Fresh parsley, chopped

1. Render the bacon in a heavy medium saucepot over medium heat until it just begins to brown. Add the onions and salt; cook until translucent and slightly browned, about 10 minutes. Lower the heat. Add the squash, carrots, and anise seeds; cook slowly, stirring the browned bits from the bottom of the pan frequently with a wooden spoon. These browned natural sugars will give the soup its caramelized complexity.

2. When the squash is soft and nicely browned, add the cognac; cook 2 minutes to steam off the alcohol. Add the stock; simmer 15 minutes.

3. In a blender, purée the soup with as much skim milk as necessary for a thick but soupy consistency. Season to taste with salt and pepper.

4. Serve garnished with toasted squash seeds and a sprinkling of chopped parsley.

Carrot Purée with Nutmeg

*Your family and friends will savor this sweet, creamy soup—
and they won't believe it contains no cream.—J.W.*

Servings: 6

2 Tbs. oil
1 medium onion, chopped
2 Tbs. white wine
*4 cups carrots, peeled, halved lengthwise, and
    sliced thin*
2 cups chicken stock or broth (canned is okay)
1 tsp. salt
Ground white pepper to taste
Pinch nutmeg
1¼ cups milk
2 tsp. fresh chives or parsley, chopped

1. Heat oil in large saucepan over medium-high heat. Add onion, sauté 5 minutes; add wine and carrots. Cook 1 minute until alcohol evaporates.

2. Add stock, salt, pepper, and nutmeg. Bring to a boil; then reduce heat and simmer for 20 minutes.

3. Ladle into a blender, add 1 cup milk, and blend until very smooth. Adjust consistency with more milk if necessary. Be careful when puréeing the hot liquid—start the blender on the slowest speed and do the job in batches. Serve garnished with a sprinkling of chives or parsley.

How to "Cream" Broth

Whipped soups have a creamy feel, even when made with skim milk. This comes from using a high-speed blender to purée. Blenders and food processors are not interchangeable. Most soup purées come out smoother with a blender. But be careful: Hot soups love to jump out of blenders.

Food tastes best when you eat it with your own spoon.

Danish Proverb

Cream of Chicken Soup

Cream soups share a simple concept: Cook a flavorful ingredient with broth, thicken it with a cooked flour/butter mixture (roux), and finish with fresh cream. Once you've mastered one, such as this cream of chicken soup, you can create your own, substituting broccoli, mushrooms, carrots, or whatever else you wish in place of the chicken.—J.W.

Servings: 8

1 chicken leg (thigh and
   drumstick)
8 cups strong chicken broth, plus
   2 cups water
Half of a medium onion (skin
   still on)
1 bay leaf

8 parsley stems
4 fresh sage leaves or ½ tsp.
   ground dried sage
4 Tbs. clarified butter or oil
4 Tbs. flour
1 cup fresh cream or half-and-half
Salt and pepper to taste

1. Place the chicken leg, the broth, and 2 cups of water in a large soup pot. Bring to a boil over medium heat and skim off any foam that rises to the surface. Add the onion, bay leaf, parsley stems, and sage. (You can tie these in a bundle with cotton twine for easy removal, if desired.) Lower heat and simmer until cooked through, about 45 minutes. Strain. Cool the chicken, discard the skin, and dice the meat.

2. In a small saucepan, combine the clarified butter and flour. Cook over moderate heat until the mixture is a smooth paste with a nutty aroma, about 5 minutes. Set aside to cool. This is your roux.

(recipe continued on next page)

3. Ladle a cup of hot soup into the roux. Over low heat, beat the mixture together with a wire whisk until smooth. Add more soup and repeat until half of the soup is thickened, bringing the mixture to a simmer between additions. Pour this thickened broth back into the rest of the soup.

4. Bring to a simmer, and cook 5 to 8 minutes. Stir in the cream and diced chicken meat, and season to taste with salt and pepper.

.... ૬ ....

When that smoking chowder came in, the mystery was delightfully explained. Oh! sweet friends, harken to me. It was made of small juicy clams, scarcely bigger than hazel nuts, mixed with pounded ship biscuits and salted pork cut up into little flakes! the whole enriched with butter, and plentifully seasoned with pepper and salt . . . we dispatched it with great expedition.

Ishmael, Moby-Dick
(Herman Melville)

How to Clarify Butter

Fresh butter smokes and burns when added to a hot pan because fresh butter is an emulsion of butterfat, water, and milk proteins. Slowly heating whole butter divides these elements, enabling you to skim off the clarified butterfat, which is a clear, golden oil. This oil tolerates the high cooking temperatures needed to brown foods in a hot pan. It also imparts that subtle buttery flavor that is comfort personified.

The Great Relief of Having Soup to Turn To

By Colleen Sell

A few days after the September 11, 2001, terror attacks in New York, Pennsylvania, and Washington, D.C., with my heart still too frozen to cry and my stomach too sickened to eat, I drove the forty-eight miles from my home to Cafe Zenon's and ordered the soup of the day: Mamma Leone's. Glancing around the unusually quiet but crowded restaurant, I noticed bowls of steaming soup in front of many of my fellow diners. As the waitress placed the soup on my table, her eyes met mine for a moment, as if to say, "I understand," instead of her usual "Enjoy!" I hesitated while yet another wave of disorientation and profound sorrow washed over me. Then, I sighed and took my first bite, cautiously, and then my second bite, slowly, and by the third, I knew that my stomach was finally going to accept what my body needed. As I ate spoonful after spoonful of the warm, savory broth, slowly and gratefully my heart began to thaw enough to provide what my soul needed. And finally, I cried.

(recipe appears on next page)

That's something I've noticed about food: whenever there's a crisis, if you can get people to eating normally, things get better.

Madeleine L'Engle

Mamma Leone's Chicken Soup

SUBMITTED BY BILL HATCH, CHEF, CAFE ZENON, EUGENE, OREGON

This rich soup was created in the early 1970s, when it was sold from a kiosk at an outdoor farmer's market. Its colors are those of the Italian flag, and it is the kind of hearty soup you'd expect your mom to serve. So, we [Hatch and his partners David Counter and David Kort] named it after the famous Italian restaurant in New York City, Mamma Leone's.

Servings: 12

1 Tbs. olive oil

2 cups diced onions

1 rib celery, chopped

4 cloves garlic, minced

1 pound boneless raw dark chicken meat, ½-inch diced (or cooked and shredded)

¾ tsp. each black pepper, oregano, thyme

2 tsp. salt

Scant 2 tsp. tarragon

Generous ¼ tsp. chili powder

Pinch cayenne

1 quart diced pear tomatoes (fresh or canned in juice)

6 cups strong homemade chicken stock

5 ounces (half of a cello bag) fresh spinach, chopped

1 cup cream

1. In a large soup pot, heat the oil over medium-high heat. Cook onions, celery, and garlic in oil until onions are soft, about 10 minutes. Add the chicken, pepper, oregano, thyme, salt, tarragon, chili powder, and cayenne. Cook, stirring, 5 to 10 minutes.

2. Add the tomatoes and stock. Bring to a simmer for 20 to 30 minutes, until chicken is thoroughly cooked. Just before serving, stir in the chopped spinach and cook 1 minute until it has wilted. Stir in the cream, and taste for seasoning.

Chinese Hot Pot (Seafood in Clear Broth)

On Chinese New Year (which comes in February), Asian families and friends gather in their homes around simmering pots of broth. Plates piled high with every imaginable food—thinly sliced pork, beef, and lamb; seafood dumplings; fish pancakes; shrimp; lobster; rare green leafy vegetables; clams and cockles—are arranged around the table. One by one, the various ingredients are simmered in the broth, dipped in a mixture of savory sauce and egg yolks, and eaten. With each new ingredient, the broth becomes more flavorful and complex. As a final course, delicate Asian "glass" noodles ("bean threads") are cooked in the broth, which is then served as soup. By the time the hot pot is finished, everyone promises that he or she will never indulge so excessively again—until next year.—J.W.

Servings: 10–12

1 bundle Asian "cellophane" noodles, or
    ¼ pound angel-hair spaghetti
6 cups diluted chicken or vegetable broth
1 dozen small (littleneck) clams
1 dozen small Chinese soup dumplings
    or store-bought small meat ravioli

12 imitation crab sticks
6 large leaves Boston lettuce, torn in half
1 dozen medium shrimp
Sesame oil

1. If using Asian noodles, soak in cold water for 10 minutes. Boil the broth in a large saucepot. Add the clams and dumplings, and simmer until the first clam starts to open, about 8 to 10 minutes.

2. Add the crab, lettuce, and noodles, and simmer until noodles are cooked (about 5 minutes). Turn off the flame and stir in the shrimp. Let stand 5 minutes, then drizzle on a few drops of sesame oil, and set the whole pot in the center of the table, with some small side-cups of various Chinese dipping sauces, such as hoisin, oyster, soy, or Mongolian barbecue.

Ruth's Split Pea Soup

SUBMITTED BY RUTH ROSENCROWN, FREEHOLD, NEW JERSEY

*This full-bodied, flavorful vegetarian soup is packed
with nutrients for the body and soul.*

Servings: 12

10 cups water
2 cups dried split peas, washed
1 onion, chopped
1 large carrot, diced
*1 handful string beans, fresh or frozen, cut into
    1-inch pieces*
1 Tbs. salt
Freshly ground black pepper to taste
Diced zucchini and fresh peas (optional)

1. Combine all ingredients in a large soup pot
with a tight-fitting lid. Bring to a rolling boil,
and skim off any foam that rises to the surface.

2. Cover. Simmer 2 hours. Adjust seasoning.

Soup breathes reassurance; it offers consolation;
after a weary day it promotes sociability . . . There
is nothing like a bowl of hot soup.

Louis P. DeGouy

Broth Got the Blahs?

If something seems to be
missing, it's usually salt!
Salt brings out the flavor
of soups. Unless you have
specific health issues (high
blood pressure, heart dis-
ease, thyroid problems),
season for flavor, not out
of fear. When a recipe sug-
gests that you "season to
taste," do it.

Winter Cabbage Soup (Borscht)

SUBMITTED BY LYNN RUTH MILLER, PACIFICA, CALIFORNIA

My mother was dedicated to providing her family with a healthy diet, and she believed that no vegetable was as good for us as cooked cabbage. "It is full of all the things you need for your bones and eyes," she would say when she placed one cabbage dish after another before me. "Cabbage is a socially unacceptable vegetable," I'd reply. "It makes me so bilious I have to stay home for at least twenty-four hours after I eat it." My mother was not about to truncate my life by omitting such a vital nutrient from my diet, and she thought long and hard about an artful disguise for this dreaded vegetable. At last, she came up with an answer so delicious even I could not refuse it: cabbage borscht soup.

Servings: 12

1 large head white cabbage
2 sour apples, peeled and cored
4 quarts water
2 Tbs. oil

4 Tbs. brown sugar
4 Tbs. white vinegar
1 Tbs. salt
1 cup sour cream

1. Quarter the cabbage through the stem end and cut out the core. Shred cabbage and slice the apples finely. Bring 4 quarts of water to a boil.

2. Heat oil in your soup pot. Add the cabbage and apples and cover with boiling water. Stir in the sugar, vinegar, and salt. Cook until tender, about 45 minutes. Taste when you think it is done and adjust seasonings.

3. To serve, garnish each bowl with a heaping tablespoon of sour cream.

···· ····

Only the pure of heart can make good soup.
Beethoven

Minestrone

*Rich and hearty, this classic Italian vegetable soup
has humble origins as a peasant dish.—J.W.*

Servings: 10–12

2 stalks celery

1 large carrot

1 potato

1 medium zucchini

1 medium yellow summer squash

1 large Spanish onion

1 Tbs. olive oil

2 leeks, washed twice thoroughly, chopped

3 cloves garlic, finely chopped

1 tsp. salt

3 tsp. chopped fresh oregano or 1 tsp.
dried oregano leaves

3 tsp. chopped fresh thyme or 1 tsp.
dried thyme leaves

1 bay leaf

2 quarts vegetable stock or water

1 can (30 ounces) diced tomatoes

2 cups cooked pasta (any small shape,
such as ditalini)

1 can (12 ounces) red kidney or white
cannelini beans

Salt and white pepper to taste

½ recipe Pesto Sauce (see page 190),
vegan pesto (no cheese), or store-
bought pesto

Grated Parmesan cheese (optional)

1. Cut celery, carrot, potato, zucchini, yellow squash, and onion into medium
(¼-inch) dice. In a large soup pot or Dutch oven over medium-high heat, heat
the olive oil 1 minute. Add all diced vegetables, leeks, garlic, salt, oregano,
thyme, and bay leaf. Cook 10 to 15 minutes until onions turn translucent.
Add stock and tomatoes. Bring to a full boil; reduce heat to a simmer and
cook 45 minutes, until potato is cooked through and tender.

2. Add cooked pasta and beans. Bring back to a boil for 1 minute. Season to
taste with salt and white pepper. Serve in bowls, topped with a teaspoon of
pesto. Pass grated Parmesan cheese at the table, if desired.

Wild Mushroom Soup with Thyme

I usually put the shallots and mushrooms though a commercial mixer's grinder attachment, but I've found that hand-chopping the shallots and pulsing the mushrooms quickly in small batches in the food processor works just as well. The final purée should definitely be done in a blender, since it guarantees a smoothness that a food processor cannot accomplish.—J.W.

Servings: 8

1 pound white mushrooms
½ pound shiitake mushrooms, stems removed
1 tsp. olive oil
4 sprigs fresh thyme or ½ tsp. dried
4–5 shallots, peeled and chopped very fine
¼ cup dry white wine
2 cups chicken stock
½ pound assorted wild mushrooms (such as chanterelle, shiitake, oyster, cremini, black trumpet, etc.), sliced into bite-sized pieces
2 tsp. butter
Salt and freshly ground black pepper
3 cups cold milk
1 Tbs. chives, chopped fine

1. Pulse the white mushrooms in about 4 small batches in a food processor, to finely chop them, stopping before they clump. Roughly hand-chop the shiitakes, and pulse them the same way.

(recipe continued on next page)

2. Heat the oil in a small saucepan over medium-high heat; toss in the thyme and allow to sizzle for a moment, then add the shallots and sauté 3 minutes until translucent. Add the chopped mushrooms. Sprinkle in a pinch of salt, and cook 5 to 7 minutes, until mushrooms are soft.

3. Add white wine and cook 2 minutes; then add the stock. Simmer 10 minutes.

4. Sauté the sliced mushrooms in butter in small batches over high heat, seasoning with salt and pepper as they cook. Set aside.

5. Put one-third of the soup and 1 cup cold milk in blender and purée until very smooth; repeat with remaining soup. Season to taste. Be careful to vent the blender to avoid dangerous splashing.

6. Serve with a spoonful of sautéed mushrooms in each bowl and a sprinkling of chives.

···· § ····

Do you have a kinder, more adaptable friend in the food world than soup? Who soothes you when you are ill? Who refuses to leave you when you are impoverished and stretches its resources to give you a hearty sustenance and cheer? Who warms you in the winter and cools you in the summer? Yet who also is capable of doing honor to your richest table and impressing your most demanding guest?

Judith Martin (Miss Manners)

Paprikash Soup (Hungarian Style)

SUBMITTED BY RENIE BURGHARDT, DONIPHAN, MISSOURI

This hearty winter-vegetable stew is redolent with Hungary's favorite spice, paprika. It's sure to perk you up on a gray November day. Jo etvagyat! (Good appetite!)

Servings: 8

1 large onion, chopped
2 Tbs. vegetable oil
2 Tbs. sweet paprika
4 carrots, thickly sliced
4 stalks celery, sliced
4 large potatoes cut up in small chunks
8 cups water
Salt and pepper to taste
10 ounces frozen corn (optional)
Noodles of choice, about ¼ pound
¼ cup half-and-half (or milk)

1. Sauté the chopped onion in the oil until translucent. Add the paprika; stir. Add the carrots, celery, and potatoes; cook covered for about 6 minutes to blend flavors. Add water, salt, and pepper.

2. Bring to a simmer and cook, covered, for about 40 minutes. Ten minutes before done, add frozen corn and noodles. Stir in half-and-half; heat through, but don't let it come to a boil.

That Old Trusty Wooden Spoon

When cooking soups, stews, sautés, and sauces, the most intense, delicious flavors often concentrate on the bottom of the pot. Scraping these tasty condensed juices off the bottom of the pot and into a dish with the wrong tool risks also scraping up burned parts and/or metal shavings. Wooden spoons gently loosen soluble concentrated juices from the bottom of the pan, without scraping up the bad stuff. They also get into corners better than metal utensils and keep your pots in good shape.

Lobster and Corn Chowder

Jasper White, whose interpretations of traditional New England dishes have breathed new life into the region's cuisine, taught this recipe to me. The flavor comes from the stock, made with shells, bodies, and corncobs often discarded in other recipes.—J.W.

Servings: 8

4 small lobsters (about 1 pound each)

5 ears corn on the cob, kernels cut off
  with a knife, cobs reserved (about
  3 cups kernels)

½ pound thick-cut bacon, cut into
  ½-inch pieces

½ bunch fresh thyme, leaves picked off,
  stems reserved

1 tsp. black peppercorns

4 bay leaves

1 whole onion, peeled

3 medium onions cut in large (¾-inch)
  cubes (3 cups)

2 ribs celery, medium-chopped (¼-inch
  pieces)

4 Tbs. unsalted butter

8 small red bliss (new) potatoes, cut
  into ½-inch slices

1½ cups heavy cream

Salt and freshly ground black pepper
  to taste

Chopped chives for garnish

1. Boil lobsters in 5 quarts strongly salted water for 5 minutes. Cool and remove tail, claw, and arm meat from shells. Cut meat into bite-sized pieces and refrigerate. Put shells and bodies into a large stockpot with the corncobs and 3 quarts fresh water. Add 1 tablespoon of the cut bacon, thyme stems, peppercorns, bay leaves, and whole onion, and bring to a boil. Simmer 1 hour and 15 minutes. Strain the stock.

2. Render remaining bacon in a soup pot until crisp, then add diced onions, celery, thyme leaves, and butter, and cook until onions soften (5 minutes). Add the corn, potatoes, and stock. Simmer until potatoes are cooked through, about 20 minutes. Add the cream and lobster meat. Season with salt and pepper, and garnish with a sprinkling of chives. Serve with crackers or biscuits.

Zucchini-Basil Soup

SUBMITTED BY LYNN RUTH MILLER, PACIFICA, CALIFORNIA

When I moved to California, I planted a whole packet of seeds of my favorite vegetable, zucchini, with visions of the marvelous meals the tiny vines would bring. Those vines soon put Jack's beanstalk to shame. They filled my yard and threatened to break down my patio doors. They climbed over the woodshed into the garage. They crept across the fence and suffocated my rosebushes. When it came time to reap their unexpected bounty, I filled every barrel, box, jar, paper bag, plastic pot, and suitcase I had, and still I had zucchini to spare. I gave them to neighbors and friends, donated them to soup kitchens and rest homes, and still I had surplus. I hauled out my cookbooks and tried to salvage what I could not give away. I pickled them. I canned them. I mashed them and used them to garnish desserts. And then I started inventing zuke recipes—like this yummy Zucchini-Basil Soup.

Servings: 4

3 cups sliced zucchini
1 Tbs. olive oil
1 large onion, sliced
¼ cup chopped Italian parsley
1 tsp. dried basil

1 cup milk or chicken stock
1 tsp. salt
Pepper to taste
Sour cream or yogurt (optional)

1. Boil or steam the zucchini. Heat the oil in a small pan and cook the onion, parsley, and basil together until the onions are soft.

2. Combine the zucchini, onion mixture, milk, salt, and pepper in a blender, and purée until very smooth. Serve hot or cold with sour cream or yogurt on top.

···· ❧ ····

Worries go better with soup than without.

Yiddish Proverb

A Dittle Code

BY KRISTL VOLK FRANKLIN

Have you ever noticed that colds don't command much respect? My family, for instance, has a great deal of difficulty recognizing that the common cold is an illness. Take last Monday.

"Mom, why are you in bed?" my daughter, who is fifteen-going-on-thirty-five, asked. "Are you sick?"

Before answering, I grabbed a tissue from the nightstand and honked into it. "I have a dittle code," I managed to say.

"A what?"

"A dittle code, c-o-l-d."

"Oh." She leaned over me with obvious suspicion. "Are you sure it's not strep throat?" She tickled my chin. "Come on, open up, let me see."

I opened my mouth and said, "aahh." I have always been a good patient.

"It's red all right," she informed me. "But I don't see any of that white yukky stuff like I had."

"It'th jutht a dittle code," I admitted in a rather apologetic tone. "All I need ith a dittle retht."

I grew up in a time when a cold was a perfectly respectable ailment. At the first cough or sneeze, my mother would press her lips against my forehead to assess my temperature. If I was hotter than her lips, I had a fever. She'd change my bedding, smoothing the fresh linens with her hands so no wrinkles could irritate my feverish body. I never knew what medicinal value clean sheets had, but they felt wonderful against my aching muscles, and the coolness of the pillowcase eased the fever in

Vera Czapka Volk Robertson Harding, mother of Kristl Franklin, models a coat she made from an American army blanket in Weisbaden, Germany, in 1951

my cheeks. Next, she'd throw together the ingredients of her special potato soup, a recipe brought with her from Germany.

I would snuggle down in my bed, knowing the warm soup, which I actually couldn't taste because of my congestion, would be wonderful. I could hear my mom outside my darkened room, whispering, "Shh, she has a cold, let her rest," to the other members of the family. As I got better, each person would tiptoe to my bedside to see how I felt, leaving a little something—a book, tissues, an orange.

But that was another time. Last Monday, no sooner had my daughter inspected my throat than my six-year-old slipped in to check on me.

"Let me see, Mom," he commanded. With brisk efficiency, he climbed up next to me, drew my head down, and puckered his lips against my forehead.

"A thousand degrees," he said with authority. He pulled down my lower eyelashes and inspected my eyeball. "And your blood is low," he concluded.

"You can't have a fever with a virus, and the common cold is caused by a virus," said my thirteen-year-old son, who had joined us at bedside. Evidently, he'd heard about the thousand-degree fever. "Therefore, you can't have a cold."

"Who thays," I retorted. "I do tho have a code."

"I say it's type-B flu," said my husband, who came in next.

"I'll bet it's a sinus infection." This was from my oldest son.

"Has to be tonsillitis." My daughter would not be outdone.

"Iron-poor blood," said my youngest.

"Why can't I be thick with a plain ode code!" I wailed.

My family, or paramedical team, contemplated me for one long quiet moment.

Okay, so maybe I was being a little childish at that point. But I couldn't help it. After all, where was my cool, clean pillow? Where was my potato soup? I broke the silence by sneezing violently into a tissue.

"Shhh," said my husband. "Let's give her some rest."

"Here, Mom, I'll turn over your pillow," said one child.

"How about some vitamin C and antihistamines?" asked another.

"I'll read you a story later if you want," said the third.

Then, one by one, they tiptoed out. My husband paused at the door. "How about some soup?" he asked.

Soup? My heart gave a little lurch. "You're going to make me potato soup?" I ventured.

A look of confusion came over his face. "Potato soup? You must be feverish. Sweetheart, it's either a can of chicken with rice or split pea with ham."

"Thicken thounds nice," I said and answered the phone on the first ring. "Heddo."

"Hello? Who is this?"

"Me . . . your thisther."

"How come you don't sound like my sister?"

"I have a dittle code."

"Come on. Are you sure it's just a cold? Sounds more serious."

"I do tho have a co—," I started to protest hotly. Then, I took a deep breath. There comes a time in everyone's life when the will to fight for the truth is weak. "Actually, thith, there'th a very good chance I have a thinuth infection or tonthillithith with iron-poor blood."

Colds command such little respect these days.

Omie's Potato Soup
(Old German Potato Soup)

SUBMITTED BY KRISTL VOLK FRANKLIN, THE WOODLANDS, TEXAS

I have included this recipe exactly as it was worded when my mother brought it with her from Germany and as it was handed down to me.

Servings: 4

500g potatoes (Kartoffeln), about 5 medium

1 small piece of leek (kleine Stange Porree)

2 medium carrots (mittelgroße Karrotten)

1 stick of celery (Stück Sellerie Knolle)

1 small kohlrabi (Stück Kohlrabi)— could use a small turnip

1. Chop the vegetables and cook them in salted water (or stock cube or chicken stock). Vegetables must be covered a little bit with the water. When it is done (about 25 to 30 minutes), press it through a colander. Add a little bit more water if necessary. Add salt and pepper to taste.

2. Chop one small onion and chop 100g (a couple of slices) smoked bacon in little pieces. In a separate pan, roast the onion and bacon together until crispy.

3. Sprinkle over the ready soup. Serve the soup in pretty soup cups with a teaspoonful of sour cream. *Guten Appetit!*

Corn and Potato Chowder

Chowder comes from the Acadian (French) word for "soup pot." But corn chowder is an American original, developed in New England during Colonial times.—J.W.

Servings: 12

8 ears sweet corn, shucked

2 slices bacon, chopped

2 large onions, chopped

2 stalks celery, chopped

1 pound red potatoes, cut into 1-inch chunks

3 sprigs fresh thyme or 1 tsp. dried thyme leaves

1 bay leaf

3 tsp. salt

1 smoked chili (optional)

4 ounces (1 stick) unsalted butter

3 quarts vegetable stock or water

4 tsp. cornstarch, dissolved in ¼ cup water

1 quart cream or milk

Salt and white pepper to taste

2 Tbs. chopped fresh chives

1. Cut corn kernels from the cob using a slicing motion with a kitchen knife. Reserve the cobs, and set kernels aside. In a large soup pot over medium-high heat, render the bacon. (The resulting oil will add flavor to the vegetables as they cook.) Add the corncobs, onions, celery, potatoes, thyme, bay leaf, salt, and chili if using. Cook until onions are translucent, about 5 minutes. Add the butter, and cook gently, allowing the vegetables to stew in the butter, for about 5 more minutes.

2. Add the vegetable stock. Raise heat to high and bring to a full boil. Lower to a simmer and cook 10 minutes more. Remove the corncobs. Add cornstarch mixture and simmer 5 minutes more. Stir in the cream, and adjust seasoning with salt and white pepper to taste. Serve sprinkled with chives.

Vichyssoise (Potato Leek Soup)

Elegant, classic French soups like this make the right first course for a formal occasion. Serve chilled or warm, and make sure to use the prettiest leek pieces, cut very precisely, for the garnish. People will notice.—J.W.

Why Make It If We're Only Gonna Mess It Up Again?

If everything just boils to mush anyway, why cook the vegetables slowly in oil before adding liquid? Because only lipids can dissolve the rigid cell walls of many veggies, which lock inside the flavor and nutrients. Carrots, for example, are high in fat-soluble beta-carotene. To extract this aromatic essence, the carrot must cook slowly in fat or oil to dissolve the cell walls without burning the carrots, so that the flavors and nutrients become part of the broth. If veggies are just thrown in with the liquid, the broth is bland and less nutritious and colorful.

Servings: 10–12

1 Tbs. olive oil
1 medium onion, chopped
1 pound (about 3 or 4) potatoes, any variety, peeled and cut into 1-inch chunks
2 bunches leeks, washed twice thoroughly, chopped (set aside 1 cup of the best parts for garnish)
1 tsp. dried sage leaves
1 bay leaf
¼ cup white wine
2 quarts vegetable stock or water
Salt and white pepper to taste

1. In a large soup pot over medium heat, heat olive oil 1 minute. Add onion, potatoes, and all but 1 cup of the chopped leeks; cook 10 minutes until onions turn translucent.

(recipe continued on next page)

2. Add sage, bay leaf, and wine. Cook 1 more minute. Add stock and bring to a full boil.

3. Reduce heat to a simmer and cook 45 minutes, until potatoes are very tender and start to fall apart.

4. Carefully purée the soup in a blender in small batches. Season to taste with salt and white pepper.

5. Steam, boil, or sauté the remaining cup of leeks, and serve the soup garnished with a spoonful of leeks in the center. This soup may be served either hot or chilled.

.... ❧ ....

If a man counts at the tops of his fingers how many things in his life give him enjoyment, invariably he will find food is the first one.

Lin Yutang

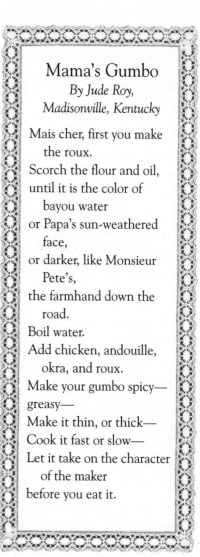

Mama's Gumbo
By Jude Roy,
Madisonville, Kentucky

Mais cher, first you make
   the roux.
Scorch the flour and oil,
until it is the color of
   bayou water
or Papa's sun-weathered
   face,
or darker, like Monsieur
   Pete's,
the farmhand down the
   road.
Boil water.
Add chicken, andouille,
   okra, and roux.
Make your gumbo spicy—
   greasy—
Make it thin, or thick—
Cook it fast or slow—
Let it take on the character
   of the maker
before you eat it.

Onion Soup

The rich caramel coloring of this soup comes from slow-browning the onions before adding the stock. A heavy-bottomed pot is essential to prevent scorching.—J.W.

Servings: 8

2 Tbs. butter
2 Tbs. olive oil
4 sprigs fresh thyme or 1 tsp. dried
6 large onions, thinly sliced
2 tsp. salt
2 Tbs. dry sherry or white wine

8 cups brown beef stock, veal stock, or chicken stock
16 slices French bread, toasted or dried overnight until crisp
1 pound Gruyère cheese, grated

1. Heat the butter and olive oil in a large, heavy-bottomed soup pot over medium heat until the butter is melted. Add thyme sprigs (if using fresh), and allow them to sizzle for 15 seconds. Add the onions, thyme (if using dried), and salt, and toss to coat with oil.

2. Cook over a medium-low flame, stirring occasionally with a wooden spoon, until the onions have given up their juices and begin to caramelize (turn brown). Lower the flame a bit more, and cook until the onions are mahogany-brown and nearly disintegrated. Some brown will stick to the bottom of the pot; this is okay, as long as it doesn't go black.

3. Add the sherry or wine, letting the alcohol evaporate for a minute, and then add the stock. Simmer 20 minutes. Remove the stems, if any, from the thyme. Season to taste.

4. Heat the broiler element of your oven and arrange the rack 4 inches from the element. Ladle soup into ovenproof bowls or crocks. Place 2 slices of dried or toasted French bread onto each portion, and sprinkle a generous amount of cheese on top. Broil the soup until the cheese on top is brown and bubbly. Serve at once.

Cuban Black Bean Soup

Cubans flavor this soup with smoked pork bone. You can use smoked ham hocks or keep it vegetarian by substituting a smoked chili (chipotle) in place of the bone.—J.W.

Servings: 10–12

1 Tbs. olive oil

1 medium onion, chopped

1 large leek, white part only, finely chopped

4 cloves garlic, finely chopped

1 tsp. cumin seeds, toasted lightly then ground, or 1½ tsp. ground cumin, heated in a dry pan until fragrant

1 bay leaf

¼ tsp. paprika

1 smoked pork bone, about 4 inches long

3 quarts chicken stock or water

2 cups black beans (soaked overnight, if desired)

½ bunch fresh cilantro, chopped (optional)

Salt and pepper to taste

Sour cream for garnish

1 Tbs. chopped cilantro

1. In a large soup pot over medium heat, heat olive oil 1 minute. Add onion, chopped leek, and garlic; cook 5 minutes until onions turn translucent, stirring frequently. Add cumin, bay leaf, and paprika. Cook 5 minutes more. Add stock, pork bone, and beans. Bring to a full boil. Reduce heat to a simmer and cook 45 minutes. Add cilantro and continue simmering until beans are very tender and start to fall apart, about 45 minutes. (Cooking time will vary, depending on the age of the beans and whether they were soaked—assume 30 minutes less for soaked beans.)

2. Remove the bay leaf. Carefully purée two-thirds of the soup in a blender, then add back to the rest of the soup in the pot. Season to taste with salt and white pepper.

3. Serve topped with a teaspoon of sour cream and a sprinkling of chopped cilantro.

New England Clam Chowder

This creamy, fragrant soup has a rich history. French-speaking Acadians in Maine and Canada adapted methods and pots brought by their ancestors from Europe to make a warming dish with local seafood. To be a true chowder, the soup must contain a pork product (bacon or salt pork), onions, and potatoes.—J.W.

Servings: 8

6 large cherrystone clams, or 12 small littlenecks, or 2 cups canned chopped clams
4 slices (about ¼ pound) bacon, chopped
2 sprigs fresh thyme, or 1 tsp. dried
2 large onions, roughly chopped (about 4 cups)
2 ribs celery, roughly chopped
1 pound red-skinned potatoes, roughly cut into 1-inch chunks
4 ounces (1 stick) butter
2 Tbs. flour
2 cups water or chicken stock
2 cups half-and-half, cream, or milk
Salt and pepper to taste

1. Steam open the clams in a covered pot with 2 cups of water. Chop the clams finely, and strain the broth. Set aside.

2. In a large, heavy-bottomed soup pot over medium heat, cook the bacon until it just begins to brown. Add the thyme, onions, and celery to the rendered bacon, allowing them to cook in the bacon's oil 1 minute. Add the potatoes and butter.

(recipe continued on next page)

3. Allow the mixture to gently stew, stirring occasionally with a wooden spoon, for 10 minutes, until the onions are very soft. Stir in the flour until all lumps are dissolved.

4. Add the water and reserved clam broth. Raise to high heat, and cook until potatoes are very soft. Remove from the heat, and stir in the chopped clams and cream.

.... ⸹ ....

Chowder breathes reassurance. It steams consolation.

Clementine Paddleford

He Ain't Heavy . . . He's My Soup Pot

When a recipe calls for a "heavy-bottomed" pot, that's your clue that a thin pot may result in a burned flavor. Thick bottoms conduct heat more evenly and retain heat better, causing fewer "hot spots" where the flame or electric element contacts the pan. Hot spots burn certain foods, no matter how carefully you stir. Today, many pans are made with alloys, which are bonded ("clad") to stainless steel interiors.

These pans offer the best of both worlds: Stainless is the best food-contact surface, and alloys containing aluminum are excellent heat conductors. Cast iron is good for even heat, but certain foods acquire an off flavor when they touch the iron. Enamel-coated cast-iron pots, such as those made in France, are very good. But most American makers now produce lines with good, bonded bottoms.

Lentil Soup with Cumin

This is the fastest bean soup you can make, ready in about an hour, without any soaking of beans. It gets better as it sits overnight, when the flavors marry, so make enough for two or more meals.—J.W.

Servings: 8

1 large carrot, peeled
1 stalk celery
1 medium onion
1 potato, peeled
2 cloves garlic
1 Tbs. olive oil

1 tsp. ground cumin
2 tsp. salt
1 cup lentils
8 cups water or chicken stock
Salt and pepper to taste
Sour cream (optional)

1. Chop carrot, celery, onion, and potato into bite-sized pieces; cut garlic into very small slices.

2. Heat the oil over medium heat in a pot large enough to hold everything. Add the cut vegetables, garlic, and cumin, plus 2 teaspoons of salt. Cook 5 minutes.

3. Add the lentils and water or stock. Raise heat and bring to a boil. Reduce heat to medium-low and simmer 1 hour. Season with salt and pepper, and serve with a dollop of sour cream, if desired.

···· &ref; ····

Everyday happiness means getting up in the morning, and you can't wait to finish your breakfast. You can't wait to do your exercises. You can't wait to put on your clothes. You can't wait to get out—and you can't wait to come home, because the soup is hot.

George Burns

Red Bean and Pasta Soup

*Italians call this "Pasta e fagioli." You can use other beans for this soup,
such as cranberry beans, white beans, or borlotti beans.—J.W.*

Servings: 8

1 medium onion, chopped
3 cloves garlic, sliced
3 Tbs. olive oil
1 tsp. oregano
2 bay leaves
1 8-ounce can tomato sauce
2 tsp. salt
1 Tbs. soy sauce

1 16-ounce package red beans soaked
    overnight in 1 quart cold water,
    drained
10 sprigs Italian parsley, including stems
6 cups vegetable stock or water
2 cups cooked pasta (any small shape)
Sour cream (optional)

1. In a pot large enough to hold all ingredients, cook onion and garlic with olive oil over medium heat for 5 minutes, until onion is translucent. Add oregano, bay leaves, tomato sauce, salt, and soy sauce. Bring to a simmer and add beans, parsley, and water.

2. Bring to a boil; then reduce to a low simmer and cook 90 minutes, until beans are tender enough to mash between two fingers.

3. Remove the bay leaf. Purée one-third of the beans in a blender and add them back to the soup. Add cooked pasta and bring the soup back to the boil for 1 minute more. Serve garnished with a dollop of sour cream, if desired.

In the childhood memories of every good cook, there's a large kitchen, a warm stove, a simmering pot, and a mom.

Barbara Costikyan

Chicken and Oyster Chowder

Savory oysters add a pleasing texture to this hearty meal-in-a-bowl. Make quick potpies by placing chunky portions of this soup into ovenproof crocks or a pie plate, covering with store-bought puff pastry dough, and baking in a hot (400°) oven for half an hour.—J.W.

Servings: 8

4 strips bacon, chopped
2 large onions, roughly cut into 1-inch pieces
2 tsp. mixed herbs such as dried thyme, oregano, rosemary, or sage
1 pound potatoes, peeled and cut into 1-inch pieces
2 carrots, peeled and cut into 1-inch pieces
10 ounces mushrooms, quartered
2 tsp. salt
¼ cup flour
8 cups chicken broth
3 cups cooked chicken, cut into 1-inch pieces
2 cups shucked oysters
Salt and pepper to taste
2 ounces butter, chopped into pea-sized pieces
Chopped parsley for garnish

1. In a large soup pot over medium heat, cook the bacon until it just begins to crisp and brown. Add the onions, herbs, potatoes, carrots, mushrooms, and salt. Cook until the vegetables have given up some liquid and the onions are translucent, about 10 minutes.

(recipe continued on next page)

2. Sprinkle in the flour, stirring to combine well. Add 1 cup of the chicken broth and stir until it thickens and simmers. Repeat with remaining broth, adding 1 cup at a time, until soup is smooth and bubbling. Cook until potatoes and carrots are very tender, about 30 minutes.

3. Stir in the cooked chicken and oysters. Bring back to a simmer, and season to taste with salt and pepper. Finish by stirring in the butter. Serve sprinkled with chopped parsley.

Moon in June?

Serve fresh oysters only in months containing the letter R, from September through April. During late spring and summer (May through August), oysters are in their reproductive cycle, which turns their once-plump bodies flaccid and watery. Warmer-season waters also breed higher concentrations of unwanted bacteria. The waters are at their cleanest in the fall, when water temperatures drop. By then, the oysters are fattened up and ready for harvest again. For a summer oyster fix, used canned oysters for fried oysters or in stews, chowders, sautés, and fritters. But wait until the R months to eat them raw.

Tuscan White Bean Soup

Tuscans serve this northern Italian classic with a hunk of rustic bread at the bottom of the bowl, which soaks up soup and becomes a velvety reward waiting to be found.—J.W.

Servings: 10–12

1 Tbs. olive oil

1 medium onion, chopped

1 large leek, white part only, finely chopped

3 cloves garlic, finely chopped

3 tsp. fresh rosemary leaves or 1 tsp. dried

1 bay leaf

3 quarts vegetable stock or water

2 cups large white (Great Northern) beans (soaked overnight if desired)

Salt and white pepper to taste

1 Tbs. very high quality extra-virgin olive oil

1. In a large soup pot over medium heat, heat olive oil 1 minute. Add onion, chopped leek, and garlic; cook 10 minutes until onion turns translucent, stirring frequently. Add rosemary and bay leaf. Cook 5 minutes more. Add stock and beans, and bring to a full boil.

2. Reduce heat to a simmer and cook 90 minutes, until beans are very tender and start to fall apart. (Cooking time will vary depending on the age of the beans and whether they were soaked—assume 30 minutes less for soaked beans.)

3. Remove bay leaf. Carefully purée two-thirds of the soup in a blender, and then add it back to the soup in the pot. Season to taste with salt and white pepper. Serve with a few drops of fine extra-virgin olive oil sprinkled on top.

···· ৡ ····

It was one of those mornings when a man could face the day only after warming himself with a mug of thick coffee beaded with steam, a good thick crust of bread, and a bowl of bean soup.

Richard Gehman

Tomato Soup

What would a comfort-food cookbook be without this simple but glorious classic?
Served with grilled cheese sandwiches in fall and winter or with BLTs in spring
and summer, tomato soup is a four-seasons favorite for kids of all ages.—J.W.

Servings: 6

2 Tbs. olive oil
1 medium onion, chopped
2 cloves garlic, finely chopped
4 pounds ripe tomatoes, peeled, seeded,
   and roughly chopped
1 tsp. salt
Freshly ground black pepper to taste
   (about ¼ tsp.)

1. In a large soup pot over medium heat, heat olive oil 1 minute. Add onion and garlic; cook 5 to 10 minutes until onions are translucent but not browned. Stir in tomatoes; simmer 25 to 30 minutes, until tomatoes are submerged in their own juices.

2. Purée in a blender or food processor until smooth. Season with salt and black pepper. May be served hot or cold. Add cream, if desired, for cream of tomato soup.

The Whole Truth and Nothing but the Truth . . . About Tomatoes

In season, use fresh vine tomatoes. Off-season, use quality canned rather than greenhouse tomatoes. Tomatoes should be aromatic; tomatoes with no aroma will have no taste. Avoid tomatoes with leathery dark patches, a sign of blossom-end rot. To bring out what flavor greenhouse tomatoes have: cut in half, put open-side up on oiled baking sheet, drizzle a little oil over tomato, and roast slowly (275° for 2 hours) before adding to recipe. Cooking tomatoes in an aluminum pot can make them taste bitter. Add a pinch of sugar to bring out tomato flavor.

Pumpkin Caraway Soup

Butternut squash or even acorn squash substitute very well for pumpkin in this soup. Each imparts its own character, which makes this three recipes in one. Chipotle chili or Spanish paprika (both in gourmet stores) gives it a subtle smokiness for added dimension. This is the kind of soup you'd expect your mom to serve on a rainy day or when someone's health or spirits are flagging.—J.W.

Servings: 6
2 Tbs. unsalted butter or olive oil
1 medium onion, chopped
1 large carrot, peeled and sliced thin
2 cups fresh pumpkin, peeled and cubed
¼ tsp. whole caraway seeds
½ dried chipotle chili or ½ tsp. smoked Spanish paprika
1½ cups chicken stock or broth (canned is okay)
3 cups cold milk
Salt and pepper to taste

1. Melt the butter in a heavy-bottomed soup pot over medium heat. Add the onion, carrot, pumpkin, caraway seeds, and chili or paprika. Sauté, stirring occasionally, 8 to 10 minutes, until pumpkin becomes tender and begins to brown (some may stick to pan).

(recipe continued on next page)

2. Add stock or broth and simmer 20 minutes. Remove from heat and stir in 2 cups of milk.

3. Purée in batches in a blender until smooth, adjusting consistency with remaining milk. Season with salt and pepper.

.... 🝔 ....

We eat until our souls rise up sighing and the most hidden virtues of our wretched humanity are renewed as that blessed soup seeps into our bones, sweeping away with one stroke the fatigue of all the disappointments gathered along the road of life.

Isabel Allende

Heaven on Earth

BY AMY MAIDA WADSWORTH, SALT LAKE CITY, UTAH

When I sit at a table in heaven with all the angels and saints, I believe we will break bread together and dunk it into a steaming bowl of soup. Is there any more comforting food when cold weather sends us indoors or when our stomachs are queasy from the frailties of life? On cold winter days, when my husband comes home exhausted from work and the children are tired of being cooped up in the house, soup warms us up and makes us feel like everything is all right with the world. Soup is surely the food of the gods and a heavenly food on Earth.

chapter two

Friends Gathering
Appetizers and Nibbles

Kota Comfort

BY KARA L. C. JONES, VASHON ISLAND, WASHINGTON

Our pregnancy had been perfect, full term with no complications and no indication that anything could go wrong. So, we were completely shocked and absolutely bereft when our son, Dakota, died at birth on March 11, 1999. When your parents die, you are an orphan. When your spouse dies, you are widowed. When your child dies . . . there is no word to describe childless parents. When our family and friends could find no other words to comfort us, they sent cards, flowers, and food.

Those first few days are a blur. After the memorial service, my parents had to return almost immediately to their home 3,000 miles away. People went back to their lives—except for my good friend Heather, who had flown in after the service. She planned to stay a week, her mission to feed our souls and our bodies.

My first distinct memory after my baby's death is of waking on the first night of Heather's stay. I had slept all day long. Still sore from the cesarean section, I had been moving slowly and still needed help getting into and out of bed. But that night I woke with an almost-clear head. Standing in the doorway of our bedroom at the end of the long dark hallway, I could see lights in the living room at the other end of the house and could hear Heather in the kitchen.

As if in a dream, I made my way down the hall, and as soon as Heather saw me, she came into the living room and took my hand.

The author, on the left in white, and her friend Heather

Her touch seemed to ground me, to bring me suddenly back into my body. She asked if she could do anything for me. I told her I was hungry and remember feeling surprised at that. She walked with me to the kitchen.

There were flowers and cards everywhere, and on the kitchen counter was a box from Heather's mom, Eileen, a care package of food. Heather had been putting it away in the refrigerator and cupboards, but a bevy of delicious treasures still covered every surface: honey-baked ham, several types of cheeses, three kinds of mustard, fresh fruit, fresh bread, and

several pieces of dark chocolate. It was all finger food, tasty and yet easy to just pick up and eat without much fuss or thought. And the physical sensation of touching the food—of the water running over the fruit as I washed it off and the soft spring of the fresh bread as we cut it, even of holding the food in my hand and bringing it to my mouth as I bit in—seemed to reconnect me with my body, with life.

As we stood there in my kitchen, coming to terms with the death of my son and feasting on all that food, Heather turned to me and said, "Well, of course, we eat! It only makes sense that when we are in pain, we should at least not be hungry!"

I will never forget that amazing gift of food and friendship from my dear friend Heather and her mother, Eileen. It was an abundance that was simple and basic, physical and real, and very healing.

Eileen's Meatloaf

Submitted by Kara L. C. Jones, Vashon Island, Washington

Servings: 4

1 yellow onion, chopped
3 cloves garlic, chopped
2 Tbs. olive oil
1 pound ground beef
Fresh basil, oregano, parsley (minced)

Bread crumbs (enough to bind)
1 egg
¼ cup ketchup
Salt and pepper to taste

1. Sauté onion and garlic in olive oil until golden and then transfer to a small bowl and cool in the fridge or freezer.

2. Heat oven to 350°. Combine beef, herbs, chilled onion, garlic, bread crumbs, egg, and ketchup. Shape into 2 loaves.

3. Cover with a little ketchup on top of each loaf and bake 30 to 45 minutes.

When I was in mourning for my father I was taken home by my best friend, who sat me in a chair, gave me a copy of *Vogue*, and told me not to move until called. I sat like a good girl while she busied herself in the kitchen. When I got to the table I realized that this angelic pal had made shepherd's pie. My eyes swam with tears of gratitude. I did not know what I wanted, but it was just what I wanted.

Laurie Colwin

Potato Puffs

*Talk about simple elegance! Make with leftover fresh
mashed potatoes or powdered instants.—J.W.*

Servings: 8
Oil for frying
1 cup mashed potatoes (or instant)
1 egg, beaten
1½ tsp. baking powder
½ cup flour
½ tsp. salt

1. Heat fry oil to about 350°. (A piece of
onion should sizzle when added.)

2. In a mixing bowl, combine the mashed
potatoes and egg.

3. Sift together the baking powder, flour, and
salt. Fold this mixture into the potatoes, mixing only enough to incorporate.

4. Drop tablespoons of the potato mixture
into the fry oil, and cook until golden brown
and steamy hot inside. Serve with tartar
sauce or tomato sauce, if desired.

Testing Potatoes for Doneness

To check a potato for
doneness, poke the tip of
a knife into the thickest
part, then lift the knife up,
handle first. If the potato
falls off, it's done. If it
hangs on, then it needs
more time.

To err is human, to digest divine.

Mark Twain

Asparagus Wrapped in Prosciutto

Here's one way to get the kids and veggie-resistant guests to gobble up their greens: Wrap them in tangy cheese and savory ham.—J.W.

Servings: 10

40 pencil-thin asparagus

4 ounces plain goat cheese, room temperature

¼ pound domestic prosciutto (Italian ham), thinly sliced

1. Trim the bottom part of the asparagus, leaving a stalk that measures 4 inches long.

2. Boil very briefly (3 minutes) in salted water. Cool immediately in ice water and drain.

3. Spread each asparagus with a thin layer of goat cheese and wrap with a single layer of prosciutto.

Food is not about impressing people. It's about making them feel comfortable.

Ina Garten

Enough, Already!

With appetizers, how do you know how much is enough? It depends on when you're serving them. For a before-dinner snack, six one-bite hors d'oeuvres per person is fine. For a cocktail party followed by a late dinner, figure nine to twelve pieces per person. But if the cocktail party is during normal dinner hours, make at least twelve pieces per person. I usually count on people making a meal out of my hors d'oeuvres, so I prepare three pieces each of four types of hors d'oeuvres per person. Serve some hot and some cold (easy to store and quick to serve), with at least one vegetarian item. Also, don't put everything out at once. Save one special appetizer to serve halfway through the event to add a little flair.

Cucumbers Galore

BY LEANN R. RALPH, COLFAX, WISCONSIN

"I thought I told you not to plant very many cucumbers this year," my mother grumbled one summer afternoon when I was a kid.

"I didn't," Dad replied, as he set down a calf bucket filled with cucumbers, most of which were just about the right size for making dill pickles.

"Well," my mother continued, "you *must* have planted a lot. That's the second bucket. And they just started."

Every year when I was growing up on our Wisconsin dairy farm, my father planted a garden. And every year, he planted cucumbers.

Dad looked at Mom for a moment. "I only planted one hill," he said.

My mother laughed. "And how big is it? Half the garden?"

Dad's face took on an injured expression. "No, it's *not* half the garden. Last year you said I planted too many—"

"And you did," Mom interrupted. "That's all I got done for a while was make pickles."

"And that's why this year I figured I'd only put in one hill," Dad replied.

By the look on my mother's face, I knew she didn't believe him. Of course, with a whole bucket of cucumbers sitting there, I could sort of see why.

"If you don't want them, then throw 'em away," Dad said.

My mother was aghast. "Throw them away? I can't do that. They're perfectly good cucumbers."

"Suit yourself," Dad said. Then he shrugged. "They'll probably slow down pretty soon. They can't keep on producing like this for long."

"I hope you're right," Mom said.

But the cucumbers kept producing. Soon Mom had ten quarts, then twenty. When she hit thirty, she was getting exasperated.

"All of these just *cannot* be from one little patch," Mom said, when Dad brought in another bucket.

"I can cut 'em off with the lawn mower," Dad suggested. "It'd just be a little more fertilizer . . . for the garden . . ." His voice trailed off. He looked at my mother and blinked.

"Roy," Mom said, "you didn't put fertilizer on those cucumbers, did you?"

LeAnn Ralph as a young child, among the cows

Dad shrugged. "Well, no. Not specifically. But one of the fertilizer bags had a rip in it when I was planting corn. Spilled out in the back of the truck, so I swept up that little bit and . . ."

The author's father, who taught her that cows can be friends

"Tossed it on the garden," Mom supplied.

Dad nodded. "And now that I think about it—it was right where I planted the . . . " He threw a sheepish look in my mother's direction.

"Cucumbers," she said. By the time the cucumbers were finished, Mom had canned fifty quarts.

"I can't win," she said to me, after I'd taken the last quart of dill pickles down to the basement.

"What do you mean?"

"Dad plants lots of cucumbers, and I end up canning fifty quarts. Dad plants one hill—I still end up canning fifty quarts."

All I can say is: Good thing we liked to eat dill pickles. Otherwise, Dad never would have lived it down. Although, come to think of it, he didn't. Not for a few years, anyway . . .

(recipe appears on next page)

Dill Pickles

SUBMITTED BY LEANN R. RALPH, COLFAX, WISCONSIN

When I was growing up on our farm in west-central Wisconsin, just about everyone I knew planted a garden. And gardens meant cucumbers. And cucumbers meant dill pickles. Lunch was the highlight of any event at our church, but no lunch was complete without dill pickles. In fact, our holiday dinners at home, Sunday dinners, or even an ordinary supper were not complete without dill pickles.

Servings: 8 quarts

8 quarts pickling-sized cucumbers
Dill (either seed or fresh sprigs)
8 small onions
Alum
Garlic (powder or fresh cloves)
1 quart cider or white vinegar

3 quarts water
¼ cup sugar
1½ cups pickling salt (be sure to use
    pickling salt and not table salt; table
    salt will make the pickles mushy)

1. Thoroughly wash and rinse 8 1-quart canning jars. Wash cucumbers.

2. If you are using fresh dill, place the sprig of dill (or 1 teaspoon of dried dill seed) in the bottom of the jar. Pack the cucumbers into the jars, alternating with slices of fresh onion.

3. To each jar add ¼ teaspoon of alum (helps keep the pickles crisp), and ¼ teaspoon of garlic powder or garlic clove.

4. When the jars are packed, place the vinegar, water, sugar, and pickling salt into a large pan and bring to a boil. When the brine is hot, pour it into the packed jars.

5. Seal each jar with a new canning lid and a ring, and place the jars in a boiling water bath for 10 minutes to ensure that the jars seal. Allow the pickles to cure for at least 2 weeks before eating them.

Artichokes with Melted Butter

Never underestimate the therapeutic effects of lazily eating an artichoke, leaf by leaf. The ritual of dipping the edible nubs into lemony drawn butter and working up to the luxurious reward at the heart is a half hour of building joy.—J.W.

Servings: 1

1 large artichoke, stem trimmed to 1 inch
1 lemon, cut in half
2 ounces salted butter, melted

1. Place the artichoke in a lidded saucepan with enough water to cover it (usually about 2 quarts). Squeeze the juice from half of the lemon into the water; toss the squeezed lemon into the pot. Bring to a boil.

2. Lower the flame to a simmer, cover the pot, and cook until a fork comes easily out of the stem when poked, usually about 45 minutes. Drain.

3. Squeeze the remaining half of the lemon into the melted butter, and mix well with a fork or whisk. Peel off the outermost 6 or 7 leaves and discard them.

4. Dip remaining leaves in butter, eating edible parts, working your way in to the entirely edible heart.

Cleaning and Trimming Artichokes

To get to the "heart," or bottom, of an artichoke, use a very sharp knife to cut off most of the leaves and trim around the solid core attached to the stem. This part forms a concave well in the center that is filled with fibrous, inedible material ("choke"), which can be scooped out with a spoon. Cleaning artichokes is especially easy after they have been cooked in water with lots of lemon juice in it.

Flaky Tomato-Cheese Squares (Baked Phyllo)

SUBMITTED BY LYDIA URE, WINDSOR, ONTARIO, CANADA

Any survey of the most popular comfort foods will surely find pizza in the top twenty. For an uptown takeoff on this hometown favorite, try this extra-special, but easy to prepare, mouthwatering treat.

Servings: 8–10

4 large tomatoes
1/3 cup warm, melted butter or margarine
7 sheets phyllo dough
1/2 cup grated Parmesan cheese
1 1/4 cups mozzarella cheese, grated

1/4 large sweet onion, thinly sliced
  (Vidalia is excellent)
1 tsp. fresh or dried thyme or parsley
1/2 tsp. crumbled dried oregano
Salt and pepper to taste

1. Cut the tomatoes into 1/4-inch slices. Drain on paper towels.

2. Brush some of the melted butter on a baking sheet large enough to fit a sheet of phyllo. Lay 1 sheet of phyllo on baking sheet, keeping remainder covered with a damp cloth. Brush lightly with more of the butter. Sprinkle with 1 tablespoon of Parmesan cheese. Repeat layering with remaining phyllo, ending with phyllo. Reserve 2 tablespoons of Parmesan cheese.

3. Sprinkle top sheet with mozzarella cheese and onion. Arrange tomato slices in a layer over top. Sprinkle with remaining Parmesan cheese, thyme or parsley, and oregano. Season with salt and pepper.

4. Bake in 375° oven for 30 minutes or until golden.

5. Cut into squares and serve warm.

Eggs of an hour, bread of a day, wine of a year, a friend of thirty years.

Italian Proverb

Daisy Deviled Eggs

SUBMITTED BY SHARON PALMER, BRADBURY, CALIFORNIA

I remember warm summer afternoons from my childhood, the grownups sitting lazily in the shade while the kids kicked up their bare feet like ponies. Mom would bring out a large round platter of deviled eggs for a premeal snack. We could devour them in one bite, letting the creamy filling burst in our mouths. There's just something about these melt-in-your-mouth standbys that makes you want to go Mmmmm and reach for another!

Servings: 12
1 dozen large eggs
⅓ cup mayonnaise
½ tsp. salt
½ tsp. black pepper
1 tsp. prepared yellow mustard
1 tsp. white vinegar
4 iceberg lettuce leaves
1 bunch green onions

1. Prepare hard-boiled eggs according to the instructions on the next page. Cool in refrigerator or under running water.

2. Set aside 1 egg. Peel remaining eggs and slice into halves horizontally. Scoop out egg yolks, keeping whites intact.

(recipe continued on next page)

3. Place egg yolks in mixing bowl; stir in mayonnaise, salt, black pepper, prepared yellow mustard, and white vinegar with a fork, whipping until fluffy. Refill each egg white with yolk mixture.

4. Peel reserved egg and slice into cross-sectional slices. Arrange iceberg lettuce leaves to cover the surface of a platter. Arrange clusters of deviled eggs in the shape of a flower, with the deviled eggs as the petals and 1 slice of plain hard-boiled egg as the center. Use green onion for the stem of the daisy. Chill until serving time.

My family gathered around the family station wagon in search of a summer picnic spot

The Secret to Perfect Hard-Boiled Eggs

Bring eggs to a rapid boil in enough water to cover them by 1 inch. Boil 1 minute only, then remove from heat, cover the pan, and let sit undisturbed for exactly 15 minutes. Transfer the eggs to an ice-water bath for 15 to 20 minutes. Voilà! Perfect hard-boiled eggs: easy to peel, delicate whites, and fully cooked yolks, without a hint of the gray shadow characteristic of an improperly cooked egg.

Stuffed Mushrooms

My mother used to make stuffed mushrooms for her friends when they came over. I thought I'd improved the recipe when I sautéed rather than baked them, but they made for messy fingers—an hors d'oeuvre no-no. Sometimes Mother really does know best.—J.W.

Servings: 8

24 small white mushrooms
1 Tbs. butter
2 cloves garlic, very finely
   chopped
1 shallot, very finely chopped, or 1
   tsp. very finely chopped onion
½ tsp. dried oregano

½ tsp. salt
1 Tbs. white wine or sherry
   (optional)
1 Tbs. finely chopped parsley
2 Tbs. grated Parmesan cheese
2 Tbs. bread crumbs
1 tsp. butter, room temperature

1. Heat oven to 375°. Remove the stems from the mushrooms and chop them finely. Line up the caps, stem side up, on a greased baking sheet, and sprinkle with a pinch of salt.

2. In a small skillet, heat the melted butter over medium heat. Add the garlic, shallot, oregano, salt, and chopped mushroom stems. Cook 5 minutes, until the shallots are soft but not browned. Add the wine and cook 1 minute more, until almost dry. Add the parsley, remove from heat, and transfer to a mixing bowl. Stir in the grated cheese and half of the bread crumbs.

3. Combine the remaining bread crumbs with the soft butter. Spoon the cooked filling into the mushroom caps, and top each with a pinch of the buttered bread crumbs. Bake 15 minutes, until the mushroom caps are soft and the tops are browned. Serve hot.

Batter-Fried Zucchini Sticks

SUBMITTED BY LYNN RUTH MILLER, PACIFICA, CALIFORNIA

The perfect Super Bowl snack food, these sticks go great with any sauce—barbecue, honey-mustard, marinara, blue cheese, ranch, or herb/garlic-flavored olive oil with a splash of balsamic vinegar. Oh, yeah! Three cheers for zukes!

Servings: 4

4 medium zucchini	*2 eggs*
1 tsp. baking powder	*⅔ cup milk*
1 cup flour	*1 Tbs. oil*
Salt and pepper to taste	*Oil for frying*

1. Cut zucchini into 3-inch sticks, about ½ inch in diameter.

2. Sift together the baking powder, flour, salt, and pepper. Beat together the eggs, milk, and oil. Whisk the flour mixture into the egg mixture.

3. Heat the oil in a heavy skillet or pot to about 360°. (A piece of zucchini should sizzle when added.) Dip the sticks into the batter and fry them in small batches until golden brown. Drain on a rack or on paper towels. Serve with warm marinara or other sauce.

Oil-Righty Then!

The best oil for frying is peanut oil. Its neutral flavor and ability to withstand high heat without burning make it an excellent medium. But most vegetable oils are suitable. Submerge foods in oil partially (panfrying) or fully (deep frying). When frying breaded foods, crumbs fall off and settle to the bottom. If allowed to stay there and burn, everything will taste like burned toast. One way to avoid this is to have a second pot ready, and when you notice buildup, pour off the good oil into the new pot. When foam appears during frying, it means some components of the oil have deteriorated, and at that point the oil will begin to seep into foods. Discard it and start over with fresh oil.

Seven Layer Fiesta

SUBMITTED BY LORETTA KEMSLEY, SYLMAR, CALIFORNIA

Quick and easy, Seven Layer Fiesta is perfect for an impromptu gathering or potluck. Use as a dip with tortilla chips, as a filler for burritos and tacos, or as a casserole.

Refried beans
Ground meat, cooked and finely crumbled,
    seasoned with taco spices and well drained
Sliced avocado or guacamole
Mild salsa, preferably in a thick or chunky paste
Sour cream
Shredded cheese: cheddar and Monterey jack
    mixture
Diced green and red peppers
Sliced black olives, for garnish (optional)
Cilantro, for garnish (optional)

1. In a large shallow bowl or glass baking dish, spread warmed refried beans in a ½-inch layer across the bottom. Repeat layering with other ingredients, as desired, making effective use of the variety of colors and flavors.

2. Garnish with sliced ripe olives and/or cilantro sprigs. Chopped lettuce, onions, salsa, and/or jalapeño peppers also make welcome toppings. Serve immediately with taco shells, flour tortillas, or tortilla chips.

Pitting an Avocado

For both types of avocado, start by cutting through the skin, down to the pit, and scoring the fruit lengthwise. Gripping both halves, give a quick twist to separate one half from the pit, leaving the other half holding that large nut. If you plan to use only half of the avocado, it's best to leave the pit in the unused portion, since it prevents the fruit from turning brown overnight. To remove the pit, hack into the middle of it with the blade of your knife, gripping the fruit in the palm of your other hand; twist the knife clockwise to loosen the pit. It should fall right out of a ripe avocado.

Grandma's Traveling Lace Tablecloth

By Judith Lynn Gyde, Toledo, Ohio

My grandma left some treasures for me when she passed away in 1988: depression glassware from her wedding, a faded teacup and saucer, Grandpa's radio that pulled in stations from overseas, a few favorite recipes, and her ivory lace tablecloth. These mementos were dear to me when I was younger, but mean even more to me now.

While I was growing up, I spent a week each summer with my grandparents in the sleepy little town of Marblehead, Ohio. Every morning, I would awake to the *bong, bong, bong* of church bells and the blare of the ferryboat horn as it left the dock for Kelley's Island. I'd jump out of bed, get dressed, and hurry downstairs. Sometimes, Grandpa would be outside already, mowing the yard with his old-fashioned push mower, or in his shop working on a new project. Grandma was always in the kitchen.

Grandma loved to bake and cook, but her special gift was hospitality. Often, the neighbor ladies would stop in to visit, and Grandma was never too busy to sit and talk with "Kid" or "Bronco." Although she was diabetic, Grandma always had homemade cookies on hand. Her friends loved her molasses cookies; so did I. We all enjoyed Grandma's sweet spirit.

My grandparents lived simply. They didn't have lavish possessions, but what they had, they cherished. Though decades old, their furniture looked relatively new. In the dining room sat their dining room table, covered with Grandma's ivory lace tablecloth. For holiday meals, the table was laden with home-cooked foods: stuffed cabbage, poppy seed bread, and yellow cake with coconut frosting. Grandma never seemed too concerned about spills, and I felt so special being a dinner guest and eating on that pretty tablecloth.

When I inherited Grandma's lace tablecloth, at first I tucked it away in a drawer for safekeeping. I didn't want any stains or snags to mar it. One day I thought about what Grandma would think of my hoarding her tablecloth, and I could almost hear her say, "Use it! Enjoy it!" So, I started bringing it out for special family and holiday meals.

Then, the husband of one of my dearest friends was transferred out of state. After the moving van left with all of their belongings, Twila called from her empty house, where she had to sit by herself for an hour or so until

Judy Gyde having tea on the tablecloth

the new owners came to pick up the keys. When I heard that, I knew I needed to be with my "Bronco," my "Kid." So, I packed a picnic basket with a thermos of tea, two teacups and saucers, molasses cookies, and Grandma's lace tablecloth. I spread the tablecloth on the living room carpet, and we sat on it and had our last tea party together. We talked about fun memories and about her new future in Chicago. We reminisced, and laughed, and cried a little. When the new owner arrived, we offered him some tea and cookies.

Another time, I took Grandma's tablecloth to a hotel, where another good friend, Gloria, was staying. I had met Gloria in France years before, under less-than-ideal circumstances. She and her husband had planned our itinerary for our stay in France, but our arrival had come at a time when Gloria was very tired from an overwhelming schedule. We did our best to be supportive and make the best of it, but ever since, I had wanted to do something special to thank her.

When I heard that Gloria and her husband were in town, I called to ask him if I could surprise her with breakfast the following day. He was delighted. So, I packed a candle, fresh fruit, pastries, my china, and Grandma's lace tablecloth. My, was Gloria surprised! What a wonderful time we shared!

Grandma's lace tablecloth has gone many places with me over the years.

I brought it along the day our pastor's family moved into their new condo. I spread it over their table and served warm vegetable soup with homemade bread to their family and the moving crew, who had worked hard that chilly November morning. Another time, after three new families had moved onto our street, I invited all the neighbor ladies to my home one evening. It was a great way to get acquainted with one another. On my dining room table was Grandma's lace tablecloth, and plates of cookies and other refreshments.

These days, that old lace tablecloth gets plenty of use, and I look forward to many more years of enjoying and nurturing family and friends around this heirloom of love. If there is anything left of Grandma's tablecloth at the end of my life, I will pass it on. ⟡

.... ⟡ ....

May your home be warmed by the love of family and friends.

Irish Toast

Ants on a Log

SUBMITTED BY LISA C. ODAFFER, BRADENTON, FLORIDA

My Brownie troop leader taught me how to make this kid-pleasing appetizer when I was seven. From then on, whenever there was a family get-together, I'd make my special contribution. I'd sit at the kitchen table with all my ingredients and implements, feeling very important as I assembled each sticky treat and arranged it prettily on a party tray.

Peanut butter

Celery sticks, 3 inches long

Raisins

Dried cranberries

1. Spread peanut butter into the groove of the celery with a butter knife.

2. Arrange three or four dried fruit "bugs" on top of the peanut butter.

Mini Potato Cups

As a change of pace from the old standby sizzling potato skins, try these refreshingly cool bite-sized spuds. Garnish with your favorite toppings.—J.W.

Servings: 8

14 baby red potatoes (about the size of a walnut), halved

¼ cup sour cream

Chives, finely chopped

Bacon, cooked and crumbled (optional)

Fresh dill (optional)

1. Use a small melon baller to make the potatoes into cups by scooping a divot from the cut side of each half. Shave a tiny bit off the opposite end, so the potato cups will stand up straight. Boil them in salty water (should be as salty as a teardrop) until tender, about 5 minutes at a rapid boil. Drain and cool.

2. Fill the cups with sour cream. I like to use a pastry bag for this, but you can use a zipper-lock bag with a corner cut off, or just spoon it in. If desired, garnish each with bacon bits or the tiniest bit of fresh dill. Serve chilled.

Guacamole and Chips

The first Mexican place I fell in love with when I moved to New York City was a hole-in-the-wall in Greenwich Village where they made guacamole at your table in a stone mortar shaped like a pig. After tasting the real McCoy, I quickly forgot all of the store-bought, made-ahead, refrigerated versions I'd ever considered "not bad." They were. Make this just before serving.—J.W.

Servings: 8

2 cloves garlic, chopped
¼ cup chopped red onion
1 small jalapeño pepper, finely chopped
4 ripe Hass avocados, halved, pitted, and scooped
    from the skin
2 Tbs. lime juice
½ tsp. salt
Freshly ground black pepper to taste
¼ cup chopped cilantro
1 plum tomato, seeded and chopped (optional)

1. In a mortar and pestle or in a mixing bowl with a fork, mash together the garlic, onion, and jalapeño. Add the avocado and mash until it forms a chunky paste. Add lime juice, salt, pepper, and cilantro, and stir to combine.

2. Garnish with chopped tomato if desired. Serve with tortilla chips or as an accompaniment to spicy food.

Homemade Tortilla Chips

Crisp fresh tortilla chips are simple to make. Just quarter a dozen high-quality store-bought corn tortillas and fry them in two cups of corn oil at 375°. Cook them in small batches until they're golden brown and sprinkle with salt. *Arriba!*

Momos (Chinese Beef Buns)

SUBMITTED BY JOSEPH LAKE, PORTLAND, OREGON

One of my favorite comfort foods is from a country I never visited. My mom got the recipe from a friend. This dish is an Americanization of the traditional Tibetan meat-and-bread "hand meal." I don't know how the tulpas haunting the Himalayas feel about it, but just writing about momos makes my mouth water.

Servings: 8 (about 32 buns)

1 envelope yeast
2 Tbs. sesame oil
1 Tbs. sugar
1 tsp. salt
2 to 3 cups all-purpose flour
1 pound ground beef

1 Tbs. soy sauce
1 beef bouillon cube in a little water
½ tsp. salt
Freshly ground black pepper to taste
3 to 4 green onions, finely chopped
Oil for frying

1. Dissolve the yeast in ¼ cup very warm water. Separately, mix the sesame oil, sugar, and 1 teaspoon salt with ¾ cup very warm water. Combine yeast, water mixture, and flour to make a stiff dough. Turn out onto floured board and knead until smooth, elastic, and very stiff (10 to 15 minutes). Cover loosely, put in a warm place, and let the dough rise to double (about 1 hour).

2. Mix meat together with soy sauce, bouillon, ½ teaspoon salt, pepper, and chopped green onions. *Note:* The bouillon in the meat is to simulate the richer taste of yak meat. Consider substituting buffalo meat without the bouillon.

(recipe continued on next page)

3. Divide risen dough into quarters. Roll each quarter into a long, thin log. Cut or pinch off about 1 to 1½ inch of each log. Roll out into a rectangle. Place approximately 1 tablespoon of meat filling onto each rectangle. Fold corners inward (like the back of an envelope) and roll flat so there is no open seam. (Don't worry if a little meat is exposed.)

4. Heat thin coat of cooking oil in a frying pan. (Add a dash of sesame oil for flavor, if you wish.) Fry each momo until golden brown. Turn oven to "warm." Stack cooked momos in layers on a baking sheet with paper towels under each layer to keep warm until serving. Do this even with the last batch—it helps drain the oil.

5. Serve hot with a dipping sauce of equal parts soy sauce and vinegar. May be frozen and reheated later, if you have leftovers, for approximately 60 seconds on medium power in the microwave.

Hostess is speechless!
Guest at the cheese tray eats the
radish mouse garnish!

By Reisfeld Boutté,
Houston, Texas

Cheese Board

Back in school, the chefs would give us rules for cheese platters. "One hard, one semihard, one semisoft, one soft." "One goat's milk, one sheep's milk, two cow's milk." "Diverse heights." "Arrange to flow counterclockwise." And on and on . . . The bottom line, though, is build an interesting cheese platter, and they will come. Here's one possible combination.—J.W.

Servings: 8

1 pound grapes
½ pound each of four cheeses
   (Example 1: A block of cheddar, a wedge of Brie, a wheel of Gouda, and a log of soft goat cheese. Example 2: A block of Italian Parmesan, a wedge of French Morbier, a chunk of Havarti, and a portion of good blue cheese.)

Sliced crisp fruits (optional) such as apples, pears, or star fruit
1 French bread
2 kinds of plain crackers (such as table water crackers and stoned wheat thins—at least 24 of each)
A large cutting board or serving tray on which a knife can be used (at least 12 inches × 18 inches)

1. Place the grapes in a solid bunch on the upper left-hand corner of the board.

2. Place the softest cheese on the lower right-hand side of the board. Use a kitchen knife to break off irregular, bite-sized pieces of the hardest cheese, leaving at least half of it uncut (in the business, we call this a "gross piece"—appealing, isn't it?). Arrange that block in front of the grapes, with the broken pieces leaning against it. Place the other cheeses anywhere on the board; cut the first 4 small pieces from each, and lean them against the gross pieces. Place a knife next to each cheese.

(recipe continued on next page)

3. If you are using a very large board, you can arrange small piles of additional fruits. If not, serve them separately. There should be some blank space on the board.

4. Just before serving, slice the French bread and arrange it with the crackers in a napkin-lined basket or bowl.

···· ❧ ····

Many's the long night I've dreamed of cheese—toasted, mostly.

Robert Louis Stevenson

Step Up from Cheez Whiz?

A beautifully composed cheese board is a great way to start or end a meal or dinner party. Three basic principles make selecting and displaying cheeses easy: various textures, various strengths, and various cuts.

Textures of cheese are based on firmness—Parmigiano Reggiano is hard, aged cheddar is semihard, Havarti and Gouda are semisoft, and Brie is soft. You should have at least three cheeses on a board, and they should be of different textures.

Strengths range from mild to very sharp. Sometimes very pungent cheese, such as raclette, is very mild in flavor.

You should have at least one strong cheese, such as cheddar, blue, or goat cheese (chèvre), and one mild, like the beautiful Morbier (which is decorated with a central layer of ash).

Finally, some of the cheeses should be left whole, uncut, until all of the cut pieces are gone. This creates an especially nice look with cheeses bearing an attractive rind, such as Parmigiano Reggiano or Stilton (an English blue cheese). The rest may be cut into attractive slices, crumbled for easy access (as in Roquefort), or left alone (as with soft, ripened cheeses like Camembert or Brie).

Party Meatballs

SUBMITTED BY ANN KIRK, SUTHERLIN, OREGON

My recipe file does double-duty as a memory box. It's filled with reminders of places I've lived and people I've known. I received this recipe from a friend, who received it from a friend, who probably received it from another friend. In our home, the word "Get-Together" is capitalized because of the sheer numbers of us sharing food and conversation. My husband comes from a close-knit family of fourteen children, and we've been known to host as many as sixty or more people at special celebrations. Everyone always enjoys this easy-to-prepare appetizer.

Servings: 8–10

2 pounds extra-lean ground beef
1 cup Italian-style dried bread crumbs
1 package dried onion soup mix
3 eggs
1 12-ounce bottle chili sauce

1½ cups water
1 cup brown sugar
1 cup drained sauerkraut
1 can whole cranberry sauce

1. Combine beef, bread crumbs, dried onion soup mix, and eggs in a bowl. Mix well. Form into meatballs.

2. Place uncooked meatballs in a glass 9- × 13-inch baking dish. Set aside while preparing sauce.

3. Put chili sauce, water, brown sugar, sauerkraut, and cranberries in a medium saucepan. Stir and simmer until ingredients are well combined. Pour sauce over uncooked meatballs.

4. Bake in 350° oven for 45 minutes.

5. Serve on a plate with toothpicks. Can also be served over rice as a main dish for 6 to 8.

Coconut Shrimp

These crunchy, scrumptious prawns can be prepared in advance and fried just before serving.—J.W.

Servings: 8–12

Oil for deep-frying (2 quarts)
3 cups plain bread crumbs
1 cup shredded coconut
45 medium (46–50 per pound) shrimp, peeled
1 cup all-purpose flour
6 eggs, beaten
45 8-inch bamboo skewers
¼ cup honey
¼ cup Dijon mustard
1 Tbs. whole grain mustard

1. Heat oil to 350° in a 2½-quart saucepan. Mix bread crumbs and coconut together.

2. Dredge each shrimp in flour, then egg, then the coconut–bread crumb mixture. Skewer each one as it is breaded so that the point of the skewer does not show.

3. Fry in small batches, being careful not to overload the pot (the oil can bubble over). Drain on paper towels and keep warm.

4. Make dip by whisking together honey and mustards.

Gone Shrimpin'!

Smaller shrimp are usually more economical, but size doesn't generally affect taste and texture. Freshness and origin do. Most shrimp are frozen within hours of being caught. Stores thaw just what they think will sell that day. You want shrimp with a clean, oceanlike smell. Even a hint of ammonia means stay away. Frozen shrimp are fine, but buy them frozen and keep them frozen until you're ready to cook them. Never buy and then freeze fresh (or partially thawed) shrimp, and never thaw and refreeze shrimp.

Crab Ball

SUBMITTED BY MARY L. MACLAY, COTTAGE GROVE, OREGON

Family gatherings are always special: Even when Uncle George starts talking politics. Even when Aunt Betty declares that her pie crust is better than Aunt Clara's. Even when the children quibble over the Monopoly game, and the grandchildren chase the cat. One thing the whole clan always agrees on is how much they love nibbling on this Crab Ball.

Servings: 8

1½ tsp. Worcestershire sauce
2 tsp. minced onion
1 cup crabmeat (fresh or 7-ounce can)
1 8-ounce package cream cheese, softened

1. Blend the Worcestershire sauce, onion, and crab into the cream cheese.

2. Line a small bowl with plastic wrap. Press the cream cheese mixture firmly into the bowl. Cover with more plastic wrap and chill at least 1 hour.

3. When ready to serve, remove the plastic wrap from the top, and place a chilled plate over the top of the bowl. Holding the plate to the bowl, quickly flip it over, and gently lift the bowl as you ease the crab ball onto the plate.

4. Serve with crackers and topped with cocktail sauce.

Cocktail Sauce

Blend together ½ cup ketchup, 2 tablespoons horseradish, 1 teaspoon lemon juice, and Tabasco to taste.

Baked Stuffed Clams

When I was growing up, for one week every summer my family went to a beach house on Fire Island and broke all of our regular culinary rules. My sister and I dug for clams in the bay with our feet, and we used a typical island recipe to make these forbidden treats.—J.W.

Servings: 8

16 cherrystone (medium-sized) clams or 24 littlenecks (small)

½ cup water or white wine

½ cup seasoned bread crumbs

1 cup chopped onion, sautéed in butter until soft

4 Tbs. melted butter

1 egg, beaten

1 tsp. Old Bay seasoning (or mixture of paprika, onion powder, and dried thyme)

¼ cup chopped Italian (flat leaf) parsley

Paprika

Lemon wedges

1. Heat oven to 425°. Steam the clams open in a covered pot with ½ cup water or white wine. Remove meat from shells and chop roughly. Reserve broth. Set aside 8 to 10 of the best shells.

2. In a mixing bowl, combine chopped clams with bread crumbs, onion, melted butter, egg, Old Bay, and parsley. Moisten with a few teaspoons of clam broth, if desired. Fill the reserved shells with the clam mixture and place in a baking dish. Dust lightly with paprika. Line up stuffed clams in a baking dish.

3. Bake 20 to 25 minutes, until tops are golden brown. Serve with lemon wedges.

····⑤····

Life is like an onion, you peel off one layer
at a time, and sometimes you weep.

Carl Sandburg

Stuffed Eggplant Rolls

These spinach-and-ricotta-filled rolls are great alone or served atop a heap of tomato-sauced spaghetti, garnished with a sprig of fresh basil. Have the deli counter at your supermarket slice the eggplant for you on the machine—it's almost impossible to do with a knife. The finished rolatine keep well for several days and are delicious at room temperature or as sandwich fillings.—J.W.

Servings: 8

1 large eggplant, sliced lengthwise into even ⅛-inch slices (as thick as the cover of a hardcover book)

Flour for dredging

Egg wash of about 6 beaten eggs, mixed with ½ cup water

4 cups bread crumbs

Oil for frying

1 pound ricotta cheese

8 ounces shredded mozzarella cheese

½ cup grated Parmesan (good quality, like Parmigiano Reggiano or Grana Padano)

Salt and pepper to taste

½ pound thinly sliced top-quality ham or Italian prosciutto

1½ pounds fresh spinach, washed and cooked, or 1 pound frozen spinach, thawed

4 cups tomato sauce

1. Dip a slice of eggplant in the flour to coat both sides. Shake off excess flour, submerge in egg wash, and shake off excess. Coat in bread crumbs, pressing to make sure they adhere well. Place on a holding tray, and repeat with remaining slices. Heat oil to about 350°. (A piece of vegetable should sizzle visibly when dropped into the oil.) Fry the breaded eggplant slices, dripping off any excess oil before stacking them between layers of paper towels.

(recipe continued on next page)

2. Heat oven to 350°. Combine the three cheeses in a mixing bowl, and season lightly with salt and pepper. Place 1 slice of ham on a slice of cooked eggplant. Spoon 1 teaspoon of cooked spinach onto the ham slice and then a generous teaspoon of cheese mixture at the wide end. Roll away from yourself, jellyroll-style, and place into a baking dish, with the seam on the bottom. Repeat with remaining eggplant and fillings, lining the finished rolatine close together in the baking dish. Bake until cheeses are visibly hot and the edges begin to brown lightly.

3. Serve on a pool of tomato sauce, garnished with basil leaves. One piece per appetizer portion, two per main course.

A real friend will tell you when you have spinach stuck in your teeth.

Anonymous

Eggplant's Bitterness

When sliced eggplant is sprinkled with salt it sheds some of its inherent bitterness along with the salty droplets that form along its surface. Eggplants vary widely in flavor and intensity, and some delicate bitter edge helps define this beautiful vegetable's character. Therefore, many people choose not to take the step of salting an eggplant and rinsing the extracted juices at all. Those who do leave the eggplant for ten to twenty minutes, then rinse the eggplant and use it according to their recipe. Long, slender, violet-hued Japanese eggplants contain none of the bitterness of America's large black variety. Pear-sized Italian-style eggplants are similar to our regular ones, but white-skinned varieties are milder.

Roasted Garlic Dip

SUBMITTED BY JUNE BURNS, APACHE JUNCTION, ARIZONA

Who says nobody loves a garlic-lover? You'll get hugs all around when you whip up a batch of this scrumpdelilicious garlicky dip. Add roasted bell pepper for an extra zing!

Yield: 1 cup (about 4 servings)

1 head of garlic, roasted
¼ cup roasted red pepper, canned
    (pimento) or fresh, roughly chopped
    (optional)
1 cup plain yogurt (or mayonnaise)

1 Tbs. cream cheese, room temperature
2 Tbs. finely chopped parsley
¼ tsp. salt
¼ tsp. black pepper
Dash Tabasco

1. While the garlic and red pepper are roasting, put the yogurt into a fine mesh strainer suspended over a bowl. Discard the liquid from under the yogurt; then put the yogurt into a bowl.

2. Add the cream cheese, parsley, salt, pepper, and Tabasco to the yogurt and mix well.

3. When the garlic is done and cooled, cut the head in half laterally. Gently push the roasted garlic through the strainer with your hands. Discard the skins. Whisk together the garlic and yogurt mixture until it is smooth.

4. Season to taste. Garnish with roasted red pepper, if desired. Serve with vegetable sticks and/or bread.

How to Roast Garlic

Wrap a whole garlic in foil and bake for 1 hour in a 350° oven. Cut the head in half laterally and squeeze out the softened roasted garlic. For a smooth paste, push through a mesh strainer. Add to mashed potatoes, polenta, omelets, or whatever.

Curry Dip

Finger food pleases in a way that fork-and-knife chow never can. There's a tactile pleasure in holding a morsel of food—feeling it in your hand. Even the sensation of swiping a carrot stick through a delicious dip adds to the comfort of the ritual. This dip is excellent for raw vegetables, chips, and bread sticks.—J.W.

Servings: 12

1 tsp. unsalted butter

½ cup finely chopped onion

½ medium jalapeño pepper, chopped fine (about 1 tsp.)

2 tsp. finely chopped red bell pepper

1 tsp. Madras curry powder

1 tsp. ground cumin

½ tsp. ground coriander

½ tsp. ground turmeric

Pinch cayenne pepper

¼ tsp. salt

1 Tbs. very fresh, soft raisins (or any raisins, soaked overnight in ½ cup water and drained)

1½ cups mayonnaise

1 Tbs. chopped fresh cilantro

A few drops fresh lemon juice

Salt and pepper to taste

1. Melt the butter in a small skillet over medium heat. Add onion, jalapeño, and red pepper; cook, stirring occasionally, until onion is translucent, about 5 minutes. Add curry powder, cumin, coriander, turmeric, cayenne, and salt. Cook a minute more, until spices are very fragrant. Add raisins and about 1 tablespoon of water. Remove from heat.

2. Transfer to a food processor. Chop on high speed for 30 seconds; scrape down sides of bowl with a rubber spatula. Add mayonnaise and cilantro; process 30 seconds more, until smooth and even. Adjust seasoning with lemon, salt, and pepper.

Crisp Potato Pancakes (Latkes)

SUBMITTED BY TARA CHAPMAN, WINDSOR, ONTARIO, CANADA

Our family enjoys "baby" latkes as a late-night snack while watching movies together. Latkes can be made ahead of time and warmed just before serving.

Servings: 4

1 large egg
3 large baking potatoes (such as Idaho), peeled
1 medium onion
1 carrot, peeled (optional)
1 baby zucchini, peeled (optional)
1 tsp. salt
1 Tbs. flour
Clarified butter or vegetable oil (or olive or peanut oil) for frying

1. Beat the egg in a large bowl.

2. Using the large-hole side of a box grater, shred the potatoes in long motions, forming the lengthiest shreds possible. Quickly grate in the onion. Grate in carrot and zucchini, if desired.

3. Add the salt and sprinkle in the flour; toss with your hands to combine well.

4. Heat the clarified butter until it shimmers but does not smoke. (A piece of potato should sizzle upon entry.) Form 8 pancakes from the batter, and panfry in batches of 3 or 4, squeezing out excess water before gently sliding each pancake into the pan.

5. Cook the pancakes slowly, without moving them, for the first 5 minutes, then loosen with a spatula. Turn after about 8 minutes, when the top appears one-third cooked. Finish cooking on other side, about 4 minutes more. Drain on paper towels.

6. Serve with sour cream, jam, or applesauce, or plain sprinkled with sugar.

chapter three

Packing a Basket, Taking a Break
Salads and Sandwiches

Making Something Out of Nothing

BY LISA C. ODAFFER, BRADENTON, FLORIDA

It was just starting to get dark outside. Dad was sitting at the kitchen table with the lights off. The cheery kitchen colors that reminded me so much of my mother were turning gray in the deepening dusk. My brother and I peeked at him from the doorway.

"What's he doing?" Rusty asked.

"Shhh! He'll hear you!" I hissed.

My brother was six years old, in the first grade, and full of annoying questions. I was eight and pretty sure I knew almost everything. For one thing, I knew that Dad was probably thinking, staring off into space like that, and shouldn't be bothered.

"I'm hungry," Rusty whined softly, "When are we gonna eat?"

It had been our first day at the babysitter's house after school.

Bonnie was a small woman with close-set eyes, and she did not believe in between-meal snacks. Rusty's face had clouded with confusion as he stood forlornly in Bonnie's kitchen.

"But Mom always gives me a snack after school," his voice quivered.

"Well, I'm not your mother, am I?" Bonnie retorted, clearly annoyed.

Rusty started to cry.

This irritated Bonnie even more. She sent him to the bathroom and told him to stay there until he "stopped his sniveling."

Bonnie's daughter Amy was in my third-grade class. She and her popular friends liked to tease me when I got good grades. Knowing almost everything definitely had its downside. Later that afternoon,

Amy and I lay on her living room rug, propped up on our elbows, watching *The Brady Bunch.* She leaned over and whispered a singsong playground taunt in my ear.

"Nyah! Nyah! Your momma doesn't love you! Nyah! Nyah! She left you with your daddy!"

I knew she was trying to make me cry, so that Bonnie would order me into the now-empty bathroom. I stuck my fingers in my mouth and made a face at her, then bit my tongue to keep the tears from coming.

The Brady family smiled and frolicked on the T.V. screen. Mr. and Mrs. Brady put their arms around each other and nodded approvingly at their children. Why couldn't my family be that way?

It was almost totally dark. Rusty had slipped past me into the kitchen and was tugging on Dad's sleeve.

"Daddy? Daddy! I'm hungry!"

I switched on the light. Dad scratched his head and looked at us as though he was seeing us for the first time.

Lisa Odaffer, right, with her father and brother in 1977

"Ahh, okay. Dinner. . . . Right. What do you kids like to eat?"

"Hot dogs!" I said. "There's a brand new bottle of ketchup!"

"Pizza!" Rusty chimed in.

Dad was warming to the idea. "Hmm. Well, let's see about that."

We began to jump up and down, offering more helpful suggestions.

"Hamburgers!"

"Potato chips!"

"Ice cream!"

"Chocolate pudding!"

We all went to the refrigerator together. Rusty was still jumping around and making suggestions, while Dad pulled the door open with a laugh. It was nearly empty inside. Mom had made us a casserole for the weekend, but it now sat empty with the other unwashed dishes in the sink. I felt my heart sink in my chest. She really was gone. Who was going to take care of us?

Rusty looked like he was going to cry. "We're gonna starve!" he whimpered.

There was some milk and all the condiments, but the crisper was empty, and the only thing in the meat drawer was a package of breakfast sausage. Dad grabbed the sausage, sat down on his heels, and looked us in the eyes.

"Hey, don't worry!" he said, ruffling Rusty's hair. "I'm a great cook! Didn't I ever tell you that before you two were born I was a cook in the Yew-ni-ted States Army National Guard?"

It was quite a shock for a girl who knew almost everything to discover that her dad had done something so amazing.

"This is no problem!" he said. "In my Army days they taught us how to cook really great meals for hundreds of men out of practically nothing!"

Rusty and I looked at each other, dumbfounded.

"As a matter of fact, we have just enough of nothing to make my all-time favorite meal!"

"Pizza?" Rusty said hopefully.

Dad had a triumphant gleam in his eye. "Creamed sausage over toast!"

This was more new information than I could stand. Who ever heard of such a thing? "Creamed what over who?" I asked.

"Creamed sausage!" he said, "Over toast. It's really good!"

"Can I put ketchup on it?" Rusty asked skeptically. He liked ketchup on everything. Even pizza.

Dad handed Rusty the ketchup bottle. "Oh, definitely! As much as you want. In fact, those soldiers loved to put ketchup on everything. It's pretty much not Army food if you can't put ketchup on it."

He pulled two kitchen chairs up to the stove and set one of us on either side of him so we could watch the proceedings as he described each step. He let me stir the meat as it browned, and he helped Rusty work the toaster. Then he poured in the last of the milk from our barren refrigerator to make the creamy sauce.

It became our favorite meal. That night and for many, many nights thereafter, we sat at the table and listened to Dad tell us stories about his days in the Army and all sorts of other adventures that he had as a young man. He told us tales from our family history and about all his hopes for our futures. As an eight-year-old girl who wanted to know everything, I had my work cut out for me. I asked him to tell them over and over again, until I knew it all by heart.

Now, as an adult, whenever I make creamed sausage over toast, it reminds me of how much my dad loved us and how hard he worked to be both father and mother. Most of all, it reminds me of the way he took the three of us and made something out of nothing.

Creamed Sausage over Toast

Submitted by Lisa C. Odaffer, Bradenton, Florida

Although my little brother liked to eat this meal swimming in ketchup (yuck), it tastes much better without it!

Servings: 4

1 tube of breakfast sausage (or any variety of ground sausage that you prefer)
3 Tbs. butter
3 Tbs. sweet onions, peeled and chopped
3 Tbs. flour
2 cups hot milk

¼ tsp. paprika
Black pepper to taste
Dash of Tabasco (optional)
About ⅓ loaf of white bread for toast (your favorite bread works just as well)

1. Cook sausage, drain, set aside. Melt butter in saucepan.

2. Sauté yellow onion until translucent. Stir in flour with a whisk to make a roux.

3. Add hot milk and stir until sauce thickens.

4. Mix in cooked meat and spices. Serve over toast.

Tossed Green Salad Dressings

SUBMITTED BY JUNE BURNS, APACHE JUNCTION, ARIZONA

Tossed green salad goes with everything, and just about anything can go into a green salad. A daily salad is also good for you. So, eat your salad, but have some fun with it! Mix and match a variety of lettuces; leafy vegetables like spinach, chard, and cabbage; fresh sliced, chopped, and julienned vegetables; seeds and toasted nuts; dried and fresh fruits; blue, Gorgonzola, or Parmesan cheese; croutons or crispy rice noodles. And substitute different homemade dressings for that same-old, same-old bottle of ranch. Here are three easy and unique salad dressings that will add pizzazz to your salads!

Honey-Orange Dressing

Servings: 8

1½ tsp. ground ginger
3 ounces orange juice
3 ounces honey
1¼ tsp. orange zest
3 Tbs. white vinegar
3 Tbs. vegetable oil
½ tsp. salt and a few
    grinds black pepper

1. Moisten the ginger in a small mixing bowl with a few drops of the orange juice. Whisk in remaining ingredients.
2. Store in a jar with a tight-fitting lid, and refrigerate for up to 2 weeks. Shake vigorously before using.

Strawberry-Dijon Dressing

Servings: 4

¼ cup sour cream
3 Tbs. Dijon mustard
2 Tbs. honey
4½ tsp. strawberry vinegar
    (available in gourmet
    food shops)
¾ tsp. chopped fresh
    cilantro
¾ tsp. poppy seeds
¾ tsp. lime juice

1. Whisk together all ingredients in a mixing bowl.
2. Keep refrigerated. Use within 5 days.

Cherry Vinaigrette

Servings: 10 (2 cups)

¾ cup cherry juice
½ cup sugar
¼ cup cider vinegar
Pinch cayenne pepper
1 cup salad oil
Salt and pepper to taste

1. Combine all ingredients in a small jar or container with a tight-fitting lid. Shake vigorously.
2. Refrigerate between uses, for up to 2 weeks.

Cole Slaw

For freshness and flavor, why not whip up a batch of this creamy slaw instead of buying the over-priced stuff at the deli? Your loved ones and your palate will appreciate the little bit of extra effort. Great for backyard barbecues, a fresh-catch fish fry with angling buddies, warm-weather luncheons, cold-weather seafood dinners, and burgers anytime.—J.W.

Servings: 8

1 tsp. salt
1 Tbs. sugar
Juice of 1 lemon (about a scant ¼ cup)
1 cup mayonnaise
½ head white or green cabbage (or ¼ head each), shredded (about 8 cups)
2 cups grated carrot (about 3 carrots)
1 Tbs. roughly chopped parsley

1. Combine the salt, sugar, lemon, and mayonnaise in a mixing bowl and whisk together well.

2. Toss dressing with the cabbage, carrots, and parsley. Adjust seasonings to taste. The slaw will soften and the flavor will enhance overnight.

When hospitality becomes an art, it loses its very soul.
Max Beerbohm

A Slice of Summer
*By Helen A. Quade,
Palatine, Illinois*

We circle around daddy
who rests the cool melon
from the cellar on the table.

With sharpened knife
he pierces
    the dark green rind,
cracking it wide open.

Eagerly, we bite into
red half-moons he slices
and lightly salts.

Sweet juice
runs in rivulets
down our chins.

We spit black seeds
into the powdery dust
at our feet.

Katydids sing
in the limbs
above us.

Beefsteak Tomato and Avocado Sandwich

on Baguette with Aïoli (Garlic Mayonnaise)

It must have been after feasting on these amazing sandwiches that the French dubbed the tomato the "love apple"! 'Tis amour at first bite!—J.W.

Servings: 4

1 cup mayonnaise

¼ tsp. cayenne pepper

4 cloves garlic, finely chopped

1 baguette (crusty French bread)

2 ripe Hass avocados, peeled, pitted, and sliced
   roughly ¼-inch thick

Juice of 1 lime

Salt and pepper to taste

3 large, ripe beefsteak tomatoes, sliced ½-inch
   thick, salted

1. Make aïoli in a food processor or mixing bowl by combining mayonnaise, cayenne, and garlic. Cut the baguette lengthwise and slather generously with aïoli.

2. Toss avocado slices with lime juice, salt, and pepper. Spread into an even layer on the bottom of the French bread. Next, layer on the center-cut slices of tomato.

3. Close the sandwich, and divide with a sharp knife into 4 equal portions.

Checking Avocados for Ripeness

California (Hass) avocados should be forest green to green-black, and the small stem nub should fall out easily. The pulp should yield to gentle pressure from the palm of your hand and feel like modeling clay through the skin. Florida avocados remain green when ripe, so touch is the only indicator of ripeness. All avocados are harvested unripe. They ripen quickly at room temperature and can be rushed by storing them in a closed paper bag.

Curried Chicken Salad

SUBMITTED BY GINNIE SIENA BIVONA, DALLAS, TEXAS

What better way to celebrate spring—or a new member of the family (wee one or wedding), or a promotion or retirement—than a lovely afternoon tea party? This salad is perfect for tea sandwiches.

Servings: 8

4 chicken breasts

4 cups chicken broth

1 cup mayonnaise

¼ cup raspberry vinegar

2 Tbs. cider vinegar

2½ Tbs. sugar

3 Tbs. hot curry powder or regular plus a pinch cayenne

¼ cup diced apple

¼ cup dried sweetened cranberries, halved

½ cup diced red pepper

6 green onions, sliced

¼ cup white raisins

¼ cup slivered almonds

Pinch salt

1. Poach chicken breasts by placing them in the boiling chicken broth, bringing back to a simmer, cooking 5 minutes, and then allowing them to cool, tightly covered, in the poaching liquid for at least 30 minutes. Chill meat and dice into ½-inch pieces.

2. Meanwhile, prepare the dressing by combining the mayonnaise, vinegars, sugar, and curry powder; whisk together until smooth.

3. Toss the diced cooked chicken with the dressing, apple, dried cranberries, red pepper, green onions, raisins, almonds, and salt.

···· ❧ ····

Chicken salad has a certain glamour about it. Like the little black dress, it is chic and adaptable and can be taken anywhere. You can dress it down and feed it to a child, or dress it up and serve it at a dinner party. You can accessorize it in an interesting way and astonish your friends at lunch.

Laurie Colwin

Oceanside Picnic

By Barbara Beaudoin, Chelmsford, Massachusetts

When my friends went to the beach with their families, they usually brought along a picnic lunch of peanut butter and jelly sandwiches for the kids, boiled ham and American cheese sandwiches for the adults, hard-boiled eggs, and celery sticks. No one I knew had an Italian grandmother who cooked macaroni at the beach, and I was too embarrassed to mention that detail to most of my friends.

Rosa P.

To my grandparents, aunts, and cousins, an oceanside outing often included a driving trip to Nahant Beach near Boston, where beachgoers could cook on the stone fireplaces set up on the sand. Most people enjoyed hot dogs and hamburgers, but not us. We gathered the dry driftwood on the beach, stacked it in the open fireplace, and boiled large pots of water for the spaghetti and macaroni to be served with chicken, meatballs, or snails simmered in red tomato sauce. As the sun started to drop in the sky, we spread out huge white tablecloths (or maybe they were sheets?) on picnic tables and brought out the crockery, pasta bowls, cutlery, warm bread, and, of course, the red wine— which was mixed with orange soda and served over ice.

Oceanside picnic, circa 1950

I did not appreciate the delicacy of snails then (or now), but I treasure the memories of those summer days. I can still feel the warm shore breeze seasoned with the aromas of all that good food as we ate, talked, and simply enjoyed each other's company. Those were, indeed, such "happy days."

Panini

Submitted by Barbara Beaudoin, Chelmsford, Massachusetts

With all the goodies piled high on thick, chewy bread, happy days are truly here again! Great for a day at the beach, a picnic in the park, or a hearty lunch after a Little League game.

Servings: 4

1 loaf crusty Italian bread
Extra-virgin olive oil seasoned with salt, pepper, garlic, basil, oregano, and sage
¼ pound mortadella
¼ pound salami
¼ pound capicolla (Italian peppered ham)
¼ pound prosciutto or boiled ham

¼ pound provolone
3 thin slices fresh mozzarella
4 thin slices Fontina cheese or other Italian cheese
Olive oil
Lettuce leaves and sliced tomatoes
Thinly sliced onions
Pickled mushrooms, pepperoncini, artichokes, and black olives to taste

1. Slice bread lengthwise. Spread the inside of the bread with seasoned extra-virgin olive oil. Layer the meats and cheeses. Add your choice of condiments. Press the top of the bread firmly back onto the sandwich, and define portions with long sandwich picks or toothpicks.

2. Cut between the picks, using a sharp serrated knife.

Potato Salad à la Grieco

SUBMITTED BY BARBARA BEAUDOIN, CHELMSFORD, MASSACHUSETTS

Got a craving for the kind of potato salad Mom used to make? Try this! It's even better (or at least a close second). One bite, and it's just like being home again, sitting together at a picnic table on a warm summer day, munching and talking and watching the hummingbirds flit by.

Josie Grieco Beaudoin with her hungry men Edward and Edward Jr.

Servings: 6

2 pounds potatoes (red bliss or new)
2 Tbs. finely chopped onion
2 Tbs. finely chopped celery
2 Tbs. finely diced green, red, and/or
    yellow pepper
1 kosher dill pickle, finely chopped
1 hard-boiled egg, quartered
1 tsp. salt

Black pepper to taste
¼ cup mayonnaise
¾ tsp. granulated sugar
Pinch dry mustard or ½ tsp. Dijon
1 Tbs. cider vinegar, to taste
1½ tsp. pickle juice
2 Tbs. sliced black or green olives,
    optional

1. Peel potatoes and cook in a large pot of water until tender but firm. Cool potatoes and cut into chunks. In a large bowl, combine potatoes with onion, celery, peppers, chopped pickle, egg, salt, and pepper.

2. In small bowl, make the dressing by whisking together the mayonnaise, sugar, mustard, vinegar, and pickle juice. Add the dressing to the potato mixture. Toss lightly. Garnish with olives, if desired. Chill thoroughly before serving.

Cucumber Sandwich Spread

SUBMITTED BY BETH LYNN CLEGG, HOUSTON, TEXAS

My paternal grandmother often made me cucumber and cream cheese sandwiches. It was during the Depression, when nothing was wasted. So, when I saw Grandma cutting off the crust as she prepared them for her bridge club, I was amazed. To me, from then on, these simple yet elegant sandwiches represented better days ahead. In good times and not-so-good times, I can always count on these refreshing little canapés to satisfy both the big kids and the little ones—for brunch or lunch, afternoon or evening tea, a bridal shower or a holiday open house.

Yield: 2 cups

1 12-ounce package of cream cheese, softened

1 medium large cucumber, pared and drained

¼ cup grated onion

1 Tbs. lemon juice

½ tsp. dill weed

Salt and pepper to taste

1. Allow cream cheese to reach room temperature.

2. Place all ingredients in a blender and blend for 30 seconds. Check consistency (it should be creamy) and for lumps; if needed, scootch mixture around with wooden spoon (with blender off), and blend another 10 seconds.

3. Serve with thinly sliced high-quality white bread—with the crusts removed, if you'd like—or with mini-sandwich loaves from the deli, melba toast, or crackers.

Happiness is like potato salad: When shared with others, it is a picnic.

Anonymous

Grilled Cheese Sandwiches

While I was working on this book, my mom timidly asked me if grilled cheese sandwiches with sliced tomatoes fit the definition of comfort food. What did she think I'd say?—J.W.

Servings: 1

1 Tbs. soft butter
2 slices white bread
2 slices American cheese
2 thin slices of ripe tomato

1. Heat a heavy-bottomed skillet over medium heat. Butter both slices of bread. Place the cheese on one side, and top with the tomato slices. Close the sandwich (buttered side out on both sides).

2. Cook the sandwich, with the cheese side on the bottom, until it's golden and the cheese has melted. Turn and cook on the other side. Eat hot.

Good health is born of the earth
and the sun and the cooking pot.

French Proverb

How to "Grill" with a Toaster Oven

Instead of frying the sandwich, we used to toast the bread lightly, and place the cheese on one slice and the tomato on the other. Then we'd put both slices on a tray in the toaster oven and cook a minute more, until the cheese melted, before assembling the halves into a sandwich and eating. No butter was used.

Jim Ackland's Grilled Cheese Sandwiches

SUBMITTED BY KAREN ACKLAND, SANTA CRUZ, CALIFORNIA

My father made grilled cheese sandwiches usually on Saturdays, and they weren't anything like the American-cheese-on-white-bread diner variety. We constantly experimented with different cheeses, breads, condiments, and complements. But the most distinctive thing about Dad's grilled cheese sandwiches is that he made them with a waffle iron. For a long time, I thought that's the way they were supposed to be, and when I finally saw a friend make one in a pan, it just wasn't the same.

Servings: 4

8 slices sourdough, cracked wheat, or
   rye bread, sliced
1 stick butter, softened
Coarse mustard or horseradish
2 cups grated cheese such as cheddar,
   Monterey jack, Swiss, Gouda, or a
   combination

4 slices ham or turkey
¼ cup canned roasted green chilies,
   chopped
4 thin slices tomato, cut in half
8 strips roasted red peppers, 1 inch wide
½ cup sautéed onion (about 1 small)
¼ cup sautéed mushrooms

1. Heat a cast-iron skillet or griddle over a low flame. Butter one side of bread. Spread choice of mustard, horseradish, or other condiments on the other side. Layer on the cheese, ham, roasted chilies, tomato, roasted red pepper, onion, and mushrooms, then top with another slice of bread, buttered side out.

2. Lay 2 sandwiches at a time into the skillet, starting with the cheese side, and cook slowly until very crisp and golden brown, pressing occasionally with a spatula and turning only once. Allow to rest 5 minutes before cutting.

Follow the Yellow-Checked Tablecloth

BY COLLEEN SELL, EUGENE, OREGON

Many moons ago, when I was a newly divorced full-time working mom with three children ranging in age from three to eleven years old, I was suddenly flattened with multiple sclerosis. One dreary February afternoon, during what turned out to be a six-month leave of absence, my coworker and friend Cathy showed up at my house with a picnic basket and a videotape of *The Wizard of Oz*. She spread a bright yellow-and-white checked tablecloth (remembering, remarkably, that my favorite color is yellow) on our family room floor, and the five of us sat there and munched on turkey sandwiches, macaroni salad, her famous "Brooklyn brownies," and sun tea (a specialty of Arizona, where the two of us northeasterners had somehow ended up) as we watched Dorothy and Toto try to find their way home. When the flying monkeys scared the bejeebers out of my toddler son, Cathy picked him up and cuddled him in her lap. And when Dorothy sang "Somewhere over the Rainbow," we all sang along, just as if we knew that one day we, too, would find our rainbow and our way home again. Then again, maybe we already had, right there on that yellow checked tablecloth in the middle of my family room in the middle of the Arizona desert.

Macaroni Salad

*Follow the yellow brick road to home sweet home with
the simple magic of homemade macaroni salad.—J.W.*

Servings: 8
1 box (1 pound) elbow macaroni
1 cup mayonnaise
1 tsp. sugar
1 Tbs. lemon juice
2 tsp. salt
Freshly ground black pepper to taste
1 medium carrot, peeled and grated coarsely
¼ cup finely chopped shallot or onion
¼ cup chopped parsley

1. Boil the macaroni until quite soft. (You want it softer for
pasta salad than you would if it was eaten hot, since it firms
when chilled.) Run under cold water to cool.

2. Whisk together the mayonnaise, sugar, lemon juice, salt,
and pepper. Dress the macaroni with this mixture. Toss with
the carrot, shallot, and parsley.

···· ····

Friendships, like geraniums, bloom in kitchens.

Blanche E. Gelfant

Orange Salad

SUBMITTED BY BEATRICE SHEFTEL, MANCHESTER, CONNECTICUT

This simple recipe came down from my grandmother, who prepared it as she traveled steerage from Sicily to New York. It prevented scurvy. After she safely reached Ellis Island and began her new life in the United States, Grandma's orange salad became a delightful light lunch for her family. I learned to make it and to love it from "taking tea" with my Aunt Kit.

Servings: 2

2 large navel oranges
Pure virgin olive oil
Garlic powder (or
    2 cloves, minced)
    to taste

Pepper, to taste
2 slices of good bread

Herb Algebra

Dried herbs are stronger than fresh, and powered herbs are stronger than crumbled dried herbs. As a rule of thumb: ½ teaspoon of powered herb = ¾ to 1 teaspoon of crumbled herb = 2 teaspoons of fresh herb.

1. Peel the oranges. (If you put the orange peel on a warm stove, the heat will warm the skins and send the scent of orange wafting through your home.)

2. Separate each orange into sections, 1 orange per bowl. Slice each orange section into quarters, keeping the orange in or over the bowl to retain all the juices.

3. Add a capful of olive oil (¼ to ½ teaspoon) to each bowl. Sprinkle with garlic powder, or mix in 1 garlic clove, minced, per bowl. Sprinkle with black pepper. Mix the seasonings into the oranges.

4. Serve with a slice of warm (not toasted) bread, per serving.

5. Eat the oranges with a tea or salad fork and dip the bread into the juice.

A Perfect Three-Minute Egg

By Melissa Pasanen, Burlington, Vermont

I pulled out my favorite skillet immediately after coming home from the hospital.

For one long month, I'd eaten adequate but uninspired meals as I lay in my hospital bed, trying to keep my unripe baby inside. Choosing my meals from the menu distracted me from the monotony of each hospital day.

Anti-contraction drugs had reduced my limbs to the consistency of overcooked spaghetti and made my brain too foggy for challenges greater than *People* magazine. Juicy profiles of the stars and wide-eyed portraits of everyday heroes briefly diverted me, but I always ended up wondering how Madonna, who was also pregnant at the time, would have handled pre-term labor. To escape the magazines, I switched to television.

Soaps and daytime talk shows revealed the worst in people, so I resorted to cooking shows. As I sipped murky, gray-green vegetable soup, I watched chefs prepare seared sea bass in a sesame crust, ginger crème brûlée with candied tangerine, and lamb-sausage-stuffed poblano chilies. For a few minutes, I would almost forget how much I missed my two-and-a-half-year-old son. I would briefly ignore the constant nervous anticipation of the next round of rhythmic contractions.

Every few days my body would overpower the medication, and doctors would unleash a daylong course of powerful muscle relaxants into my bloodstream. My body would enter a dreamlike state of extreme slow motion. For the next twenty-four hours, I couldn't eat. I could barely even think.

Shortly after the last dose snaked down long plastic tubing into my arm, the doctors would give me permission to eat again. Despite nausea and exhaustion, I relished my appetizer of salty, microwaved chicken noodle soup and crisp toast with peanut butter. My husband, happy to have a task, would arrive with my requested main course: good bread with tangy goat cheese and cracked green olives, or chewy pad thai noodles twisted around fat pink shrimp.

After two weeks, my husband and I gave up our aching hope that I would go home. We were just relieved to make it through another day avoiding birth. Repeated tests could not explain why I persistently went into labor. The monitors showed a healthy baby, development appropriate for five-and-a-half months. I felt betrayed by my body.

Late one Sunday evening, my reflexes cut through the drug decoy for the final time. We were very lucky. Although he was eleven weeks early, our three-pound baby boy arrived safely. He was classified a "feeder and grower" and greenhoused in the neonatal intensive care unit.

As soon as I got my land legs back, I returned to my life and my kitchen. Across town, minute amounts of laboriously pumped breast milk dripped constantly through a feeding tube into Alex's tender stomach. My skillet weighed more than he did for the five weeks he remained in the hospital.

I juggled the needs of my older son with those of my tiny new baby in his plastic incubator bubble. While kicking the soccer ball with my rambunctious preschooler, I felt I was neglecting the fragile newborn still in the hospital.

Alex, three pounds at birth, on his favorite fourth birthday present

During the hours I spent cradling Alex's doll-sized translucent body against my chest, I recalled the wistful look on his older brother's face. Even the coldest mother-in-law would have forgiven me if our family diet had consisted of Chinese takeout and pizza during the period that I wore a path between home and hospital.

But I needed to cook. I dug out my bursting file of recipes—torn, cut, and copied. I made meals I had never cooked before. I dared to use new ingredients and flavors I had previously disliked: licorice-scented fennel, yellow and red peppers, alarming amounts of chili powder, woody lemon grass, pungent fish sauce, and sweet dusky cardamom.

New recipes distracted me; preparing old favorites provided refuge. The morning a nurse reported that Alex had lost weight two days in a row, I made creamy macaroni and cheese. Life might spin out of control, but I could still make a white sauce. Ounce by ounce, his weight crept up. When it hit a hefty four-and-a-half pounds, we brought Alex home and celebrated with a chunky ratatouille of late summer eggplant and tomatoes from the garden.

Alex enjoying his fourth birthday party

Finally, I relaxed. I even made an occasional bowl of egg salad for dinner—best when eaten by the spoonful like I did as a child.

In a quilt of soothing food memories, my ultimate comfort food has always been the egg. When I was sick, my mother cracked soft-boiled eggs into a bowl of buttered toast pieces, which became richly saturated with the yolk. Now, on the evenings when my two boys throw ketchup-soaked fish sticks at each other during the evening witching hour, I sometimes slip a couple of eggs in to boil.

The problem is that they come out right only half the time. It is a delicate balance. I can't eat a soft-boiled egg that is too soft, because a runny white makes me gag. But if it's overcooked, the yolk remains stubbornly distinct from the toast. Because I only cook soft-boiled eggs when I'm on the edge, my failure to make them right can send me over.

If I examined my successes and failures scientifically, I think I could develop the perfect method. But, as I learned in the hospital, sometimes even science doesn't have the answer. About half of all premature labor has no obvious medical explanation and responds to no treatment. An egg is not a mass-produced microwave dinner. Each one is unique, born of nature, not machinery, and nurturing one successfully requires as much good fortune as science.

"A Perfect Three-Minute Egg" was first published on Salon.com, *March 7, 2000.*

Melissa Pasanen's Egg Salad

SUBMITTED BY MELISSA PASANEN, BURLINGTON, VERMONT

During a long month of bed rest during my high-risk pregnancy, I rediscovered the meaning of nurturing and comfort food. Eaten from a big bowl by the spoonful or between slices of crisp toast, good old egg salad really soothes the tender spots.

Servings: 4 generous sandwiches

6 hard-boiled eggs, chopped

3 Tbs. finely chopped dill pickle (about 1 medium pickle)

¼ cup mayonnaise

1 to 2 tsp. Dijon mustard, to taste

1. Combine all ingredients in a bowl and mix well. Season with salt and pepper to taste.

2. If not eaten straight from the bowl, egg salad is especially good on lightly toasted white sandwich bread.

Pineapple Snow

SUBMITTED BY LINDA E. KNIGHT, WOODSLEE, ONTARIO, CANADA

My mom, the oldest of ten, was the glue that held our extended family together. She was the one who planned every family reunion and remembered every family birthday, anniversary, and milestone, which she usually honored with her incredible cooking. Among her most beloved dishes was this golden fruit salad.

Servings: 8

2 cups long-grain rice
1 1-pound bag of miniature white
  marshmallows
1 cup crushed pineapple, canned or
  fresh

1 pint whipping cream
1 tsp. vanilla extract
1 Tbs. granulated white sugar
1 6-ounce jar of maraschino cherries,
  for garnish (optional)

1. Cook rice until tender.

2. Add marshmallows to hot rice, stirring constantly until melted.

3. Drain pineapple and add to rice-marshmallow mixture. Stir to blend. Cool in refrigerator.

4. Whip cream until stiff peaks form. Add vanilla and sugar to whipped cream.

5. Fold whipped cream gently into cooled rice mixture. Refrigerate until ready to serve. Garnish with maraschino cherries, if desired.

Peace—that was another word for home.

Kathleen Norris

Hot Turkey Sandwich with All the Trimmings

The day after Thanksgiving is a journey of sinful pleasures, as millions of refrigerators turn into leftover heavens for sandwich mongers like me. I basically put the whole of last night's dinner between two slices and chow down.—J.W.

Servings: 1

¼ pound leftover turkey meat
¼ cup leftover turkey gravy
¼ cup stuffing
2 slices sturdy, crusty bread
1 Tbs. cranberry sauce
Salt and pepper to taste

1. Warm the turkey and gravy together in a saucepan or microwave. Heat the stuffing. Toast the bread extra dark. (It'll need the strength to handle this hoagie.)

2. Spread a thin layer of cranberry sauce onto a slice of toast, and layer on the hot stuffing and turkey. Season to taste and pour on any remaining gravy. Close sandwich. Don't bother trying to cut this one in half.

···· ⑤ ····

Most turkeys taste better the day after; my mother's tasted better the day before.

Rita Rudner

Even-Seasoning Secret

To avoid salty patches in some parts of your food and bland, unseasoned patches on other parts, take a cue from pro chefs: Season from a great height. Most chefs pinch salt between their thumb and forefinger and sprinkle it down onto food from a great height, more than a foot above the item being seasoned. It tends to shower broadly over the food this way, covering evenly.

Pot of Memories

BY KATE MCBRIDE, FOXBORO, MASSACHUSETTS

One of my favorite possessions is an old, gray-speckled, aluminum pot with handles on each side and the name "Guardian" etched into its heavy bottom. It sits amidst my collection of professional Calphalon pots, looking somewhat ragged and out of place. But this pot is special. It has a history. It is my "gravy" pot, and it is the *only* pot to make meatballs in.

This pot belonged to my grandmother, Velia Borsilli, known to everyone in the family as "Grandma Vee." Born in Italy, she came to America as a young married woman with her husband, "Solly" (Salvatore Borsilli), and settled in New York City. Every Sunday, my mom and dad would take my brother and me to Grandma's house, a ground-floor apartment in a six-story brick apartment building in the Bronx, for dinner. My brother, Bobby, and I would play outside while the adults cooked and talked. In those days, it was safe for children to go outside without their parents. Sometimes, an old man would come around with a pony and take pictures of the kids on it for a quarter. On lucky days, a quarter would get us a ride on "The Whip," a rickety contraption built onto the back of a wandering truck.

Most Sundays, though, my favorite place was at Grandpa's side in the kitchen. His job was to take the big hunk of Parmesan cheese out of its waxy butcher paper and grate enough for the macaroni and meatballs. I would gaze up at him with my big brown eyes, and he would smile and silently slice off a corner of the sharp cheese and

Salvatore Borsilli in 1925

*Get your picture taken on
a pony for a quarter*

slip it to me. Sometimes Grandma would catch us, and because the cheese was imported and expensive, she'd give Grandpa a stern look. Everyone knew my grandpa spoiled me.

I don't remember much of my childhood, but I remember those Sundays . . . the smell and sound of onions sizzling in olive oil . . . watching my grandma roll meatballs between her hands and drop them into hot oil. And the tastes: the tangy grated cheese, steaming macaroni and mounds of meatballs smothered in sweet and spicy tomato gravy, chunks of crusty Italian bread dipped in my grandpa's homemade red wine.

After we finished our dinner, my brother and I would linger at the table, knowing that along with a pot of fresh coffee would come a platter of Italian pastries. I always struggled to choose between the crunchy custard-filled cannoli and the equally pleasing chocolate éclair. My brother invariably picked the multilayered napoleon, a choice I never understood; there just wasn't enough creamy stuff or chocolate between the layers of flaky pastry to interest me. As the adults sipped their espresso from tiny cups and discussed the latest family news, Bobby and I quietly feasted on the sweet pastries, licking our fingers at the very end.

During the years I was married, I continued at least one part of that tradition. Every Sunday morning I could be found in the kitchen, rolling meatballs and setting up a pot of gravy to simmer. Everyone loved my meatballs (according to my grandma, the secret is the raisins), especially my husband, and I was glad that I had taken the time to learn how to make this family dish and could share it with my growing family.

Now, twelve years after my husband's untimely passing and with my teenage daughter away at school, it makes no sense to cook that huge pot of gravy and meatballs for myself. Still, I sometimes find myself reaching for that heavy Guardian pot and returning to the Sunday ritual of making gravy and meatballs.

Maybe it's the meditative comfort of mixing the ingredients, rolling the

The author and her family in their sunday best in front of Grandma's house

meatballs with my hands, forming balls just the right size and slipping them into the sizzling oil. Then, while the gravy cooks for the requisite four or more hours, filling my home with savory odors, I putter about, read the paper, relax. Of course, every hour or so I have to dunk in a chunk of bread and eat it, dripping with gravy, to make sure it is cooking properly.

Maybe it's because I *need* to do it, to convince myself that I can still make the best meatballs, that I haven't lost the touch. Or maybe I just don't want to lose touch with those memories of long-ago Sundays at Grandma's house.

(recipe appears on next page)

Grandma Vee's Meatballs and Gravy

SUBMITTED BY KATE MCBRIDE, FOXBORO, MASSACHUSETTS

Every family of Italian descent has its own secret ingredient that makes their meatballs "the best." Raisins make this recipe special.

Servings: 12

2 pounds ground beef

2 eggs

½ cup milk

1 cup Italian seasoned bread crumbs (or enough to form the correct texture)

5 cloves garlic, minced (or to taste)

2 Tbs. raisins

½ cup grated Parmesan cheese

2 Tbs. pignoli nuts

Handful chopped parsley

Salt and pepper to taste

1 cup good olive oil, for browning

1 large onion, sliced, for browning

½ Tbs. red pepper flakes

1 to 2 tsp. oregano

1 Tbs. sugar

3 large cans premium Italian tomatoes, chopped, juice and all

2 pounds imported Italian macaroni, such as rigatoni or ziti

1. Combine all meatball ingredients (first 10 ingredients) in large bowl. Mix well; form meatballs with your hands.

2. Heat olive oil in large gravy pot and add the sliced onions. Brown the meatballs on all sides; drain excess oil and lower heat. Sprinkle red pepper flakes, oregano, salt, pepper, and sugar over meatballs. Add tomatoes, including the juice. Cover loosely, leaving cover slightly askew. Lower heat and simmer for 3–4 hours.

3. Boil the macaroni in ample salted water until just tender, drain, and serve in bowls with two meatballs (per bowl), smothered in gravy and sprinkled with grated cheese.

Chicken Potpie

Velvety sauce, rich chicken flavor, and delicate vegetables make this classic supremely comforting. For fun, this recipe can be divided into eight oven-safe bowls and baked as individual pies.—J.W.

Servings: 8

1 recipe Basic Pie Crust (see page 220) or 1 package
    frozen puff pastry
4 cups stock or water
1 chicken (2$\frac{1}{2}$ to 3$\frac{1}{2}$ pounds), cut up
4 medium or 2 extra-large (horse) carrots, peeled,
    cut in 1-inch chunks
1 pint pearl onions, peeled
2 ribs celery, cut in 1-inch chunks
8 mushrooms, halved or quartered
2 medium red potatoes, cut in 1-inch chunks (2 cups)
$\frac{1}{2}$ cup flour
$\frac{1}{3}$ cup oil
$\frac{1}{2}$ cup chopped fresh herbs such as dill or parsley
1 egg, beaten, mixed with 2 Tbs. cold water

1. Roll out dough to fit the top of a baking dish large enough to hold all ingredients (about 9- × 13-inch). Bring the stock or water to a boil in a large soup pot. Season the chicken well with salt and pepper.

(recipe continued on next page)

2. Add chicken to broth and bring back to a boil. Simmer 5 minutes, then turn off, cover, and set aside 15 minutes. Spoon chicken out and set aside to cool. Add all vegetables to the broth, bring back to a boil, and then lower heat and simmer until the potatoes and carrots are tender, about 20 minutes. Remove all bones from chicken. Combine flour and oil in a small skillet and cook 3 minutes until they form a smooth paste and smell slightly nutty—do not brown.

3. Heat oven to 400°. Ladle a cup of the broth into the flour mixture, and whisk until it thickens. Transfer this mixture back into the rest of the broth, and stir until mixture is thick and smooth. Add chicken meat and fresh herbs. Taste and adjust salt and pepper. Transfer mixture to baking dish; cover with dough, and brush with egg mixture. Cut a few holes to vent steam. Bake 30 to 45 minutes on a pan to catch the drippings, until top is golden brown and sauce is bubbly.

Choose Carrots for Taste

I prefer large, loose "horse" carrots, for their sweetness and juiciness. I usually avoid so-called "baby" carrots, which are usually bland unless very fresh.

A hungry man is not a free man.

Adlai Stevenson

Roasted Cod on Garlic Mashed Potatoes

There's something exquisitely satisfying about hearing an audible crunch when your fork breaks through the golden crust on this tender, juicy fish. To ensure that your crust makes noise, don't move the fish while it's searing in the pan. Just let it brown, and turn it only once before putting the whole pan in the oven.—J.W.

Servings: 4

1 bottle dry red wine

A few sprigs fresh thyme

1 recipe Garlic Mashed Potatoes
   (see page 166)

4 very thick portions cod, haddock,
   hake, or pollock fillet, skin on

Olive oil for sauté

1 Tbs. chopped garlic (about 3 cloves)

2 large bunches fresh spinach, stems
   removed, washed thoroughly

1. Heat oven to 425°. Boil red wine with thyme sprigs in a nonreactive (steel, glass, or enamel) sauce pot, until it is reduced to a syrup consistency. Cover and set aside. Make mashed potatoes and keep warm.

2. Season cod with salt and pepper. Preheat large cast iron (or ovenproof) skillet to very hot. Sear the cod, skin side down, in olive oil, in very hot skillet, without moving the fish until the skin has formed a golden crust (about 4 minutes). Turn cod over, and place skillet into preheated oven for 3 minutes more. Remove from oven and allow to rest for 5 minutes.

3. Lightly cook garlic in some olive oil in a large skillet over a medium flame, until it just begins to brown. Add the spinach and a pinch of salt to the garlic. Cook until wilted, and drain any juices in a colander.

4. To serve, make a circle of mashed potatoes on plate, place a mound of spinach in the center, and rest the cod, skin side up, atop the spinach. Drizzle with a spoonful of red wine syrup just before service.

Fusilli with Morels and Roasted Chicken

This is a great way to utilize extra meat the day after a roast chicken dinner, and it makes a great dinner pasta The woodsy, earthy flavor of the wild mushrooms marries well with the meat flavor. Substitute other mushrooms if morels are unavailable.—J.W.

Servings: 4

½ pound fusilli (spiral-shaped pasta)
Few drops olive oil
3 Tbs. unsalted butter, cut into small pieces
½ tsp. dried rosemary, or 1 sprig fresh, chopped
¼ pound fresh morel mushrooms, sliced into rings

1 cup roasted chicken meat, broken into bite-sized pieces
½ cup strong chicken stock or broth
2 or 3 lemon wedges
Salt and pepper to taste
Grated Parmesan

1. Cook the fusilli al dente, according to directions on box. Drain, toss with a few drops olive oil, and set aside.

2. Melt 1 tablespoon butter in a large (12-inch) skillet, over medium heat. Add the rosemary, and when it starts to sizzle, toss in the sliced morels. Sauté until they are soft, then add the chicken and cook until it is warmed through, about 5 minutes. Stir in the pasta and half of the chicken stock. Simmer until pasta is thoroughly warmed through, about 5 minutes more.

3. Swirl in the butter. Adjust the sauce consistency with remaining stock. Season with squeezes of lemon, salt, and pepper. Divide into four bowls and sprinkle with freshly grated Parmesan.

···· § ····

Real abundance is found when we join hands with those we love.

Anonymous

Grandma's Chicken and Dumplings

SUBMITTED BY SHARON PALMER, BRADBURY, CALIFORNIA

Chicken and dumplings was a beloved dish from my grandmother's country kitchen. She used her trusty cast-iron kettle with legs to cook the dumplings up just right. She'd always warn, "Don't open the lid! It'll make the dumplings tough!" Once the stew was done, the chicken and gravy were served atop a heaping pile of freshly cooked mashed potatoes, with the dumpling carefully placed to the side.

Servings: 8

1 fresh chicken (2½ to 3 pounds),
   cut up
6 cups plus ½ cup water, divided
1 Tbs. plus 1 tsp. salt, divided
1 tsp. pepper

1 cup milk
2 Tbs. margarine
2 cups all-purpose flour
1 tsp. baking powder
⅓ cup shortening

My grandmother, Edith Hanson, in 1930—a hard-working Southern farm wife who kept all her pots boiling on the hottest of summer days

1. Clean chicken and remove skin. Season the chicken with 1 tablespoon salt and 1 teaspoon pepper. Place in a big pot. Cover with 6 cups water and place a tight-fitting lid on the pot. Bring to a boil, skim any impurities that float to the surface, and then reduce heat to a simmer. Cook very slowly for about 1 hour, until chicken is tender.

(recipe continued on next page)

Bottom row, second from the right, sits my great-grandmother Edna Hanson, who perfected the recipe for Chicken and Dumplings and always cautioned my mother and grandmother, "Don't open the lid, you'll make them tough."

2. Remove chicken from broth and cool slightly. Chop chicken coarsely. Add back to broth, along with 1 cup milk and 2 tablespoons margarine. Simmer 1 minute.

3. In a mixing bowl, stir together flour, baking powder, and 1 teaspoon salt. Cut in shortening, and then add about ½ cup water to make a sticky dough. Drop by heaping tablespoons into bubbling broth. Cover and boil slowly for about 15 minutes. Serve immediately.

Mama
By Helen Quade,
Palatine, Illinois

Chin in palm, I watch
your floured fingers
lift, fold, push,
lift, fold, push
mounds of dough into
   loaves
that turn gold and
release an aroma
holy as incense.
I close my eyes, Mama,
and see you lifting lids,
stirring sauces, frying
   chicken,
tasting, tossing, dicing
while billows of steam
rise to the ceiling in a swirl
that uncurls your coiled
   hair.

The fricassee with dumplings is made by a Mrs. Miller whose husband has left her four times on account of her disposition and returned four times on account of her cooking and is still there.

Rex Stout

Prime Rib with Yorkshire Pudding

SUBMITTED BY LOIS L. LEVINE, SAN CARLOS, CALIFORNIA

The most festive meal in my childhood home was inevitably Beef Roast and Yorkshire Pudding. The wonderful smells coming from the kitchen signaled something special—a birthday, anniversary, or company for dinner. My mother prepared a standing rib roast the old-fashioned way, with precise timing, which meant dinner had to be eaten exactly on schedule. I have found a more modern, forgiving method for the same cut of meat. My version allows the meat to stand for two to five hours, but still gives it that medium-rare perfection.

Servings: 8 (individual puddings, or 36 small, if using minimuffin tins)
1 standing rib roast
1 Tbs. kosher (coarse) salt
1 tsp. freshly ground black pepper
2/3 cup flour, plus additional for dredging
1/2 tsp. salt
2 tsp. butter
1 egg
2/3 cup milk
3 Tbs. melted shortening or beef drippings from the roast

1. Heat oven to 500°. Have roast at room temperature. When oven is hot, salt, pepper, and flour roast and place in oven. Leave roast in 15 minutes per rib (i.e., 2 ribs = 30 minutes, 3 ribs = 45 minutes, etc.). Turn off oven and *keep oven door closed* at least 2 hours. The beauty of this method is that the meat will hold at medium rare until you are ready to serve.

(recipe continued on next page)

2. Combine ⅔ cup flour and salt; cut in butter with two forks. Add egg and milk and beat at high speed in electric mixer or food processor for 10 minutes. Chill thoroughly. Place a muffin tin in 425° oven until very hot, about 10 minutes. Pour 1 teaspoon melted shortening or beef drippings (fat) into each of 8 cups. Fill half full with batter. Bake for 30 minutes. (These may be made in tea-size muffin cups, producing 36 small puddings. The baking time should be reduced to 15 minutes.)

.... 🔊 ....

Roast beef, medium, is not only a food. It is a philosophy. . . . Roast beef, medium, is safe, and sane, and sure.

Edna Ferber

A Cut Above

Tender cuts are not always the most flavorful. In fact, tougher, inexpensive cuts, like shoulder (chuck), have much more flavor than expensive tenderloins and rib roasts. But you wouldn't serve a chuck roast for a wedding banquet any more than you'd chop up a tenderloin for stew. Slow, gentle cooking in liquid, or braising (stewing), is perfect for tougher cuts like chuck, shank, and leg meat, and even parts of the hindquarter, such as top round, bottom round, and eye round. Straight grilling, sautéing, or roasting best highlight the buttery delicacy and juiciness of more tender cuts, like tenderloin and sirloin. Some very flavorful cuts, such as flank and parts of the chuck, are great for either steaks or stews, while some cuts, like brisket, absolutely must be slow-cooked to be delicious. Brisket, if cooked properly and long enough, makes the best pot roast.

Tuna Noodle Casserole

Yes, my mom made it, too.—J.W.

Servings: 8–10

1 pound wide egg noodles
1 can (10 ¾ ounces)
   condensed cream of
   mushroom soup
1 can (6 ounces) tuna
12 stuffed Spanish olives,
   sliced crosswise

1 package (10 ounces) frozen
   young green peas
1 cup seasoned bread crumbs
2 Tbs. butter

1. Heat oven to 350°. Butter a 9- × 13-inch baking dish. Cook the egg noodles according to package directions. Rinse under cold water to chill.

2. In a mixing bowl, combine the cooked noodles, condensed soup, tuna, olives, and peas. Season to taste with salt and pepper. Transfer to buttered baking dish.

3. Distribute bread crumbs evenly over casserole, and dot with butter. Bake 30 minutes, until browned on top.

···· § ····

Rituals are the formulas by which harmony
is restored.

Terry Tempest Williams

Shepherd's Pie

SUBMITTED BY SUZIE HIRSCHFELD, NEW YORK, NEW YORK

England's second-best import . . . next to The Beatles. You don't have to be British to enjoy this delicious meat pie. To know Shepherd's Pie is to love Shepherd's Pie.

Servings: 10

2 Tbs. olive oil

2 medium onions, chopped

3 cloves garlic, finely chopped

2 pounds ground beef or turkey

2 tsp. salt

½ tsp. freshly ground black pepper

2 packages (10 ounces) frozen peas and carrots or mixed vegetables

1 can (15 ounces) pink or black beans, with liquid included

1 Tbs. Worcestershire sauce

¼ cup red wine (optional)

2 pounds peeled potatoes, cut in 1-inch chunks

1 pound peeled parsnips (or another pound potatoes), cut in pieces

4 ounces (1 stick) butter

1 cup milk

Salt and pepper to taste

½ cup grated Parmesan cheese

1. Heat olive oil in a large skillet over medium-high heat. Cook onions in oil until translucent, about 5 minutes. Add the garlic, ground meat, salt, and pepper. Cook until the meat is browned, stirring occasionally. Stir in the frozen vegetables, beans, Worcestershire sauce, and red wine. Simmer for about 15 minutes; season to taste.

2. In the meantime, bring the potatoes and parsnips to a boil in a pot with enough water just to cover. Cook until tender, drain thoroughly, and mash with butter and milk. Season well with salt and pepper.

3. Heat oven to 425°. Place meat mixture in a 9- × 13-inch baking dish and spoon the mash on top. Sprinkle top with grated cheese. Bake on top rack for about 30 minutes, until mash is crisp.

Roasted Lemon-Thyme Chicken

Any time is a good time for lemon-thyme chicken. Winter, spring, summer, and fall, roast chicken with gravy ladled generously over egg noodles is a perfect ready-in-an-hour dish. It's especially great for weekend guests you actually want to spend time with, rather than cooking an elaborate meal.—J.W.

Servings: 4

1 chicken (3½ to 4 pounds)
1 Tbs. oil
2 tsp. dried thyme
1 tsp. salt
½ tsp. ground black pepper
½ lemon

½ head of garlic, cut in half
    laterally
1 medium onion, whole,
    unpeeled
1 Tbs. cornstarch, dissolved in
    ½ cup cold water

1. Heat oven to 450°. Rub the chicken inside and out with the oil, thyme, salt, and pepper. Place the half-lemon and half-head of garlic into the cavity. Place the chicken breast-side up in a small roasting pan, along with the unpeeled onion.

2. Cook 20 minutes on top rack of oven; lower heat to 325°. Cook 30 to 35 minutes more, until juices do not appear pink when tipped from the cavity (a thermometer should read 150° on the bone).

(recipe continued on next page)

3. Transfer chicken to a cutting board to rest for 15 to 20 minutes. Meanwhile, add 1 cup of water to the roasting pan. Use a wooden spoon to scrape up all browned bits; transfer to a small saucepan, along with the lemon and garlic from the chicken. Thicken by adding the cornstarch solution. Simmer 10 minutes, and season.

4. Serve the carved chicken with the quartered roasted onion, and ladle gravy over the chicken and/or egg noodles.

Give It a Rest!

Oven-roasted meats cook from the outside in. When you check the internal temperature of a roast just out of the oven, it will read about ten degrees less than what the final temperature will be. True readings come after the "carry-over cooking" from residual heat within the roast after you remove it from the oven. During that time, the outside of the roast relaxes a bit, and juices that have been under pressure flow back into the meat, making it moist and more delicious. Carving before this essential "rest" insults the poor roast, which deserves the chance to put its best slice forward.

Pork Chops au Gratin

SUBMITTED BY AMANDA CUDA, BRIDGEPORT, CONNECTICUT

While I was growing up, my mother was the queen of comfort foods. The recipe nearest and dearest to her heart was pork chops and scalloped potatoes, a dish she'd brought from her mother's kitchen right into ours. This dish goes in the oven every time I have a particularly long or hard day at work. Or when it's really cold outside. Or when I just want to feel good. Even though I'm eating by myself in front of the television set, it feels like I'm back at the dinner table with my parents, shoveling in comfort by the forkful.

Servings: 3

4 large russet potatoes, peeled and thinly sliced

1 large onion, thinly sliced

3 pork chops, 1-inch or more thick

Salt and pepper to taste

4 Tbs. butter or margarine, broken into pieces

Scant cup of milk

1. Heat oven to 500°. Lightly butter a 9- × 13-inch baking dish. Distribute half of the potato slices in an even layer in the prepared baking dish. Layer half of the onion slices on top of the potatoes. Sprinkle with salt and pepper to taste

2. Season chops liberally with salt and pepper on both sides, and place them into the baking dish, spaced evenly apart. Top with a layer of onion and a final layer of potato. Sprinkle it all with salt and pepper to taste. Dot the casserole with butter pieces and splash milk over the top. Cover with foil.

3. Bake 30 to 45 minutes, until potatoes are tender and pork chops are cooked through.

What one loves in childhood stays in the heart forever.

Mary Jo Putney

The Initiation

By Colleen Sell, Eugene, Oregon

When I was a single mom, attending college and working, I had little time, money, and energy for socializing. In five years, I'd had maybe a dozen dates. Then I met a nice but unlikely suitor: a childless bachelor. After a year of seeing him only when my little darlings were with their dad, I invited "that guy" over for dinner. By the time he arrived (an hour late), the kids were starving and ready to tangle.

"Smells good," he said as he walked past the kids without so much as a nod and to the living room, where he promptly turned on the television. "What's brewing?"

"Chili," I said, as I shushed my adolescent daughters, who were hissing, "What a nerd!" and "How ruuude!"

"Oh. I don't really like chili."

"Me either!" piped my son. "But I looooove my little mama's chili!"

The five of us sat in silence for ten long minutes. As my famished kids gobbled their dinner, That Guy nibbled on salad and corn bread before taking a tentative spoonful. And then another . . . and another . . . until, head bent over the bowl, sweat streaming from his forehead (as my mortified daughters rolled their eyes), he'd downed every last drop. Then he asked for seconds, saying, "You should bottle and sell this stuff!"

My son and I smiled, while my daughters giggled themselves silly, and That Guy scarfed another helping of Mamacita's Chili. Then I sent him home with a quart and an *Adios!*

(recipe appears on next page)

Mamacita's Chili

SUBMITTED BY COLLEEN SELL, EUGENE, OREGON

This chili gets better as it cooks, so take your time and cook it slowly over low heat, stirring often. Serve piping hot, garnished with shredded cheddar or jack cheese or a dollop of sour cream. For an authentic Mamacita Chili feast, add a tossed green salad with fresh mandarin orange segments and toasted pumpkin seeds, warm corn bread with creamed cinnamon-honey butter, iced "sun" tea spiked with lemon or a sprig of fresh mint, and warm gingerbread topped with whipped cream. Olé!

Servings: 8

1 pound ground beef, chicken, or turkey (dark/white mix is best)

Olive oil

1 medium onion, chopped (about 2 cups)

2 cloves garlic, finely chopped, or 1 tsp. garlic powder

3 mixed bell peppers (red, green, and yellow), chopped

1 can (28 ounces) or 3 cups fresh Roma plum tomatoes, chopped

1 can (10.5 ounces) tomato soup

1 to 2 cans (15 ounces each) dark red kidney or black beans

1 cup chopped baby carrots

1 cup fresh or frozen corn kernels

3 or 4 cups water (add/subtract to desired consistency; chili will thicken as it cooks)

1 tsp. chili flakes

3 Tbs. chili powder

2 tsp. cumin

1 cinnamon stick, or 1½ tsp. ground cinnamon

1 Tbs. granulated white sugar (optional, but recommended)

Salt (about 2 tsp.) and white pepper (about 1 tsp.) to taste

For garnish: diced raw onion, grated cheddar cheese, and fresh sour cream

(recipe continued on next page)

1. In a skillet over medium heat, lightly brown ground meat. Drain and transfer to a Dutch oven (large heavy pot). Add olive oil to the skillet, and cook the onion, garlic, and bell peppers; add to browned meat in Dutch oven. Add tomatoes (including juice), tomato soup, beans, carrots, and corn. Stir well. Slowly add water while continuing to stir, to desired consistency.

2. Add all spices and seasonings. Bring to a slow easy boil over medium heat, stirring almost constantly. Lower heat, cover pot loosely, and simmer for at least 90 minutes, stirring frequently at first. Taste after 30 minutes, adding more of whatever you think it needs. Add a little water if the chili starts to thicken up more than you'd like. This chili benefits from a long, slow cook over very low heat—up to 3 hours is great.

3. Top each serving with grated cheddar cheese, diced raw onion, and/or a dollop of sour or fresh cream.

Mamacita and her lil' chili lovers, 1982

Stuffed Peppers

Better living through science has given us bell peppers in all the colors of the rainbow. That said, my favorites are still red and green, but the other colors can add fun to the dinner table. Select peppers that stand upright.—J.W.

Servings: 8

8 large bell peppers, any color
1 Tbs. olive oil
1 large onion, chopped (about 3 cups)
1 Tbs. dried herbs such as thyme, rosemary, oregano, basil, or a combination

3 cloves garlic, chopped (about 1 heaping Tbs.)
2 pounds ground beef, pork, or chicken
3 cups cooked rice
2 tsp. salt
½ tsp. black pepper
¼ cup chopped parsley

1. Heat oven to 350°. Cut the top one-fourth cleanly from each pepper; remove seeds. Line up the peppers in a lightly buttered baking dish, with their tops beside them. In a skillet over medium heat, heat the oil; cook the onion, herbs, and garlic until soft, about 10 minutes.

2. In a mixing bowl, combine onion mixture, meat, rice, salt, pepper, and parsley. Spoon this mixture into the peppers, and cover with the tops (mix and match the tops for attractive contrast).

3. Bake 30 to 45 minutes, until piping hot and fully cooked in the center (150° on an instant-read thermometer).

Juicy, Flavorful Meat Fillings

Use meat with at least 10 percent fat content. If using ground poultry or lean beef, add a little chopped bacon for moisture.

Auntie's Casserole

Perhaps it was because my dear Aunt Prussia and Uncle Roy were childless that they doted on my brother and me like they did. After witnessing the generosity and caring they bestowed on neighbors and perfect strangers, though, during the year that I lived with them, I suspect that it had more to do with their basic goodness. Among my treasures from that year is a handwritten recipe card for my aunt's "made-up" casserole, which we made together in her bright kitchen.

Aunt Prussia

Servings: 8

1 Tbs. olive oil
1 chopped onion
1 pound ground beef
1 can (15 ounces) garbanzo
    beans (chickpeas), drained
1 can (15 ounces) whole kernel
    corn, drained
1 can (15 ounces) chili (you
    can use the spicy version if
    you like)

½ cup sliced good-quality
    olives
2 cups cooked rice
1 tsp. salt
2 tsp. dried oregano
1 tsp. dried thyme
1 cup grated cheese, such
    as sharp cheddar or
    Monterey jack

1. Heat oil in a large skillet over high heat. Cook onion and beef until browned, turning only occasionally, about 5 to 7 minutes.

2. In a mixing bowl, combine browned meat mixture with garbanzos, corn, chili, olives, rice, salt, oregano, and thyme. Put in casserole or baking pan; cover with grated cheese.

3. Bake at 300° for about 1 hour or until lightly browned on top.

Stuffed Cabbage

As with most home cooking, my mother's recipe for Stuffed Cabbage, one of my favorite childhood dinners, was charmingly vague about amounts and times. I'm thankful this book has given me reason to codify it.—J.W.

Servings: 8–10
2 Tbs. olive oil
3 medium onions, chopped (about 5 cups)
2 tsp. garlic powder
1½ pounds ground beef
3 cups cooked rice
4 tsp. salt, divided
½ tsp. black pepper
2 cans (14.5 ounces) stewed tomatoes, cut in large pieces,
    juices included
½ cup raisins, packed
1 Tbs. lemon juice
2 Tbs. brown sugar
1 large head green cabbage

1. In a saucepan over medium flame, heat the olive oil; add the onions and garlic powder. Cook until translucent, about 5 minutes. Transfer half of this mixture to a mixing bowl, along with the ground beef, cooked rice, 3 teaspoons salt, and pepper to taste; mix very well with hands and set aside.

2. To the remaining half of the onions, add the stewed tomatoes, raisins, lemon juice, brown sugar, and 1 teaspoon salt. Simmer over very low heat for 20 minutes while you assemble the cabbage rolls.

(recipe continued on next page)

2. Bring a large pot of water to a boil. Plunge the whole head of cabbage in, and boil for 5 minutes. Lift cabbage from pot, remove softened outer leaves, and return the head to the pot. Repeat until you have 20 or so wilted leaves. Trim out any particularly large stems. These pieces can be chopped and added to the sauce, as can the smaller center leaves. Chop half of the remaining cabbage center and add it to the cooking sauce.

3. Heat oven to 350°. Pour the sauce into a large baking dish (9 × 13 inches or larger). Place a cabbage leaf on a work surface, stem side facing away from you. Place ¼ cup of filling (a little more for very large leaves) on the nearest part to you, fold 1-inch flaps from the sides to lock in the filling, and roll the filling away from yourself. Place cabbage roll stem-side down atop the sauce. Repeat with remaining leaves until you have used all the filling.

4. Cover the rolls with any remaining cabbage leaves, and then cover the dish with foil. Place dish on a large baking sheet to catch any drippings, and bake 2 hours, until filling is thoroughly cooked and cabbage is very tender.

···· ❦ ····

One can say everything best over a meal.

George Eliot

Jay's Famous Staff Meal Meatloaf with Gravy

*At the restaurants where I've worked, one of the cooks always makes
dinner for the rest of the staff. This is one of my favorite and
most requested contributions to staff meals.—J.W.*

Servings: 8–10

2 Tbs. olive oil

2 cups chopped onions

2 cloves garlic, chopped

1 tsp. each dried oregano and thyme

1 Tbs. kosher salt

A few grinds black pepper

1 pound each of ground beef, pork, and
   chicken

1 cup bread crumbs

1 can (14.5 ounces) diced tomato
   (juice included)

3 eggs, beaten

½ cup chopped Italian (flat leaf) parsley

½ cup grated Parmesan cheese

¼ cup ketchup

½ cup flour

½ cup vegetable oil

4 cups cold chicken stock or water

1. Heat olive oil in a skillet over medium-high heat. Add onions; cook 5 minutes. Add garlic, oregano, thyme, kosher salt, and pepper; lower heat and cook 5 minutes more.

2. Heat oven to 375°. In a large bowl, combine the meats, bread crumbs, tomatoes, eggs, parsley, cheese, and onion mixture. Mix well, and shape into 2 loaves with your hands in a large roasting pan or baking dish. Coat the outsides with ketchup. Roast 1 hour (about 150°). Cook together the flour and oil over medium-low heat in a small saucepan for 5 minutes; set aside.

3. Transfer meatloaves to a carving board and allow to rest for at least 15 minutes. Transfer the pan drippings to the pan with the flour mixture, cook over medium heat, and gradually add the cold chicken stock. Simmer 5 minutes. Season with salt and pepper. Serve with mashed potatoes or polenta.

Louise Love's Kitchen

BY HELEN (LEN) LEATHERWOOD, BEVERLY HILLS, CALIFORNIA

My mother cooked one dish and one dish alone—spaghetti with clam sauce—but only if no one else was there to cook and we had run out of Campbell's soup and chicken pot-pies. Mom didn't clean, either; cooking and cleaning were what you hired other people to do. She had more important things to do—like giving birth seven times and playing bridge at the golf club.

Later, she got her consciousness raised and headed to graduate school. Then, even the spaghetti with clam sauce stopped. I loved my mother, but concocting delectable dishes in the kitchen just wasn't part of her repertoire. For me, the women who did cook and clean for my family became icons of home and hearth. The first one I remember was Louise Love.

Louise lived on the corner of Seventh Street and Pine in "colored town," across the street from a juke joint named Sadie's Place. Louise's house stood at a crooked angle on its small lot, like it had just been washed up by floodwaters. The small wooden house was immaculate but worn, with curling paint and jagged holes in the front porch floor where boards had rotted through. The screen door gave a high-pitched squeak when it was opened.

The heart of Louise's house was her kitchen. The linoleum floor was black in spots from wear, but spotless. I loved to walk across it barefoot, feeling the coolness on the soles of my feet. Red-checkered curtains hung on the cabinets and a matching cloth covered the small square table. Canisters of flour, sugar, and baking soda sat out on the counter, and a can of bacon grease rested on the shelf next to the gas stove. Through the single window over the yellowed porcelain sink, sunlight filtered through the bois d'arc leaves from the big tree outside. A door, resting crooked in its frame, led to the penned backyard, where chickens scratched for worms in the black dirt and a rooster sometimes flapped his wings and crowed.

The floors creaked when Louise moved her heavy body over them. She wore old house slippers with the backs trodden down. The pink underside of her feet contrasted sharply with the dark brown of her skin. She wore her black hair greased and pulled back into a short ponytail, and a clean white apron over her housedress.

"Baby, you sit in that chair while Ruby and Louise make us a little dinner, okay?"

The author at age seven

The author at her desk

The question was actually a directive, of course, designed to keep me out of the way, but I didn't care. I loved it when Louise and her daughter cooked. I'd sit in that crooked little kitchen and watch with fascination and contentment as Louise rolled out a pie crust with a floured rolling pin, then placed it in the pie pan. She could flute the edges and pour in the cherry filling in minutes, and then, as she wove thin strips of crust over and under to form a lattice top, she'd let me eat the pie-dough scraps.

While the pie baked in the oven, Louise would dredge chicken in seasoned flour and lay it in a hot pan to fry. Daughter Ruby would pour "sweet milk," as my daddy called it, and liberal doses of butter, salt, and pepper into potatoes she was mashing. A quiet efficiency and a happy banter passed between the two women as they cooked. I was satisfied to drink in the warmth of the kitchen, the aroma of the foods, and the intimacy that the mother and daughter shared in their common tasks.

Now, so many years later, the smells of fried chicken, homemade biscuits, and freshly baked pie still take me back to Louise Love and her ocean-wave house. As a child, I understood that Louise didn't have the pretty things that my family and friends had, but I also knew that she had something we didn't. She knew the joy of standing side by side with someone you love in a familiar old kitchen, cooking delicious foods with and for the people you love. And she knew that expressing love was as simple as tossing pie scraps to a waiting child. ✣

A small house will hold as much happiness as a big one.

Proverb

Aunt Judy's Pot Roast

SUBMITTED BY JUDITH GILBERT, VALLEY STREAM, NEW YORK

My aunt Judy uses only top-quality kosher meat for this dish. A kosher butcher will know the terms specified for the roast, or you can use any pot roast cut. Judy recommends making it a day in advance and slicing it cold for best results.—J.W.

Servings: 8

3 Tbs. oil

2½ pounds square-cut, round, or other
    pot roast cut of beef

3 medium onions, cut into wedges

Lawry's seasoned salt (salt, pepper, gar-
    lic, paprika)

6–8 carrots, peeled, cut into
    2-inch pieces

6 medium potatoes, peeled, cut in half

⅓ cup ketchup

⅓ cup water

1 tsp. paprika

Aunt Judy in 1951

1. In a Dutch oven over high heat, heat 2 tablespoons of the oil. Sear the meat on both sides for 10 minutes each, until well browned. Transfer to a plate.

(recipe continued on next page)

2. Add another tablespoon of oil to the pot, and cook onions 5 minutes. Remove half of the onions (to be placed on top of the meat while cooking).

3. Season the meat liberally with Lawry's seasoned salt, and place on top of the onions in the pan. Distribute the potatoes and carrots around the meat. Place reserved onions on top of the meat.

4. Combine the ketchup and water, and pour over the meat and vegetables. Sprinkle the paprika over the potatoes.

5. Cover tightly, and cook slowly for 2 to 2½ hours over low heat, until tender. It should break apart with a fork. Refrigerate overnight, and slice cold. Reheat in a covered casserole in the oven.

Knife Knowledge

Serrated-edge "bread" knives are great for cutting crumbly things that would crush under the press of a smooth blade. But for clean slices, especially when carving cooked meats, there's no substitute for a razor-sharp slicing knife.

The feeling of friendship is like that of being comfortably filled with roast beef.

Samuel Johnson

Roasted Turkey

with Giblet Gravy and Southern Corn Bread Dressing

SUBMITTED BY SHARON PALMER, BRADBURY, CALIFORNIA

Servings: 20

1 fresh turkey, 18 to 20 pounds

1 batch corn bread (page 196), or 6 cups crumbled corn bread of any kind

Salt and pepper to taste

3 cups crumbled biscuits (page 201 or store-bought)

1½ sticks (12 Tbs.) margarine, divided

1½ cups chopped onion

2 cups chopped celery stalk and tops

¼ cup chopped fresh sage, or 1½ Tbs. dried sage powder

3 Tbs. flour

1. Heat oven to 325°. Make turkey giblet broth by placing turkey giblets, neck, and liver in pot with 5 cups water and boiling for 30 minutes until tender. Season turkey liberally inside and out with 2 teaspoons salt and 1 teaspoon pepper. Rub the skin with 8 tablespoons of margarine. (You may need to warm the margarine.)

2. Make stuffing: Crumble prepared corn bread and biscuits in large mixing bowl. Melt remaining margarine in a skillet. Sauté chopped onion and celery with margarine, sage, 1 teaspoon pepper, and ½ teaspoon salt just until crunchy tender. Add to corn bread mixture. Pour 2½ cups of giblet broth into the stuffing mixture. Reserve remaining broth for giblet gravy. Toss stuffing to mix thoroughly.

3. Stuff turkey with dressing. Place in large roasting pan, breast side up. Add ½ cup water. Place an aluminum tent on top of the turkey and bake for approximately 4 to 5½ hours, until a meat thermometer inserted in the inner thigh indicates 165° and the stuffing registers 150°. Set aside to rest at least 30 minutes before carving.

(recipe continued on next page)

4. Prepare the giblet gravy by chopping the giblets and liver and pulling meat off the neck. Pour about 4 cups of turkey drippings into a small bowl. Let stand a few minutes until the fat rises. Skim off about 3 tablespoons turkey fat and cook in a saucepan over medium heat. Stir 3 tablespoons of flour into the melted fat; cook until golden. Skim remaining fat from turkey broth and discard. Add turkey broth and reserved giblet broth to saucepan, stirring until smooth. Add chopped giblets, neck meat, and liver, ½ teaspoon salt, and ½ teaspoon pepper. Stir until thickened and bubbly. Serve immediately.

Poke, Wiggle, and Tip: Checking Roasted Poultry for Doneness

For both aesthetic and health reasons, chickens and turkeys should be cooked thoroughly. There are three accepted ways to check these birds for doneness:

- Thermometer: The surest way is to poke the tip of an instant-read meat thermometer into the thickest part of the cooked bird—the thigh. It should read 150° on the bone. Remember that the internal temperature will continue to rise for 10 to 15 minutes after the roast leaves the oven.

- Wiggle the drumstick: Poultry has a springy, bounce-back reaction when the drumstick is wiggled before the meat is fully cooked. If you pull the leg bone from side to side and it gives loosely, the meat is done.

- Tip out the juices: As unstuffed poultry roasts, natural juices pool in the cavity. At first, they are pink and opaque. When the bird is cooked, these juices are clear. Simply tip the pan and observe the color of the juices that run out into the pan.

- Ducks, squab, and other game birds do not require the thorough cooking of chicken and turkey, and are best appreciated when slightly rare on the breast.

Fried Chicken

Slow cooking is one of the hallmarks of most comfort foods. This Southern classic is no exception. To make the juiciest, most flavorful chicken, soak the chicken in brine (saltwater) and then in buttermilk before coating it with seasoned flour.—J.W.

Servings: 4

½ cup kosher salt

1 quart water

1 fryer chicken (2½ to 3½ pounds), cut into 8 pieces

1 quart buttermilk

2 cups flour

1 Tbs. dried oregano

1 tsp. paprika

1 tsp. salt

1 tsp. pepper

1 pound shortening or fry oil

1. Combine the kosher salt and water. Place the chicken into the saltwater and soak for 4 hours. Drain on racks, and then transfer the chicken pieces to a container with the buttermilk. Soak 4 hours more (or, for best results, overnight).

2. Whisk together the flour, oregano, paprika, salt, and pepper. Heat the oil in a large skillet to about 325°; oil should be about 2 inches deep. Shake excess buttermilk from a piece of chicken, and dredge the piece in the flour. Dip it back into the buttermilk, and dredge it in flour a second time. Gently transfer it to the fry oil. Repeat with remaining chicken pieces, being careful not to crowd the pan. (Pieces should not touch. Work in batches if necessary.)

3. Fry slowly until crust is golden brown and chicken is cooked to the bone, about 30 minutes, turning occasionally. Drain on wire racks (not paper towels).

···· ❦ ····

Etiquette: A fancy word for simple kindness.

Elsa Maxwell

Food Woman Glazed Ham

SUBMITTED BY MELINDA FRANK, REDONDO BEACH, CALIFORNIA

Cooking makes me feel grounded and connected to family and home after a hectic workweek and commuting. I am so often found in my kitchen chopping, dicing, and simmering in an aromatic cloud of spices that I acquired the title "Food Woman" from a friend of my son. As I lean toward spontaneous experimentation, dishes from my kitchen have come to be called the "Food Woman Concoctions."

Servings: 16–20

1 4- to 6-pound fresh ham
Whole cloves
1 can (16 ounces) sliced pineapple in its own juice (unsweetened)
1 cup brown sugar
1/4 cup sesame oil
1/3 cup soy sauce
1/4 cup roasted sesame seeds

1 Tbs. ground black pepper
Dash cayenne pepper (or to taste)
1 tsp. cinnamon
1 tsp. nutmeg
1/2 tsp. Dijon mustard
2 oranges, sliced to about same thickness as pineapple (rind on)

1. Score the top of the ham, making ¼-inch slices, and stud with whole cloves.

2. Drain the pineapple, reserving the juice.

3. Mix together in a bowl the reserved pineapple juice, brown sugar, sesame oil, soy sauce, sesame seeds, black pepper, cayenne pepper, cinnamon, nutmeg, and Dijon mustard. Brush half of the mixture over the ham. Cover the exposed surface of the ham with alternating slices of pineapple and orange, secured with toothpicks.

4. Bake in 325° oven for 1½ to 2½ hours (depending on the size of the ham), until internal temperature reaches 140°. Brush remaining glaze on ham and finish baking, another 15 to 20 minutes.

Barbecued Baby Back Ribs

My friend John up in Boston is a true swine-o-phile, knowing the best ways to make pork sing. He taught me his method for making ribs, which is cunningly simple.—J.W.

Servings: 4

2 cups white vinegar

2 cups apple cider vinegar

1 quart water

2 pounds pork ribs, cut into 3-rib sections

2 cups homemade barbecue sauce (or top-quality bottled sauce)

1. Bring the vinegars and water to a boil. Add the ribs. Liquid should just cover the ribs. Bring back to a boil, and then simmer gently, stirring occasionally and moving ribs from bottom to top, for about 10 minutes. Drain.

2. Fire up a charcoal or gas grill to very low flame, or heat oven to 350°. Brush top and bottom of ribs with a thin coat of barbecue sauce, and cook slowly and evenly, meat-side down in the oven, or on an upper rack on the grill for about 15 minutes. Turn over, brush again liberally with sauce (dab it on), and cook 20 to 25 minutes more, meat-side up. Brush on more sauce and cook another 20 to 25 minutes, until the ribs attain a dark, lacquered look and some black spots appear around the edges. Brush regularly with additional sauce, giving a final coat 5 minutes before taking them off the fire.

3. Cut apart the ribs with poultry shears and serve with cold beverages.

Home is a place where teenagers go to refuel.

Anonymous

Quick and Easy Barbecue Sauce

SUBMITTED BY JUNE BURNS, APACHE JUNCTION, ARIZONA

Barbecue: synonymous with summertime and good times!

Yield: 1 quart

1 cup chopped onion

4 Tbs. minced garlic

4 Tbs. vegetable oil

2 tsp. ground cumin

½ tsp. cayenne pepper

2 cups ketchup

1 cup malt vinegar

½ cup soy sauce

½ cup brown sugar

¼ cup Worcestershire sauce

1. Sauté onion and garlic in vegetable oil. Add cumin and cayenne, and simmer 20 minutes.

2. Transfer onion-garlic mixture to a bowl, scraping the pan with a spatula to get all the spiced oil. Add the rest of the ingredients and mix well.

3. Brush over meat as it sizzles on the grill, or pour over meat in a roasting pan and bake, or transfer sauce and shredded cooked meat to a saucepan and simmer until heated through, 15 to 20 minutes.

When we lose, I eat. When we win, I eat.
I also eat when we're rained out.

Tommy Lasorda

Fatty Roast Pork Butt with Garlicky Gravy

This was a favorite staff meal for the cooks at Jasper's Restaurant in Boston, where pork with garlic and clams was a signature dish. We omitted the clams, but not the fatty pork butts! By the way, pork butt isn't the part of the pork many people think it is: It's actually the shoulder.—J.W.

Servings: 12

1 boneless pork butt roast (about
    5 pounds)
1 Tbs. salt
Black pepper to taste
½ cup olive oil
½ cup sliced garlic (about 1 head)

4 bay leaves
½ cup flour
2 cups brown stock (such as veal or
    beef—the best would be stock made
    from the roasted pork bones)
2 cups chicken stock

1. Heat oven to 450°. Rub roast well with salt, pepper, and some of the oil. Pour remaining oil into a large roasting pan, and transfer the pork into that pan. Roast 30 minutes, and then lower the oven to 350°. Roast meat for another 90 minutes, turning it to brown all sides.

2. When pork reaches 140° (check with a thermometer, or stick a skewer into the center—the skewer should feel hot when removed and touched to your lip), add the garlic and bay leaves. Continue roasting for another 30 minutes. Transfer the roast to a separate pan to cool and to catch the juices. Meanwhile, sprinkle the flour into the roasting pan, and whisk into the oil. Place back in oven for 5 minutes.

3. Add cold stock to the flour mixture and stir in with a wooden spoon, rubbing the bottom of the pan to bring up any browned bits. Transfer gravy to a saucepan and simmer 10 minutes, until thick and smooth. Add any juices that have escaped from the cooling roast. Serve sliced with mashed potatoes, stuffing, or polenta, and plenty of gravy.

Lamb Shanks with Lentils

*Skip Lombardi, an old Boston friend, taught me this warming, simple dish
that he learned form his father. As he put it, "It turns a common
cut of meat into something quite special."—J.W.*

Servings: 4

4 lamb shanks (about 4 pounds),
  trimmed of all visible fat

2 cloves garlic, slivered

2 Tbs. olive oil

2 whole cloves of garlic, peeled

1 medium onion, diced

2 cups lentils (use green or brown)

2 bay leaves

1 Tbs. fresh oregano, or 1 tsp. dried

¼ cup chopped Italian parsley

4 cups water

Salt and pepper to taste

1. Poke small pockets into the lamb shanks with a paring knife. Stuff each
pocket with a sliver of garlic. Heat the olive oil over medium-high heat in a
large skillet. When oil is very hot—shimmering but not smoking—brown the
lamb shanks on all sides. Set aside.

2. Lower the heat and add the garlic cloves to the pan. Cook until brown;
remove from the oil and discard.

3. Add the onion to the oil and cook until soft, about 5 minutes. Add the
lentils, bay leaves, oregano, parsley, and 4 cups of water. Bring to a boil, add
salt and pepper to taste, and return the shanks to the pan. Reduce heat to low
and cover. Simmer 1 hour, checking after 30 minutes to see if the lentils need
more water. Remove the lamb after an hour, and cook the lentils further until
very tender. Adjust seasoning, and serve the lamb atop beds of lentils.

When one is too old for love, one finds great comfort in good dinners.

Zora Neal Hurston

Patti's Fried Chicken

SUBMITTED BY PATTI AUSTIN, ROSENDALE, NEW YORK

This is one of my son Nick's favorite meals. We only have it two or three times a year, but it's always a treat. I serve this with mashed potatoes, country fried gravy, and collard greens.

Servings: 4

1 frying chicken, cut in 10 pieces
½ cup buttermilk (low fat)
1 cup flour
1 cup cornmeal

1–2 tsp. adobo
Salt and pepper to taste
Approximately 1 cup vegetable oil
    (use your judgment)

1. Wash the chicken pieces thoroughly and pat them dry with a paper towel. Marinate the chicken in a bowl with the buttermilk. Cover and refrigerate for approximately 1 hour.

2. Combine the flour, cornmeal, adobo, salt, and pepper in a bowl or bag. Mix well. Coat the chicken well with the flour mixture. Heat the oil in a large frying pan until hot over a medium flame. Cook for about 15 to 20 minutes on each side, until chicken juice is clear when pierced with a fork.

3. Drain chicken on paper towels or brown paper and serve.

Blessed are those who can give without
remembering, and receive without forgetting.
Elizabeth Bibesco

Roast Leg of Lamb

SUBMITTED BY JOSH MARTIN, NEW YORK, NEW YORK

When I want to entertain old friends, nothing seems more fitting than a roast leg of lamb. Everything about it says comfort: tasty, warm, tender, and special. It goes over so well that when I plan a dinner party, friends request it. Even guests on a diet will come back for seconds (or thirds). I get a Zen-like pleasure out of preparing this dish, and as it roasts, it fills my entire home with the delicious scent of rosemary and basil.

Servings: 8

1 leg of lamb, approximately 6 to 8 pounds, bone in

4 to 6 cloves of garlic, minced

1 bunch fresh basil (approximately 8 pieces), stems removed

½ cup dried rosemary, covered with about ¾ cup olive oil (prepared 1 to 2 hours before use, to allow rosemary flavor to impregnate olive oil)

1. Heat oven to 500°+. Trim fat off leg of lamb (also removing the thin layer of "fell"). Puncture the meat liberally with fork or knife. Rub with garlic (do *not* insert into the meat) and fresh basil leaves, saving the leaves. Apply a liberal coating of the rosemary-and-olive-oil mixture, rubbing well. Place the lamb on a rack in a roasting pan, and put the basil leaves on top of the meat.

2. Place in oven. Cook until you hear some sizzling, about 10 minutes, then loosely cover leg with tin foil and reduce oven to 350°. Allow 15 to 18 minutes per pound total cooking time for medium doneness (about 2 hours for a 7-pound roast). Midway through cooking, turn leg. For the last 15 minutes, remove foil to create a crisp outer coat. Meat is done when thermometer applied to thickest part registers an internal temperature of 130° (rare) or 150° (medium/well done). Alternative test: Poke meat fork in thickest portion of leg, hitting the bone; let it remain there a moment, then pull out and touch the end of the fork to your lip. If it is very warm or hot, the meat is done.

Grilled Whole Red Snapper

with Zucchini and Vidalia Onions

This barbecue requires a well-seasoned grill to keep the fish from sticking. Grillers will be rewarded with an exceptional juiciness and depth of flavor that can only be achieved by cooking fish on the bone.—J.W.

Servings: 4

4 medium red snappers (about 1½ pounds each), gutted, scaled

1 cup teriyaki marinade (or a mixture of soy sauce, honey, chopped garlic, and chopped fresh ginger to taste)

Vegetable oil

2 pounds zucchini (about 6 medium), quartered lengthwise

Extra-virgin olive oil

Salt and pepper to taste

4 medium Vidalia onions (or red Bermuda onions), each peeled and sliced into 2 thick (1-inch) slices

1. Marinate the whole fish overnight in the teriyaki sauce, turning once. Heat grill to very hot and season it with vegetable oil.

2. Toss the zucchini with a few drops of extra-virgin olive oil, salt, and black pepper. Rub a little olive oil on the flat surfaces of the onions, and season them with salt.

3. Lay the whole fish onto the grill lengthwise in line with the bars of your grill. Distribute the onions around the fish. Grill 5 minutes without disturbing. Using tongs and a long spatula, lift and turn the fish. Cook 4 minutes more until just done at the bone, testing with a fork. The fork should go in and out easily at the thickest part of the fish.

4. Remove the fish from the grill. Turn the onions, and distribute the zucchini on the grill. Cook about 5 minutes, until browned, then serve on plates with the fish.

Spectacular Shrimp for Two

SUBMITTED BY PATRICIA G. NAGLE, ALBUQUERQUE, NEW MEXICO

My husband said to write this one down. 'Nuff said?

Servings: 2
½ red onion, diced (about ½ cup)
2 Tbs. butter
20 raw large or jumbo shrimp, peeled
1 tsp. fresh thyme (or ½ tsp. dried)
1 tsp. dried cilantro, or 3 tsp. fresh, chopped
1 tsp. lemon juice
1 to 3 Tbs. sherry
¼ cup heavy cream

1. Sauté onion in butter until clear and limp. Add shrimp, cook on low/medium heat, stirring until shrimp are almost completely pink.

2. Add thyme, cilantro, and lemon; stir in sherry. Turn heat to low; stir in cream. Raise heat and cook 1 minute, until cream thickens. Serve immediately with rice or pasta.

We owe much to the fruitful meditation of our sages, but a sane view of life is, after all, elaborated mainly in the kitchen.

Joseph Conrad

A Taste of Tuscany—Braised Veal "Osso Buco"

SUBMITTED BY DAWN ALTOMARI-RATHJEN, PORT EWEN, NEW YORK

Although I am a graduate of the Culinary Institute of America, I believe I learned most of my best cooking from my aunt Gloria! For example, sample my favorite comfort meal, a hearty dish of steaming Osso Buco. Serve with crusty Italian semolina bread to mop up all the juices left on your plate.

Servings: 8

1½ tsp. olive oil

5 pounds veal shanks, sliced by butcher into 1½-inch-thick cross sections

Salt and freshly cracked or ground black pepper to taste

4 onions, peeled and sliced into large wedges

4 carrots, peeled and cut into thirds

2 stalks celery, cleaned and cut into thirds

1 leek, thoroughly cleaned and chopped large

½ bulb garlic (about 7 cloves), peeled and minced

3 fresh tomatoes, roughly chopped

1 cup red wine

3 cups rich brown stock or bouillon

2 bay leaves

¼ bunch parsley

¼ bunch fresh thyme (or 1 Tbs. dried thyme leaves)

¼ bunch fresh oregano (or 1 Tbs. dried oregano leaves)

1 Tbs. salt

Freshly ground black pepper to taste

1. Heat oven to 325°. Heat oil in a Dutch oven or an ovenproof casserole with a tight-fitting cover on the stovetop. Season veal shanks generously with salt and pepper and brown on all sides.

(recipe continued on next page)

2. Add onions, carrots, celery, leek, garlic, and tomatoes. Cook over medium heat, until lightly browned. Pour in wine; cook until it reduces to half its original volume. Add stock, bay leaves, parsley, thyme, and oregano. Liquid should come two-thirds of the way up on the meat and vegetables. Bring to a boil, and then cover and place in oven.

3. Allow to cook slowly, undisturbed in the oven for 2 to 3 hours, until the meat is very tender and falls off the bone. (This cooking method is known as braising.) Adjust seasoning with remaining salt and pepper.

Talk of Joy: There may be things better than beef stew and baked potatoes and homemade bread—there may be.

David Grayson

The Truth about Meat Thermometers

When checking meats for doneness, nothing beats an exact temperature reading. There are two types of meat thermometers; both are equally accurate. One type is inserted into the roast before cooking and remains in the roast, providing a constant reading of the internal temperature. The newer type, preferred by professional chefs because of its versatility, is the instant-read thermometer, which is inserted into a roast at any point for an up-to-the minute reading. Both are relatively inexpensive and fill an essential role in the properly equipped kitchen.

The Little Red Can

By Amy D. Johnson, Arlington, Texas

I've always loved to visit my grandparents in Cleburne, Texas, and as anyone in the family can tell you, there is always a gathering around the dining room table for meals and hilarious conversations. As the first grandbaby, though, I was at a slight disadvantage. When I sat in the dining chair, only my nose could reach the table. Cleburne is a small town, and the phone book boosted me up only an inch. So, Grandma and Grandpa came up with the idea of the little red can.

It was about ten inches high, made of tin, and painted a glorious shiny red. It worked perfectly, enabling me to bang away on the table with my little spoon and cup as I tried to keep up with the joyful banter around the table. After I finished a meal, I was placed on the floor, and the can was opened, and all sorts of surprises kept me busy while the adults visited.

My daughter, Hannah Elizabeth, is the second generation to enjoy the little red can

Pretty soon, other grandbabies started to arrive, and each had their own turn on the little red can. When the last grandbaby graduated to a "real chair," the little red can was relegated to a closet for many years. Decades later, I had a daughter of my own, and we traveled to Cleburne for one of the many family feasts. Grandma proudly pulled out the little red can. It was a little worn, bent, and slightly rusty around an edge or two, but it still worked perfectly, and my daughter loved it just as much as I had.

Betty Korbus's Tuna Croquettes

SUBMITTED BY KAREN ACKLAND, SANTA CRUZ, CALIFORNIA

In my husband's family, tuna croquettes are no joking matter, but when this cherished dish is served at family get-togethers, there seems to be plenty of laughter and conversation all around.

Servings: 6

1 can (6 ounces) tuna, drained, packing oil or water reserved

1 can cream of celery soup, undiluted, divided

1 cup finely crushed cracker crumbs (any kind of cracker)

2 tsp. lemon juice

1/4 cup chopped parsley

1/8 tsp. or less mace

1 egg, beaten

Generous 1/4 cup chili sauce or ketchup

Oil for frying

1. In a large bowl, combine tuna, 1/2 cup of the celery soup, about 1/4 cup of the cracker crumbs, lemon juice, parsley, and mace. Mix well. Add additional cracker crumbs, if necessary, until the mixture is barely firm. Chill and shape into patties or any croquette shape.

2. Combine egg and chili sauce or ketchup. Dip croquettes in egg mixture, then roll in additional cracker crumbs. Fry in small amount of oil over low heat until nicely browned on both sides and hot in the center. Finish in a moderate oven if desired.

3. Make a sauce by combining the remaining soup with some of the reserved tuna oil or water. (We use the tuna in water and don't put any oil in the sauce and it tastes fine.) Add 1/4 cup chili sauce or ketchup. Add a little extra water if you want it thinner. Cook over low heat until hot.

Chicken and Rice Casserole

with Bacon and Mozzarella

SUBMITTED BY DENISE LITTLE, GREEN BAY, WISCONSIN

One day, my younger sister Julie called me up almost in tears. Her baby girl had a mild fever and had been cranky all day. She'd been too busy with the sick baby to go to the store, and her pantry and fridge seemed to have nothing in them for a meal. She wanted something delicious and comforting—it had been a rough few days for both young parents—and it had to be quick and easy to fix. After she gave me a quick inventory of the ingredients she had on hand, I came up with this chicken casserole.

Servings: 8

3 Tbs. olive oil

1 small onion, finely chopped

8 boneless, skinless chicken thighs

8 ounces grated mozzarella cheese

8 slices bacon

8 wooden toothpicks

1½ cups uncooked white rice

Salt, pepper, and seasonings to taste

1½ cups canned chicken broth (12-ounce can)

1½ cups white wine (*if preferred, use water or more chicken broth instead*)

Julie and her daughter Lauren

1. Heat oven to 350° F. Place the olive oil and onion in the bottom of a glass casserole dish at least 8 × 8 × 3 inches in size, and place casserole in oven.

(recipe continued on next page)

2. While onion is cooking, season the boneless chicken thighs with salt and pepper and stuff the cavity where the bone was in each thigh with grated cheese, about 1 ounce per thigh. (This is about what will fit naturally. A little more or less won't matter.) Wrap each cheese-stuffed thigh with a slice of bacon, and use a toothpick to hold together the opening on the thigh and to keep the bacon in place.

3. Carefully remove casserole dish with onion and oil in it from the oven. Stir the cooked onion and hot oil to prevent it from sticking to the bottom of the pan, and stir in dry white rice. Arrange bacon-wrapped chicken thighs, split side down, on top of rice. Season thighs with salt and pepper. Pour in chicken stock and white wine (or other liquid, to make a total of 3 cups). Place uncovered casserole dish in preheated oven, and cook until rice is fluffy and chicken is cooked through—about 45 minutes.

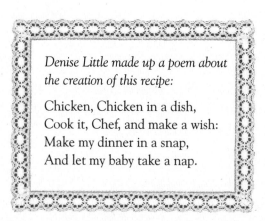

Denise Little made up a poem about the creation of this recipe:

Chicken, Chicken in a dish,
Cook it, Chef, and make a wish:
Make my dinner in a snap,
And let my baby take a nap.

Hobo Casserole

SUBMITTED BY TINA A. SHRADER, BLUEFIELD, WEST VIRGINIA

I came up with this recipe when I was a newly divorced mom with little money. Now, when I fix this simple casserole, my family is reminded of how a dish made from next to nothing brought us a heaping helping of comfort during a difficult time—and of how fortunate we are to share a meal and a home together today.

Servings: 12

1 can (16 ounces) tomato juice

2 cans (15.5 ounces each) pinto beans

5 to 6 large potatoes, peeled and sliced very thin (about 6 cups)

1 large onion, peeled and sliced (about 3 cups)

Salt and pepper to taste

2 pounds ground beef, shaped into 12 thin patties

1. Heat oven to 400°. Pour about one-third of the tomato juice into a 9- × 13- × 2-inch glass baking dish; tilt to coat. Distribute 1 can of the pinto beans evenly; make a layer with half of the potatoes. Spread on half of the onions, and season with salt and pepper. Repeat the layers until the pinto beans, potatoes, and onions are all used. Pour a third of the tomato juice evenly over the casserole.

2. Distribute the beef patties over the top of the casserole, trying to cover the top completely. Shingle them if they are too large. Pour remaining tomato juice over the top.

3. Cover with foil, and bake for 90 minutes. Remove cover and bake another 30 minutes, until potatoes in center are tender and cooked through. Remove from the oven and cool slightly before serving.

chapter five

All *the* Trimmings
Pasta and Side Dishes

Red Sauce

BY DANIELLE ANNE CAMPBELL, STATELINE, NEVADA

When I think of my grandfather, I see him in the kitchen, creating, savoring, alone in his element with his God. In his sanctuary, the dark oak cabinets glisten from the sweat of his cooking. The polished copper pots shimmer on their racks, clanging shoulder to shoulder next to satin-finished stainless steel. Pots of red sauce bubble and churn on the stove. Steam rises all around, carrying sweet herbs and red wine. Dark meat simmers in the marinade on the fire.

Grandpa made red sauce better than anyone in the family, man or woman. His sauces would take days, sometimes weeks to make. The process began with marinating the meat. "Aged meat has the best flavor," he'd say. Red meat with patches of brown had the character he preferred. The local butcher always kept a package for Grandpa in the back.

I would sit at the small kitchen table and silently watch his masterful movements. I'd sip Grandpa's rich hot chocolate, never too sweet or too bitter, topped with hand-whipped, silky cream and freshly grated dark chocolate. I liked to pretend I was in a small Italian village, watching a great European chef cooking in his restaurant.

Grandpa reminded me of a dancer. Like Fred Astaire, he'd glide across the tiled brick floor to where the herbs hung. Grown in his garden in summer and dried for the winter months, the season of the herbs gave the winter and summer sauces their unique flavor.

Ceremoniously, with eyes closed, he'd place a dried leaf into his mouth. He'd move the herb with his tongue, sashaying his jaws from side to side, swirling it, resuscitating it, as if it were Communion.

Then, his decision made, he'd swiftly pluck the perfect number of leaves from the stalk. Mercilessly, he crumbled them between his index finger and thumb, dropping them into the hot liquid. What remained on his hands was added, too, with a rub and one decisive *clap*!

On a small turquoise and olive flowered plate, he'd offer me a few of the exotic anisette cookies from his pantry, the kind of cookies I only ate there. I'd nibble and dip, the way I thought the ladies of Italy might do with their thick, dark coffee.

The pots would simmer and shake, the sauces making popping sounds here and there, while Grandpa and I talked. Grandpa was a handsome man with a

The author with her grandfather on her second birthday

boyishly round face, backlit by silky brown eyes, framed in thick, curly, chestnut hair, but what I loved most were his hands. I'd watch them as he spoke, thick, rugged and strong, capable of anything.

He'd season, taste, add a touch of red wine. Season, taste, simmer, throw in a pinch of basil. Season, taste, simmer, drizzle a sweep of olive oil on top. He'd reach for the jar of dried mushrooms kept in the cupboard over the stove: portobellos and porcinis, Italian mushrooms. The mushrooms were one of the secrets of his sauce. In the past,

Grandpa had lived near moist, wooded areas, where he picked his own mushrooms, awakening them from their sleep nestled under fallen logs. In Carson City, he had to purchase mushrooms from the grocery store, but still he did so by hand, examining each and every one. Meticulously, he'd dry them every summer outside in the hot desert sun.

I'd watch his large hand, graceful and sure, armed with his wooden tasting spoon, plunge deep into the steaming pot. Before long, the reddened spoon reappeared, carrying with it the thick crimson liquid. Grandpa took it in, breathing deeply the aroma of his creation, his first taste of the sauce.

Then lightly he'd sip, ceremoniously, eyes closed. I scrutinized the slow movement of his Adam's apple as he'd swallow and the odd sound his tongue made, pushing and pulling against the roof of his mouth. A giggle would tickle at my chest. A mouthful of Chianti and then another taste.

I'd watch while he spoke into the sauce and stirred. Steam rising around his face and head, Grandpa became a wizard, the creator of a magical potion. I believed that his stained spoon carried with it special powers, magic that made his sauce the best.

To this day, Grandpa's sauces have never been duplicated. No matter how closely we follow his recipes, they never taste quite the same. His sauces were flavored with the taste of his hands and his heart, his labor and his love. No one could ever replicate that.

Grandpa accompanies me each and every time I dance my dance in the kitchen. Armed with my wooden tasting spoon, his spirit moves me to season and taste, to simmer and stir, to lean over the steaming red, hot liquid and murmur my prayers into the pot.

···· ⸹ ····

It occurred to me that when people are tired and hungry, which in adult life is much of the time, they do not want to be confronted with an intellectually challenging meal. They want to be consoled.

Laurie Colwin

Fresh Fruit Cocktail

SUBMITTED BY STEPHANIE SARNOFF, EUGENE, OREGON

This soul-satisfying dish is a refreshing way to include essential nutrients in your kids' (and your own) diet. Great as a side dish, it can also be used as a topping for cereal, yogurt, or cottage cheese.

Servings: 8

2 large oranges
1 large red apple
1 can (20 ounces) crushed pineapple in
   its own juice

1 cup white seedless grapes
½ cup maraschino cherry juice
½ cup maraschino cherries, sliced
1 large banana

1. Peel the oranges. Separate segments and cut each in half, cutting over the bowl to reserve the juice.

2. Core and dice the apple. (It is not necessary to peel, but if you prefer peeled, go ahead.)

3. In a ceramic bowl, mix together the fruit juices and all of the fruits—except for the banana.

4. Cover and chill (overnight is okay), or serve immediately.

5. Spoon into individual bowls and slice banana on top.

Variations: Substitute Chambourd raspberry liquor and fresh raspberries for maraschino juice and cherries. Substitute (or just add) fresh sliced strawberries, kiwi, mangoes, peaches, or pears.

I once believed that eating healthy meant eating food that was missing something—TASTE. I once believed eating healthy meant being unsatisfied. I once believed eating healthy meant no security, no comfort, no love.

Oprah Winfrey

Spinach Lasagna Rolls

SUBMITTED BY KATE MCBRIDE, FOXBORO, MASSACHUSETTS

*This meatless lasagna is lighter than the usual layered style and is
a hit with kids (in spite of the spinach) and vegetarians (because of it)!*

Servings: 12

1 onion, chopped

¼ cup good-quality olive oil

3 cloves garlic, chopped

¼ tsp. red pepper flakes

1 Tbs. sugar

2 cans (28 ounces) peeled plum
   tomatoes, chopped

1 carrot, grated

1 zucchini, grated

Salt and pepper to taste

1 2-pound container part skim
   ricotta cheese

1 egg

½ tsp. salt

½ tsp. white pepper

¼ tsp. nutmeg

1 16-ounce package shredded
   mozzarella cheese

1 cup grated Parmesan cheese

1 package frozen chopped spinach,
   cooked and drained well

1 box lasagna noodles, curly edge
   preferred, cooked and drained

1. Sauté chopped onion in olive oil until soft. Add garlic, red pepper flakes, sugar, and tomatoes, juice and all. Stir in grated carrot and zucchini. Salt and pepper to taste. Simmer the sauce for at least 1 hour, until the shredded vegetables have dissolved and the flavors have blended.

2. Put ricotta cheese in a large mixing bowl. Crack and stir the egg into the cheese. Add salt, pepper, and nutmeg. Add two-thirds of the shredded mozzarella and all of the Parmesan. Add chopped, drained spinach. Mix the filling well.

(recipe continued on next page)

3. Once sauce and filling are done, spoon a ladle full of the cooked sauce to cover the bottom of a lasagna pan.

4. Place a generous ¼ cup portion of the filling on one end of a lasagna noodle and roll it up, and place the roll in the pan. Repeat until the pan is full. Cover the rolls with sauce and sprinkle the remaining shredded mozzarella on top.

5. Bake in a 300° oven, covered, for 45 minutes, and uncovered for an additional 10 minutes. Let sit for 15 minutes to settle before serving. Serve 2 rolls per person in a warmed bowl.

Caitlin McBride, at 2½, learned to love spinach because of this dish

Now, That's Italian!

Not all pasta is created equal. If your pasta comes out gummy or has a sour, bitter, or floury taste, try switching brands. There can be a significant difference between the quality of pasta brands and only a few cents' difference between the prices. If you're wondering why your pasta isn't coming out as nicely as someone else's you like, find out what brand they use and try it. And remember: Just because it's imported from Italy doesn't mean it's better. You'll find variations in quality in both domestic and imported dried pasta brands.

Macaroni and Cheese

SUBMITTED BY JANE PARKS-McKAY, SANTA CRUZ, CALIFORNIA

When I was learning to type at the junior high school I attended in Huntsville, Alabama, in the 1960s, I typed this recipe as a homework assignment using an old Underwood manual typewriter. In true Southern belle tradition, I'd started a hope chest and filled it chock-full with things I would eventually use when I left home and married. I tucked this recipe into the recipe box in my hope chest. Years later as a newlywed, not knowing how to cook and loving anything with cheese in it, I pulled this out of my recipe box. To this day, making this dish brings back tender memories, and eating it creates new ones. Use good-quality cheddar for this recipe, and the flavor will shine through.

Servings: 4

8 ounces (half a box) elbow macaroni	1 tsp. salt
2 Tbs. oil	¼ tsp. black pepper
2 Tbs. flour	3 cups grated cheddar cheese, divided
3 cups milk	½ cup dry bread crumbs

1. Cook macaroni until tender; drain well.

2. In a medium saucepan over moderate heat, whisk together the oil and flour; cook 5 minutes. Gradually whisk in the milk, in three additions, allowing mixture to thicken between each addition. Season with salt and pepper; cook over low heat 1 minute. Fold in 2 cups of the cheese; remove from heat.

3. Combine the cheese sauce and cooked macaroni, and spread into a lightly buttered 1½-quart baking dish. Spread the remaining 1 cup of cheese over the macaroni. Sprinkle bread crumbs over casserole. Add salt and pepper. Bake at 350° for 30 minutes, until bubbly and golden on top.

Boston Baked Beans

SUBMITTED BY SHERRIL STEELE-CARLIN, RENO, NEVADA

My family has lived "out West" since 1949, but we're still New Englanders at heart—and in the kitchen. Throughout my childhood, Saturday-night suppers were often homemade Boston Baked Beans with Boston Brown Bread. I learned this recipe from my mom, who learned it from her mother. They're both gone now, and I miss them terribly. Even though I've never lived in New England and have only visited once, whenever I make this meal, I feel a sense of belonging, a connection to New England and to my mother and my grandmother.

Servings: 24

*2 cups pea beans or navy beans, soaked
    overnight in 1 quart water*
1 onion, peeled and quartered
*¼ pound salt pork, scored in crosshatch
    pattern, ¾ of the way through*

¼ tsp. baking soda
1 tsp. dry mustard
½ cup molasses
½ tsp. salt
2 Tbs. brown sugar

1. Place presoaked and drained beans, along with onion, salt pork, and baking soda, in a large saucepan. Cover with boiling water. Simmer until outer layer of beans begins to split, 1 hour. Drain.

2. Heat oven to 300°. In mixing bowl, blend mustard, molasses, salt, and brown sugar; add to beans. Transfer to a covered casserole dish; add enough water to almost cover. Bake for about 3 hours, until the beans are very soft, bubbly, and browned through. Uncover for the last half hour of baking. If beans appear too dry, add extra water during baking; they should be saucy.

Savory Bread Stuffing

Just about every American kid has had a nightmare experience with "green" stuffing—so heavily endowed with sage that it nearly gets up off the platter and walks outside to join its brethren grass. But for every Stupefying Sage stuffing, there is one from our childhood that is so delicious we dream about it the rest of our lives. Here's one of those memorable dressings—with just the right amount of sage!—J.W.

Servings: 8

¼ pound slab bacon, cut in ½-inch dice

2 cups roughly chopped onions

1 rib roughly chopped celery

1 Tbs. chopped garlic

1 tsp. rubbed sage

1 stick (4 ounces) plus 1 Tbs. butter

1 Granny Smith apple, peeled and
   roughly chopped

¼ cup raisins

2 cups cold chicken stock

8 cups day-old bread, cut up

½ cup chopped Italian (flat leaf) parsley

1 tsp. salt and a few grinds black pepper

2 eggs, beaten

1 chicken (3½ to 4½ pounds)

1. Render the bacon over medium heat in a large skillet until halfway cooked (slightly browned, but still soft). Add onions, celery, garlic, and sage, and raise heat to high. Cook 5 minutes, until translucent. Add butter, apple, and raisins, and cook an additional 5 minutes. Remove from heat. Add the cold stock.

2. In a large mixing bowl, combine the bread cubes, parsley, onion mixture, salt and pepper, and eggs. Mix well. Let stand 5 minutes to soak up liquid. (Mixture should be pretty saucy when ready.)

3. Stuff chicken or turkey cavity, and bake as directed (page 135). Or spread the stuffing into a lightly greased baking dish and bake covered in a 350° oven for 30 minutes. Remove the cover and bake another 15 minutes to brown the top.

Evelyn's Marinated Carrots

SUBMITTED BY EVELYN BRISBOIS, RIFTON, NEW YORK

These are always a hit and fun to enjoy anytime. They should marinate at least overnight in the refrigerator, but remember that the longer they marinate, the better they taste!

Servings: 12–24

2 pounds of carrots, sliced on the diagonal, cooked until just tender
1 large red bell pepper, sliced
1 large green bell pepper, sliced
1 large onion, sliced thinly
1/2 cup white vinegar

1/2 cup sugar
1/3 cup vegetable oil
1 Tbs. dry mustard
1/2 tsp. salt
1/2 tsp. pepper
2 small cans tomato paste

1. Place the carrots, peppers, and onion together in large bowl.

2. In a small saucepan, bring the white vinegar and sugar and to a boil. Add the vinegar and sugar mixture to the vegetables. Then add the vegetable oil, mustard, salt, pepper, and tomato paste.

3. Toss with the vegetables and let sit until cool. Place in the refrigerator. Marinate overnight in the refrigerator.

···· ····

From quiet homes and first beginnings,
Out to the undiscovered ends,
There's nothing worth the wear of winning,
But laughter and the love of friends.

Hilaire Belloc

Sausage-Potato Stuffing

SUBMITTED BY BARBARA BEAUDOIN, CHELMSFORD, MASSACHUSETTS

In our family, holiday turkey always means dressing made with mashed potatoes instead of bread. The original recipe was passed on to me not only by my mother but also by my mother-in-law. Whoever would have guessed that my husband's mom and my mom (both of Italian parents) would serve this French Canadian–inspired dressing as their traditional holiday recipe? They had each been given the recipe by their mothers-in-law. Until I met my husband, I didn't know anyone else who'd had this stuffing. Fate must have brought us together. Holiday dinners now include our children, their spouses, and our grandchildren, and we all look forward to "our stuffing." It is our connection to family members who came before us, and I hope this dish will continue to appear at the Thanksgiving dinners of my future great-grandchildren.

Servings: 10–12

4 Italian pork sausage links (casings removed)

½ roll (about 6 ounces) of pork sausage

Salt and pepper to taste

2 tablespoons olive oil

1 medium onion, finely chopped

3 medium celery stalks, finely chopped

6 ounces cremini or similar mushrooms, sliced

½ tsp. each of dried sage, thyme, and oregano

1 egg, beaten

¾ cup low-sodium chicken broth

5 pounds potatoes, peeled, boiled, and mashed

1. Combine sausage meat in a large bowl and break up with a fork; season with salt and pepper. In a large skillet, add oil and sauté onion, celery, and mushrooms for about 10 minutes, or until vegetables are soft. Season to taste with fresh or dried sage, thyme, and oregano. Add meat mixture and cook over medium heat until sausage is cooked and lightly browned. Drain excess fat.

(recipe continued on next page)

From left to right: Edward and Anna Hamilton,
Barbara and Edward Beaudoin Jr.,
and Josie and Edward Beaudoin

2. Add beaten egg and the chicken broth to the mashed potatoes and mix well. Add the meat/vegetable mixture to the potatoes. Mix well (a potato masher is helpful for this) and refrigerate. If using to stuff a turkey, chill thoroughly before filling the bird.

3. If baking on the side (recommended), proceed as follows. Heat oven to 350°. Bake the dressing in a large covered casserole for 1 hour. Remove the cover and bake for another 20 minutes to brown the top.

Variations: Add finely chopped walnuts, grated carrots, golden raisins, or chopped apples to the vegetable mixture.

> ### To Keep Potatoes from Budding
>
> Place an apple in the potato bag.

There's nothing like a dishtowel for wiping that contented after-dinner look off a husband's face.

Anonymous

Garlic Mashed Potatoes

The only thing more comforting than buttery mashed potatoes is buttery mashed potatoes with the round, vegetal flavor of garlic, especially roasted garlic. I like to place a helping of them in the center of the plate, lean a steak, chop, or slice of meatloaf against it, and pour gravy over the whole shebang.—J.W.

Servings: 4

1½ pounds (about 4) peeled potatoes, cut
    roughly into 1-inch pieces
1 head garlic (about 10 cloves), peeled
1½ sticks butter
½ cup cream
2 tsp. salt

1. Boil potatoes and garlic cloves together in enough water to cover them until very soft, about 25 minutes. Drain well, and return to pan on stove to dry for 1 minute. Melt together the butter and cream (can be done in microwave).

2. In a standing mixer, using the whip attachment, or in a large mixing bowl with a stiff whisk, mash the potato-garlic mixture with salt. Gradually mash in the butter mixture. Mash only enough to achieve a smooth consistency and mix ingredients. Season to taste.

Variation: Roast the garlic before adding to the potatoes. (See page 76.)

Less Is More . . .

Overwhipping potatoes turns them into gluey gluten. The key is to mash (or whip) spuds by machine just enough to break up the lumps, then to fold in the butter, milk, and seasonings by hand. For really smooth spuds, press cooked potatoes through a ricer, which looks like an oversized garlic press, then fold in the milk, butter, and seasonings by hand. For a more homestyle (lumpy) texture, use either a stiff whisk or a good ole potato masher.

Green Boats

SUBMITTED BY GORDON KELLEY, EUGENE, OREGON

When I first made these, I thought the finished potato halves looked like boats. So, in a silly Dad moment, I was inspired to cut thin slices of cheddar into triangles and insert them into the top of each potato to make a sail. I delivered the plates to our kids (ages four and seven at the time), humming a brisk little tune and making steamboat noises ("Toot! Toot!"). Aradia and Zane thought it was hilarious and dubbed them Green Boats on the spot.

Servings: 4

4 large baking potatoes
2 cups finely chopped broccoli
    (steamed)
1 cup grated white cheddar cheese

Splash of milk
Pinch of salt
4 small triangles, about $1/8$ inch thick, of
    white or yellow cheddar cheese

1. Make a shallow lengthwise cut around the edge of each potato. Bake in a 400° oven for 1 hour.

2. Scoop the cooked potato into a bowl, being careful not to tear the skins. Place the empty skins on a baking sheet.

3. Mash the potatoes; add and blend in the other ingredients. Fill the skins. Return the filled skins to the oven and bake for another 5 to 10 minutes.

4. Stick the triangular cheese sails into the potato boats.

···· ❦ ····

My idea of heaven is a great big baked potato and someone to share it with.

Oprah Winfrey

Spicy Stuffed Comfort Potatoes

with a Heart-Healthy Option

SUBMITTED BY FAITH BRYNIE, BIGFORK, MONTANA

After my husband and soul mate underwent open-heart surgery, our lives and our diets changed forever. In time, my husband's health improved, and we were grateful for the added years we could now spend with one another and our loved ones. Though we adjusted to the life changes, it was a challenge and a disappointment trying to cook heart-healthy and tasty meals . . . until I found some flavorful new dishes for us to enjoy together. Inspired by a recipe I saw in a magazine while sitting in the cardiologist's waiting room, I went home and concocted a modified, low-fat version of spicy twice-baked potatoes for my hubby and me.

Servings: 4
2 large baking potatoes (about 1 pound each)
3 Tbs. sour cream
¼ cup skim milk
2 Tbs. margarine or butter
1 can (15 ounces) red kidney beans, drained and rinsed
1 small onion, minced
1 Tbs. minced fresh cilantro or 1 tsp. dried Italian spices
4 Tbs. tomato salsa
½ cup shredded cheddar cheese
Salt and pepper to taste

(recipe continued on next page)

1. Bake the potatoes in the oven (90 minutes at 350°) or microwave, cool them enough so you can handle them comfortably, and cut in half lengthwise. Scoop the insides of the potatoes into a mixing bowl. Reserve the skins.

2. Heat oven to 400°. Mash or whip the potatoes with the sour cream, milk, and margarine. Stir in remaining ingredients and return the contents to the skins. Bake for 30 minutes. Serve with extra salsa, sour cream, and margarine, as desired.

Variation for Heart-Healthy Comfort Potatoes: Substitute fat-free sour cream (not so-called "imitation sour cream," which is high in sodium); use a cholesterol-lowering spread, such as Benecol or Take Control brand, in place of regular butter or margarine; use fat-free shredded cheese; season with a salt substitute. Also, draining and rinsing the beans well removes much of their salt content.

The dinner table is the center for the teaching and practicing not just of table manners but of conversation, consideration, tolerance, family feelings, and just about all the other accomplishments of polite society except the minuet.

Judith Martin ("Miss Manners")

Home Fries

On my way home from junior high school, a generally unpleasant time in any adolescent life, I found daily comfort at the counter of my town's old-fashioned luncheonette in the form of a $1.25 plate of crisp, bacon-scented home fries just like these.—J.W.

Servings: 4

1 pound (about 3 medium) peeled white
   potatoes, halved

4 slices bacon

2 medium onions, sliced thinly
   (about 3 cups)

1 tsp. salt

Black pepper to taste

1. Boil potatoes until medium-tender but *not* falling apart. Chill 1 hour or overnight. Slice into ½-inch slices.

2. In a large heavy skillet or on a griddle, cook the bacon until crisp. Remove from pan, leaving the grease in the pan. Add the onions to the bacon oil and cook over moderate heat until soft, about 10 minutes.

3. Add the potatoes and cook slowly, adding a nugget of butter if necessary, until nicely browned, about 20 to 25 minutes. The trick to great browning here is not to disturb them while they're cooking, until a crisp crust has formed. Scrape up and turn only once or twice with a spatula.

4. Crumble in 1 slice of the bacon; reserve the rest for another use. Season the fries well with salt and pepper.

···· ❦ ····

What I say is that, if a fellow really likes potatoes,
he must be a pretty decent sort of fellow.

A. A. Milne

A Cookbook for Allie

BY SANDY KEEFE, EL DORADO HILLS, CALIFORNIA

When I was a little girl, Friday night was always macaroni and cheese night at our house. Mom would boil the elbow macaroni, chop mild cheddar cheese into cubes, and grate peppercorns with a hand mill. With seven children at home, the casserole went fast—no seconds, no leftovers!

Before leaving home, I carefully copied my mom's recipe onto an index card. A little more adventurous than my mother, I would stir in a can of tomatoes or some fresh dill from time to time. When my oldest daughter, Shannon, turned ten, we spent a rainy afternoon creating *Shannon's Cookbook* in a blue loose-leaf binder, and "Grandma's Macaroni and Cheese" was the first entry.

Then my youngest daughter, Allie, came along. Born with Down syndrome, Allie had visual impairments and a number of physical limitations. She was also impulsive and lacked awareness of basic safety rules. When she turned ten, I sat down to begin *Allie's Cookbook* in yet another loose-leaf binder. I chose an easy-to-read felt-tip marker and colorful paper, and thought about the wonderful recipes handed down in our family.

Picking up the old faded index card with my mom's original macaroni and cheese recipe, I stared in silence. It would be a long time before Allie could handle a sharp knife to cube the cheese, and her little hands lacked the fine motor skill required to turn the pepper mill.

The markings on our measuring cups were too small for her to see, and the hot stove was a definite danger.

Determined to adapt the macaroni and cheese recipe for Allie, I stood up and put on my favorite red-striped apron. Rifling through cupboards and drawers, I gathered equipment for a simpler version of our beloved casserole. A safe, easy-to-handle plastic grater replaced the sharp knife. A tin of ground pepper substituted for the pepper mill. A bright red strip of masking tape marked the one-cup level in an unbreakable plastic measuring cup. As

Allie grates cheese

a final preparation step, I boiled a batch of elbow macaroni and let it cool to room temperature.

Using the felt-tip marker and a sheet of lilac paper, I wrote the recipe for "Allie's Macaroni and Cheese." Then, I placed the paper inside a clear plastic sheet protector and inserted it into the binder labeled "Allie's Cookbook."

When Allie came home from day camp, she immediately noticed the new cookbook on the counter. "Allie's!" she shouted joyfully. With only a little help, she gathered her ingredients and went to work. Tongue clenched between her teeth in concentration, she grated cheese and stirred it into the noodles.

Three generations: (clockwise from top right) Sandy Keefe; her two daughters, Allie and Shannon; and her mother, Lois Horton Brown

Chuckling happily over the bright red tape on the measuring cup, she added milk to the pasta. A sprinkle of pepper, a quick stir, and her masterpiece was ready for the oven.

At dinner that night, Allie bounced in her seat and laughed aloud as we sampled her macaroni and cheese, and her dad testified that it was "the best macaroni and cheese ever!"

Allie's Macaroni and Cheese

SUBMITTED BY SANDY KEEFE, EL DORADO HILLS, CALIFORNIA

Help your kids make this easy dish for the family and watch them burst with pride as the compliments come rolling in!

Servings: 4

1 pound cooked macaroni (cooled)
2 cups grated sharp cheddar cheese
1 cup milk

½ stick (¼ cup) margarine or butter
5 shakes pepper

1. Wash your hands with soap and water.
2. Rinse and dry your hands.
3. Dump the macaroni into the big red bowl.
4. Grate the cheese on the cutting board.
5. Pick up the cheese and put it in the red bowl with the macaroni.
6. Pour the milk into the red bowl, too.
7. Cut the margarine into small pieces and put it into the red bowl.
8. Shake the pepper into the red bowl 5 times.
9. Stir everything in the red bowl with your hands.
10. Ask Mom to put the red bowl in the oven.

Note for Mom or Dad: Bake covered at 350° for 1 hour.

Noodle Nut Noodles

SUBMITTED BY SUSAN BILLINGS MITCHELL, TAYLORSVILLE, UTAH

Homemade egg noodles are fun to make and scrump-deli-icious!
No wonder our family is nuts for noodles!

Dad dries his homemade noodles
with Mom's hair dryer

Happiness is homemade.
Anonymous

Servings: 3 cups cooked noodles
1 egg
2 Tbs. cream or milk
1 Tbs. melted shortening or vegetable oil
¼ tsp. baking powder
¼ tsp. salt
1 cup of flour, or enough to make stiff
  dough

1. In a large bowl, mix together egg, cream or milk, and shortening. Slowly stir in baking powder, salt, and enough flour to make a stiff but workable dough. Wrap dough in plastic film and let stand for 30 minutes.

2. On a floured surface, roll dough as thin as possible—at least as thin as a computer floppy disk. If it is too elastic, cover and let it rest another 10 minutes before rolling further.

(recipe continued on next page)

174

3. Starting at one end, roll dough up into a loose tube, and then cut into thin strips, about ¼ inch wide. Gently unroll the noodles and spread them out on a flat dry surface. Let dry 2 hours (or less, if you blow with a hair dryer).

4. Drop the noodles into a pot of boiling broth (chicken or vegetable stock or stew) or lightly salted water, stirring constantly while adding noodles. Cook uncovered about 10 minutes, or until tender but not limp. Serve steaming hot.

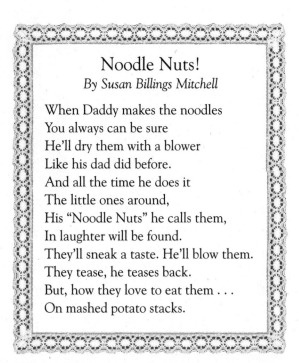

Noodle Nuts!
By Susan Billings Mitchell

When Daddy makes the noodles
You always can be sure
He'll dry them with a blower
Like his dad did before.
And all the time he does it
The little ones around,
His "Noodle Nuts" he calls them,
In laughter will be found.
They'll sneak a taste. He'll blow them.
They tease, he teases back.
But, how they love to eat them . . .
On mashed potato stacks.

Black-Eyed Peas

SUBMITTED BY SHARON PALMER, BRADBURY, CALIFORNIA

In the South, black-eyed peas are considered lucky, and so they are often served on New Year's Day to provide good fortune for the year to come. Black-eyed peas are made thick and soupy, a perfect accompaniment ladled over a fresh batch of corn bread.

Servings: 6

2 cups dried black-eyed peas
6 cups water
1 onion, chopped
2 Tbs. vegetable oil
1 tsp. salt
1 tsp. pepper
1 small ham hock

1. Sort and wash the black-eyed peas. Place in a pot and cover with water. Sauté onion in oil until tender and add to pot. Add salt and pepper and the ham hock. Cover pot and bring to a boil; reduce heat to simmer.

2. Cook for 2 hours, checking water level and stirring frequently. May need to add water, if the level reduces. Serve with corn bread.

My great-grandmother Pemberton, born in 1863, is sitting at the upper left side of the chair.

Anyone who believes for one second that the nouvelle cuisine has had any impact on the way Americans eat in their homes is crazy.

Nora Ephron

Creamed Corn

Now that sweet corn of good quality is available much of the year, celebrate with a rich, comforting dish of creamed corn accompanied by dark greens and crispy fried onion rings.—J.W.

Servings: 4

6 ears sweet corn, shucked
1 Tbs. butter
¼ cup finely chopped shallots or onion
½ cup heavy cream
Salt and freshly ground black pepper to taste
Freshly chopped chives (optional)

1. Using a knife, cut the kernels from the cob with a tip-to-stem slicing motion. You should have about 3 cups.

2. Melt the butter in a skillet; add the shallots and cook until soft, about 3 minutes. Add the corn and cream; cook until thickened, about 2 minutes; season with salt and pepper. Garnish with chives, if desired.

Spring Thaw
By Colleen Sell

Food is more than food
when spring blossoms,
baby vegetables,
and warm hearts
are so near

Basic Polenta (Grits)

Polenta, otherwise known as grits, is about as down-home as you can get. One of the great things about polenta—in addition to simplicity and economy—is its versatility. You can serve good old basic grits like this, or add in some spices and beans, use it as the base of a vegetarian casserole, or leave out the Parmesan and eat it for breakfast topped with warmed fruit and a sprinkling of sugar.—J.W.

Servings: 8

6 cups water

2 cups coarse ground cornmeal

2 tsp. salt

4 Tbs. butter

1 cup grated Italian Parmesan cheese (such as Parmigiano
   Reggiano)

1. Bring water to a rapid boil in a heavy saucepot. Whisk in cornmeal in a steady stream. Lower heat to very low.

2. Cook, stirring with a wooden spoon, for 20 minutes, until polenta has reached its full thickness (it should be as thick as oatmeal, and a wooden spoon should stand upright for a few seconds when placed in the center of the pot) and is smooth. Beware: Polenta is like molten lava at this point and can splash.

(recipe continued on next page)

3. Season with salt and pepper. Stir in the butter and cheese. Polenta will become thicker as it cools. Portion onto plates or serving platter and top with garnish of your choice. Some excellent toppings for polenta include:

- Tomato sauce and sliced cheese
- Sautéed mushrooms
- Stewed meats such as chicken or rabbit
- Meatballs

The child gathers the food on which the adult feeds to the end.

Ralph Iron

Crisp Grilled or Fried Polenta

Polenta and its Southern U.S. cousin, grits, gel into firm cakes when chilled. These cakes can be brushed with oil and placed on a hot grill to form a nice crust or panfried to crisp, golden perfection. Spread hot polenta on sheet pans to cool. Then use cookie cutters to create shapes for frying or grilling, making individual polenta cakes that, when cooked again, will be crisp outside and saucy inside.

Herbed Cabbage Medley

SUBMITTED BY JUDITH GILBERT, VALLEY STREAM, NEW YORK

This light, warmed slaw makes an excellent side dish for hearty meals, especially when the vegetables are in season and purchased fresh from the farmer's market or plucked from your own kitchen garden.

Servings: 4
1 large onion, sliced thinly (2 cups)
2 Tbs. butter or margarine
½ head cabbage, shredded (5 cups)
3 medium carrots, shredded (about 2 cups)
1 tsp. salt
1 tsp. dried oregano

1. In a medium skillet or saucepan, cook the onion in butter for 5 minutes over medium heat, turning only once. Stir in the cabbage, carrots, and salt.

2. Cover and cook over medium heat for 10 minutes more, until tender, turning only once. Stir in crushed oregano.

I was a vegetarian until I started leaning toward the sunlight.

Rita Rudner

Monster Zucchini Mash

SUBMITTED BY LYNN RUTH MILLER, PACIFICA, CALIFORNIA

I love zucchini. I really do. I always have. And I always will. But the first year I grew not one, not two, but several zucchini plants, I ended up with enough zucchini to feed my entire suburb for a year. So, I had to do some creative cooking to make good use out of all those good zukes. This delicious side dish—or vegetarian comfort entrée, if you'd prefer—is a product of that summer of zucchini madness. I hope you'll enjoy it as much as I and all my family, friends, and neighbors still do.

Servings: 4

3 medium zucchini, sliced	½ tsp. soy sauce or tamari
½ head cauliflower, broken into pieces	2 Tbs. wheat germ
9 cloves garlic	2 Tbs. butter

1. In a large pot of rapidly boiling water, cook the zucchini until tender, 5 to 7 minutes. Remove with a slotted spoon. Boil the cauliflower pieces and garlic together until cauliflower is very tender, 10 to 15 minutes.

2. Mash steamed zucchini with cooked cauliflower, garlic, and soy sauce. Spread into an 8-inch square casserole. Top with wheat germ and dot with butter. Bake in a 350° oven for 1 hour.

It is not really an exaggeration to say that peace and happiness begin, geographically, where garlic is used in cooking.

Xavier Marcel Boulestin

Potato and Cheese Dumplings

Pyrohi (Varenyky)

SUBMITTED BY CAROL M. HODGSON, GIBSONS, BRITISH COLUMBIA

My Grandma Josephine helped Grandpa run the farm, and she ran a Polish kitchen with all the traditional Old World foods: cabbage, sausage, and potato dumplings. Most days, there was food cooking on her pot-bellied stove from before sunup till sundown. If a stranger turned up at her door hungry, he'd leave with a full stomach and a bag of vittles for the road. That's just the way she was. I learned a lot about life and cooking and kindness in Grandma's kitchen.

Servings: 6–8 (about 30 dumplings)

2 cups flour

1 tsp. salt

2 eggs, beaten, divided

⅔ cup cold water

4 large potatoes, peeled and boiled until
    tender

1 large onion, chopped

1 Tbs. oil

Salt and pepper to taste

2 cups grated cheddar cheese

2 Tbs. sour cream or plain yogurt

Sour cream and applesauce for garnish

(recipe continued on next page)

Josephine Zatylny, the author's grandmother

1. Mix flour with 1 teaspoon of salt. Add 1 beaten egg and cold water. Knead lightly, then cover with a lid and set aside.

2. For potato filling, mash the hot boiled potatoes. Sauté the onion in the oil until soft, about 5 minutes, and add to mashed potatoes. Season well with salt and pepper and allow to cool. For cheese filling, combine 2 cups of grated cheddar cheese with 1 beaten egg, a little salt, and 2 tablespoons of sour cream or plain yogurt.

3. To form pyrohi, roll dough out thin and cut circles with a cutter or inverted water glass. Holding the cut round in your palm, place 1 teaspoon of filling in center, fold in half, and press the edges to seal. When you press, wetting your finger-tips in cold water will help the dough to seal. Lay pyrohi on dry kitchen towel and cover.

4. When all the pyrohi are made, drop a few at a time into a pot of boiling water and boil for 4 minutes. Lift out with a slotted spoon, drain, and place in a bowl.

5. Add a little melted butter and serve with sour cream, apple-sauce, and/or small pieces of fried bacon. If you wish, pyrohi may also be fried gently until golden brown before serving.

If you can't feed a hundred people, feed just one.

Mother Teresa

Green Bean and Potato Casserole

SUBMITTED BY B. J. LAWRY, COTTER, ARKANSAS

This is a wonderful side dish or a meal in itself. In the Ozark mountain country, where I live, this meal serves as a welcome tummy warmer, especially on those rainy, chilly spring and fall days. Whenever I make it, my neighbor catches the aroma and always finds a reason to visit. My daughter even comes home early from work!

Servings: 4

1 1/2 cups cooked fresh or frozen (10-ounce package) green beans, whole or cut (not julienned)

1/4 cup diced celery

1 cup cooked white potatoes, diced

5 slices bacon, fried crisp and crumbled into bits, divided, drippings reserved

1 small onion, chopped

4 1/2 Tbs. all-purpose flour

1 cup evaporated milk, undiluted

1 cup shredded cheddar cheese

1/3 cup bread crumbs made from toasted seedless rye bread

1. Heat oven to 350°. Combine the green beans, celery, potatoes, and 3 slices crumbled bacon in a casserole dish.

2. Sauté the onion in the bacon drippings. When the onion has softened, add the flour and stir until smooth. Add the milk slowly and cook, stirring constantly, until thickened. Add the cheese and stir until melted.

3. Mix the sauce with the vegetables in the casserole. Sprinkle the top with the toasted rye bread crumbs and the remaining crumbled bacon. Bake for 30 minutes.

Hospitality is one form of worship.

Jewish Proverb

Biz's Too-Good Sweet Potato Casserole

SUBMITTED BY GINNIE SIENA BIVONA, DALLAS, TEXAS

When something is just out-of-this-world great, my kids (five of them, all grown) used to say that it was "too good!" Now, my grandchildren (six of them, all nearly perfect) join the chorus. Nothing pleases me more than when one of my little (or big) ones takes a bite of something I've prepared just for them and says, "Too good!" This recipe for sweet potatoes is my daughter Biz's creation, and if I must say so myself, it is just toooo good!

Biz and her sons, Davis and Spencer

Servings: 8

3 large sweet potatoes
1/4 cup sugar
1/3 teaspoon vanilla
2 eggs, beaten
2 (yes, two!) sticks butter (the real stuff!)
1 tsp. cinnamon
3/4 cup brown sugar

1/3 cup flour
1 cup pecans, coarsely chopped
Pinch salt
1 stick butter, melted, divided

1. Heat oven to 350°. Butter a 1½-quart baking dish. Cook the sweet potatoes on high in the microwave for 15 minutes. Remove from skins and mash. In a small bowl mix sugar, vanilla, eggs, butter, and cinnamon. Add the sugar mixture to the potatoes. Mix well, and transfer to a prepared baking dish.

2. In a mixing bowl, combine the brown sugar, flour, pecans, salt, and melted butter. Mix well and sprinkle on the potatoes. Drizzle the remaining melted butter over the topping. Bake for 30 to 40 minutes. Do not let your teenage son start picking at this before dinner or you won't have any topping left!

Food Woman Baked Veggies

SUBMITTED BY MELINDA FRANK, REDONDO BEACH, CALIFORNIA

Cooking is like meditation to me. Even when all I'm doing is scrambling eggs, it helps me to unscramble after a hectic day. I've also found that sharing a meal brought our family closer together. As my sons got older and started bringing home friends for dinner, I was surprised to learn that some of them rarely had a home-cooked meal with their families. In all these years of sharing all those meals with all those kids, not one of them ever failed to clean his or her plate and to thank me. Now, isn't that something?

Servings: 8

¾ cup olive oil

1 Tbs. balsamic vinegar

1 small red pepper, finely chopped

2 cloves fresh garlic, finely chopped

1 large or 2 medium onions, finely chopped

Dash ground cloves

½ tsp. salt

Ground black pepper, to taste

1 medium eggplant, cut into ¼-inch slices, rinsed in salted water and patted dry

Basil leaves, snipped finely with kitchen scissors

4–6 zucchini, sliced in half and then lengthwise

2 large tomatoes, sliced

Unseasoned bread crumbs (enough to sprinkle over top of casserole, about 1 cup)

1–1½ cups of mozzarella cheese, grated

1. Heat oven to 400°. Mix together oil, vinegar, red pepper, garlic, onions, cloves, salt, and pepper.

2. Lightly coat the bottom of a 9- × 13-inch baking dish with olive oil.

(recipe continued on next page)

"Food Woman" and her sons

3. Place a layer of eggplant in the baking dish, brush with the seasoned oil-and-vinegar mixture. Sprinkle with basil.

4. Add a layer of zucchini slices, and brush with the seasoned oil-and-vinegar mixture.

5. Add a layer of tomato slices, and brush with the seasoned oil-and-vinegar mixture.

6. Sprinkle the top with bread crumbs.

7. Cover the stacks with whatever of the mix is left. Sprinkle lightly with bread crumbs.

8. Bake until fork tender, about 20 minutes. Remove from the oven and sprinkle mozzarella cheese on top. Return to the oven and bake until cheese is melted, about 5 minutes.

···· ····

What I love about cooking is that after a hard day, there is something comforting about the fact that if you melt butter and add flour and then hot stock, it will get thick! It's a sure thing! It's a sure thing in a world where nothing is sure.

Nora Ephron

Rome Applesauce with Cranberry Chutney

Rome apples, named for Rome, New York, not Rome, Italy, make excellent chunky applesauce because they don't disintegrate when cooked.—J.W.

Servings: 8

1 cinnamon stick, about 2 inches long
8 Rome apples, peeled and cut into
   1-inch pieces

¼ cup water
¼ cup sugar
1 recipe Cranberry Chutney (optional)

1. Warm the cinnamon stick, dry, in a heavy-bottomed pot large enough to hold all the apples. Reduce flame to low, and add the apples, water, and sugar. Cover tightly.

2. Simmer gently for 40 minutes, then uncover and simmer 10 minutes more.

3. Either mash gently with a fork, or leave very chunky. Cool and serve with a dollop of Cranberry Chutney.

Cranberry Chutney

My grandmother, who made this sauce every time she made applesauce, felt applesauce was incomplete without cranberry sauce in it. I concur.—J.W.

Servings: 8

2 cups fresh or frozen cranberries
¼ cup very finely diced red onion
1 cup sugar

6 whole cloves
¼ cup water

1. Combine all ingredients in a small heavy-bottomed saucepot.

2. Simmer 10 to 15 minutes, until all cranberries are broken and have a saucy consistency.

Papa's Sea Foam Salad

SUBMITTED BY JANET L. WALBAUM, BAKERSFIELD, CALIFORNIA

This wonderfully light gelatin salad has been served at my family's holiday feasts for four generations. Originally simply named Lime Salad, my grandfather began referring to it as "Sea Foam," because of its color and weightless, fluffy consistency. A great addition to almost any meal, this gelatin and fruit salad goes wonderfully with holiday dinners, adding a festive sea green accent to the plate.

Servings: 6

1 small (3-ounce) package lime Jell-O
1 (29-ounce) can pears in heavy syrup

1 (8-ounce) package cream cheese,
   softened to room temperature
½ pint whipping cream

1. Pour Jell-O into heat-resistant serving bowl (approximately 2½ quarts) or mold. Strain pears, reserving syrup

2. In a small saucepan, bring 1 cup of the pear syrup to a gentle boil. When done, pour hot pear syrup over Jell-O and stir until completely dissolved. Chill in refrigerator until slightly thickened.

3. In the meantime, blend pears in food processor or blender until smooth. Slowly add cream cheese to pears, continuing to process until well combined.

4. Stir cream cheese mixture into thickened Jell-O. Beat whipping cream with electric mixer; then gently fold into gelatin mixture. Refrigerate until set and serve cold.

Stay, stay at home, my heart and rest: home keeping hearts are happiest.

Henry Wadsworth Longfellow

Fusilli with Pesto Sauce

SUBMITTED BY LISA HUGHEY-UNDERWOOD, DANVILLE, CALIFORNIA

To me, comfort food means one thing: pasta. As I've matured, my preference has moved from my childhood favorite of macaroni and cheese to fusilli with pesto sauce. Although store-bought pesto will do in a pinch, the absolute best pesto comes from your own kitchen. You don't need a fancy food processor; a regular high-speed blender works just fine. Start with the freshest basil you can find. This sauce will keep in the refrigerator for months if covered with a light layer of oil. So, whenever I need a dose of comfort, I'm just a pasta boil away from contentment.

Servings: 8

2 cups basil leaves
¼ cup pine nuts
2 cloves (or more to taste) garlic, chopped
½ cup extra-virgin olive oil

¾ cup Parmesan cheese (Parmigiano Reggiano is great, or you can use a mix with Romano)
1 pound fusilli or other pasta shape

1. Wash the basil leaves well. Toast the pine nuts either on a cookie sheet in a moderate oven or in a dry skillet over medium heat until lightly browned. In a blender or food processor, pulse all the ingredients into a smooth paste, scraping down the sides of the blender or food processor. Season to taste.

2. Cook the fusilli according to package directions. Drain the pasta, then toss with as much pesto as you would like. You may want to add a few drops of olive oil to the pasta mixture, or you can keep the concentration of pesto really high.

···· ❦ ····

Is it not delightful to have friends coming from distant quarters?

Confucius

chapter six

The Staff of Life
Breads, Rolls, and Quickbreads

Dutch Breakfast Bread

By Annemarieke Tazelaar, Seattle, Washington

When my mother's cancer progressed to the stage that she was too weak to cook or to take care of the house, she spent most of her day on the living room couch. From there, she scheduled my father's time with housekeeping tasks to be done, grocery lists to be purchased, and meals to be cooked.

Dad's only culinary skill in the kitchen was boiling water for tea, but Mother dictated recipes and cooking directions from her perch. Although she had little appetite herself, she was determined to make sure that my father could still enjoy his favorite Dutch meals and snacks.

When Mother died after an eight-year battle with her illness, my father met his new life with a mixture of grief, loss, and relief in being released from his role of caretaker. He could finally experience some freedom from the responsibility of years of worry, anguish, and frustration. But he missed her terribly. In spite of her pain, she had always remained cheerful and interested in the world around her. Now, for the first time in his life, he was alone.

At first, he was at a loss about organizing his time. Meals were the biggest challenge. He had never written anything down, preferring to let my mother direct their joint endeavor to put food on the table.

The author,
Annemarieke Tazelaar

Annemarieke's Mom and Dad,
Lester and Nell, in 1975

So, it took considerable courage for him to call me, two weeks after her death, and invite me over for dinner. When I arrived, he met me at the door, wearing a handwoven apron. A cookbook lay open on the kitchen counter, and the familiar aroma of almost-done potatoes wafted from the stove.

We settled down to a creditable meal of boiled potatoes, green beans, and fried pork chops, satisfying and basic. I heaped praise on my father, and his eyes filled with tears, something he was still prone to at odd times.

It was his gift at the end of the meal that touched me the most. It was a family favorite: Dutch breakfast bread, which he had baked the day before.

In the years to come, it became his signature gift. At family get-togethers, his contribution was his bread. Whenever friends invited him to dinner, he brought the bread, wrapped in foil and tied with weaving yarn.

My dad is gone from my life, too, now. But his bread still comforts me on the mornings when I miss my parents.

Dutch Breakfast Bread

SUBMITTED BY ANNEMARIEKE TAZELAAR, SEATTLE, WASHINGTON

For best-tasting results, allow to rest 2 days before consuming.

Yield: 3 small loaves

3 cups self-rising flour
1 cup honey
1 cup sugar

1 cup milk
1 tsp. baking soda
1 tsp. anise seed

1. Mix all ingredients into a large bowl.

2. Pour into 3 well-greased 1-pint bread forms, or line the forms with wax paper and let stand overnight at room temperature. The next day, bake for 40 minutes at 350°, testing with a toothpick to make sure the loaves are done.

3. Take out of oven and remove paper immediately, or, if greased, take loaves out of forms after 20 minutes.

···· 🍮 ····

The smell of good bread baking, like the sound of lightly flowing water, is indescribable in its evocation of innocence and delight.

M. F. K. Fisher

Original Iowa Pumpkin Bread

SUBMITTED BY JANIS M. STILES, SARATOGA, CALIFORNIA

For some real comfort, spread the bread with cream cheese to make sandwiches and serve with cups of cinnamon-spiced tea shared with a friend.

Yield: 1 loaf, about 10 to 12 servings

2 eggs
1 cup pumpkin purée (or canned)
1/2 cup vegetable oil
1/3 cup water
1 1/2 cups sugar
1 2/3 cups flour
1/4 tsp. baking powder
1 tsp. baking soda

1/2 tsp. cloves
1/2 tsp. cinnamon
1/2 tsp. allspice
1/2 tsp. ginger
1/2 tsp. nutmeg
3/4 tsp. salt
1/2 cup raisins (optional)
1/2 cup chopped nuts (optional)

1. Heat oven to 325°. Prepare a loaf pan with cooking spray and a dusting of flour.

2. Mix all the wet ingredients and the sugar in a bowl.

3. Mix all the dry ingredients in another bowl (no sifting necessary).

4. Stir the dry mixture by thirds into the wet mixture. Forget your electric mixer. This is a spoon-and-muscle operation.

5. Bake for 1 hour, 15 minutes. The bread is done when a wooden toothpick inserted in the center comes out clean.

6. Cool 10 to 15 minutes in the pan, remove, and cool at least 15 minutes more. Wrap and refrigerate before slicing.

Hix Family Corn Bread

SUBMITTED BY JUDY HIX ABERCROMBIE, IRVING, TEXAS

One of my jobs during middle school was to make corn bread for our evening meal. My mom taught me the way her mother had taught her: a handful of this and a pinch of that. After I'd gone off to college, my mom called one day to ask for the corn bread recipe. It had been so long since she'd made it, she'd forgotten how. My son ended up being the child of mine interested in family recipes, but he wasn't comfortable cooking by touch and taste alone. One day, he measured the ingredients as I made a batch of corn bread and wrote down the recipe for future generations, and now to share with you.

Servings: 12 servings

¼ cup shortening or vegetable oil
1 cup flour
1 cup cornmeal, plus a little extra
1 Tbs. baking powder

¼ tsp. salt
¼ cup sugar, plus a little extra
2 eggs, beaten
1 cup milk

1. Heat oven to 400°. Place shortening or oil in a 10-inch iron skillet and place in oven until melted and hot, about 10 minutes. If you do not have an iron skillet, a cake pan or casserole dish will work fine.

2. Mix the flour, 1 cup of cornmeal, baking powder, salt, and sugar in a large mixing bowl. Stir in the eggs and milk until well combined, but do not overmix.

3. Remove the skillet from the oven and add the hot oil to the batter, whisking it in quickly to prevent eggs from curdling. If the mixture is too thick at this time, add a little more milk until the consistency is like a thick cake batter.

4. After all of the oil has been poured out of the skillet into the batter, sprinkle enough cornmeal on the bottom of the skillet to cover it. Return the skillet to the oven to brown the cornmeal.

(recipe continued on next page)

The Hix family portrait, taken at Christmas, 2001

5. Pour the batter into the skillet. Sprinkle a light layer of sugar on top of the batter. Bake in a 400° oven for about 20 minutes. A toothpick inserted in the middle should come out clean when it's done.

6. Cool slightly before running a table knife around the edge of the pan and turning the corn bread out onto a plate or rack.

From morning till night, sounds drift from the kitchen, most of them familiar and comforting. . . . On days when warmth is the most important need of the human heart, the kitchen is the place you can find it; it dries the wet socks, it cools the hot little brain.

E. B. White

Sacrament

BY SHULLA SANNELLA, WOONSOCKET, RHODE ISLAND

The package came by priority mail to a small rural post office far from my home, where I had gone to care for a son recovering from a life-threatening illness. I smiled when the postal clerk handed me the small box bound meticulously in brown paper and masking tape with my name perfectly inscribed in the familiar backward-slanting cursive. It was from my ninety-year-old mother in Florida.

When I got back to my son's home, I immediately opened the gift and slid the perfectly formed loaf of homemade bread from its wrapper. I cut two thick slices, toasted them to a golden brown, and slathered them with creamy unsalted butter. I slid into a chair by a window overlooking the gray northern day and feasted. As oatmeal and bran mixed with molasses melted on my tongue, the texture and taste released a childhood memory of my mother and grandmother in the kitchen, wearing aprons, baking bread. They pulled hot loaves from the green-and-beige claw-footed stove with heavy, stained oven mitts and place the loaves by the window to cool. Chattering sweetly, they handed me the first warm buttery slice heaped with jam.

As tears slipped gently down my cheeks, I once again received the age-old sacrament of fresh bread made with caring hands.

(recipe appears on next page)

.... § ....

In 1920, 70 percent of the population baked their own bread.

Oatmeal Bread

SUBMITTED BY SHULLA SANNELLA, WOONSOCKET, RHODE ISLAND

This venerable recipe gives comfort and says love one slice at a time.

Yield: 2 standard loaves

2 packages active dry yeast
¾ cup warm water (110°)
3 cups milk, scalded
3 Tbs. shortening
3 Tbs. blackstrap molasses

1 Tbs. salt
1½ cups "quick" oats (do not substitute
    instant oatmeal)
7 to 8 cups flour

1. Sprinkle yeast over water. Set aside to soften.

2. Combine milk (scalded), shortening, molasses, and salt. Cool to lukewarm.

3. Stir in the softened yeast, oats, and 1 cup flour. Add enough of the remaining flour to form a soft dough. Knead on a floured board until very smooth and elastic (8 to 10 minutes).

4. Place in a lightly greased bowl, and turn once to grease surface. Cover and let rise until double in size (about 1 hour).

5. Punch down and let rest for 10 minutes.

6. Shape into 2 loaves and place in greased 9- × 5-inch loaf pans. Cover and let rise for 1 hour.

7. Bake at 375° for 45 minutes or until golden brown.

The best smell is bread, the best flavor salt, the best love that of children.

Proverb

Boston Brown Bread

SUBMITTED BY SHERRIL STEELE-CARLIN, RENO, NEVADA

My mom, a New Englander transplanted to Southern California, made it a tradition to serve this bread with Boston Baked Beans for Saturday-night supper. The scent of the bread baking meant supper was almost ready. Dad, too, was a Boston native, and this was one of his favorite suppers. He loved to make cold bean sandwiches the next day. Mom shuddered, but Dad lived for those sandwiches.

Yield: 3 loaves (about 24 servings)
2 cups graham or whole-wheat flour
½ cup all-purpose flour
2 tsp. baking soda
1 tsp. salt
2 cups buttermilk
½ cup molasses
1 cup seedless raisins

1. Heat oven to 350°. Combine all ingredients; mix well. Spoon mixture into three well-greased 1-pound coffee cans. Let stand 30 minutes before baking.

2. Bake for 45 to 50 minutes or until a toothpick comes out clean when inserted into the center.

Jean White Steele, fresh from her kitchen, poses in front of one of her beloved New England covered bridges—she loved them nearly as much as she loved cooking

There is no chiropractic treatment, no Yoga exercise, no hour of meditation in a music-throbbing chapel that will leave you emptier of bad thoughts than this homely ceremony of making bread.

M. F. K. Fisher

Powder Biscuits

SUBMITTED BY MARLENE COCHRANE, WHITEHORSE, YUKON, CANADA

Growing up, I spent every summer on my grandparents' farm. While Grandpa and my two bachelor uncles worked the fields, Grandma and I would try to get the milking, baking, gardening, and household chores done before it got hot. The men would return at noon for "dinner"—a full-course meal of meat, vegetables, potatoes, salad, and fresh bread. At around 6:00 P.M., they would come home for "supper"—another full-course meal. In late August, the men would harvest into the late hours of evening, and Grandma and I would take meals to them. One of the dishes we hauled out to "our men" was beef stew and biscuits.

Servings: About 2 dozen small biscuits

2 cups flour	*2 tsp. sugar*
4 tsp. baking powder	*¼ cup margarine*
1 tsp. salt	*1 cup milk*

1. Heat oven to 400°. Sift or whisk together flour, baking powder, salt, and sugar. Blend in margarine with a pastry blender, or by rubbing it in between your fingers until the mixture clumps easily.

2. Add enough milk to make a soft dough. Knead lightly, and then pat or roll to 1-inch thickness. Cut into desired shapes, using a knife, cookie cutter, or the rim of a glass or can.

3. Bake on greased sheet 15 to 20 minutes, until golden brown on top.

Mixing Quickbreads

Muffins, biscuits, banana breads, and other non-yeast baked goods are called quickbreads because they rise quickly, usually from the action of baking powder or soda. Unlike yeast-risen breads, which require kneading, quickbread batters should be stirred as little as possible. Stir only enough to combine wet ingredients, even when using special cake or pastry flours. Otherwise, the pastry will be crumbly or tough.

The Hanukkah Blintz Blitz

By Lynn Ruth Miller, Pacifica, California

Every holiday of my childhood in Toledo, Ohio, all my aunts, uncles, and their families would gather at our house. My mother would create a spectacular banquet, each one more delicious than the one before. The year the war ended, however, there was dissension in the ranks.

Mom's two younger sisters decided it would be more fair to rotate holiday feasts from one family to the other. My mother was horrified. Then, my Aunt Tick suggested that the family meet at her home for the first night of Hanukkah.

"But you can't make blintzes, and that's what everyone serves for the Festival of the Lights," my mother protested.

"Well, I can," said my Aunt Hazel. "So, we can all eat at my house."

"Girls, girls," said my father, a born mediator. "We can settle this very easily. We will have a blintz contest. The one who gets the largest number of blintzes out of one cup of batter can have all eight dinners at her house."

Before anyone could say a word, my mother cried, "What a marvelous idea! We can have the contest here this weekend."

Aunt Hazel opened her mouth to object, but my mother silenced her. "I have the gas stove," she said. "And the pan."

Now, my mother's blintz pan was a seasoned frying pan black with soot. She insisted that the secret to her blintzes resided in that magic pan, which she never washed. Her blintzes were so thin, she had been known to get thirty-two pancakes out of one recipe.

The three Blintz Queens: Aunt Tick, Aunt Hazel, and the author's mother, Ida

Aunt Hazel exchanged a significant look with Aunt Tick. "Fine," she said. "But I will use my own recipe."

"And I'm bringing my own pan," said Aunt Tick.

The next Friday evening, the three sisters donned their aprons and gathered around my mother's stove. Each had prepared her own batter and greased her own pan. The tasting committee consisted of the three husbands, the children, and our dog.

"You're first, Tick," said my father.

My aunt nodded, her color high. She set out a paper towel on the counter to catch the pancakes, and then she began flipping. Although the recipe set the yield at a dozen pancakes, my tiny aunt managed to turn out thirty—just two short of my mother's record. Triumphant, she held one up to the light: It was as thin as tissue paper. A smashing success!

"Good work, honey," said proud Uncle Harry. "I'll go home and start polishing the silver for next week."

"Not so fast," said my feisty Aunt Hazel. "I wasn't ping pong champion of Warren High School for nothing."

"What does that have to do with it?" said my mother. But her face paled, and I could see her hand shaking as it clutched her weathered pan.

"Watch," said Aunt Hazel.

Those pancakes flew through the air, thin as cirrus clouds. When they landed, we counted them. Thirty. Even Steven!

Aunt Hazel brushed the drops of sweat from her brow and smiled. "I'll take the first four nights, Tick. You can have the last."

My mother squared her shoulders. "My turn," she said, and a silence fell over our kitchen.

My mother walked to her stove and took the stance of the champion she was. We all stood back to give her elbow room, and she began.

I can still see the rapid-fire of those floating pancakes, so light they landed all over the counter and floated over to the kitchen table. One drifted and came to rest on top of the dog; another hit my father on the arm. Two landed on top of the icebox, and we found ten scattered like broken balloons in the dining room across the hall. In seconds, all the batter was gone, and we rushed from room to room collecting the results.

"I count forty-two," said Uncle Harry.

"You forgot the one hanging from the kitchen light and the seven in the dining room," I said. "There were five on the dining room chairs and two under the buffet."

"What about those three on the bread box?" said my mother. "And I see two on the dining room chandelier."

"The dog ate four of them," said my father. "So the grand total is sixty-five."

He put his arms around my defeated aunts. "Sorry, girls," he said.

Well, we had the eight-day celebration at our house that year and every Hanukkah after that until I married. That year, I took my mother's recipe and tried my hand at making blintzes. I got eight from the recipe, and they were so thick I could have sold them to Goodyear Tire. I called my mother.

"How did you ever manage to get sixty-five pancakes out of so little batter?" I asked.

"How did Judah Maccabee get that light to burn for eight days?" asked my mother.

"God knows," I said.

"Right," said my mother.

(recipe appears on next page)

My Mother's Magic Blintzes

SUBMITTED BY LYNN RUTH MILLER, PACIFICA, CALIFORNIA

The secret to perfect blintzes: Never wash the pan!
And the magic? Ah . . . that's in the soul of the cook.

Servings: 12

1 tsp. salt	¼ tsp. vanilla	2 egg yolks, beaten
1 cup flour	1 Tbs. butter	1 Tbs. melted butter
4 eggs, well beaten	1½ pounds cottage	1 Tbs. sugar
1 cup milk	or ricotta cheese	

1. Make the batter by beating the salt and flour into the eggs until smooth, and then whisking in the milk and vanilla.

2. Lightly grease a 6-inch nonstick skillet with butter and heat the pan over medium-low heat. Pour in only enough batter to make a very thin pancake (about 2 tablespoons). Tip the pan from side to side to cover the bottom, and cook until the pancake blisters and is golden brown, about 3 minutes. Toss on a board, fried side up. Repeat with remaining batter. You can stack these pancakes one atop the other—they won't stick. Wipe frying pan with a paper towel when finished.

3. Count pancakes. If you don't have 24, you need more practice. If you have 30, you are ready for the next step. Beat together the cottage or ricotta cheese, egg yolks, melted butter, and sugar until smooth. Place a rounded tablespoon of filling mixture in the center of each pancake and fold into an envelope (a simple three-fold will make a nice cigar shape, if you don't plan to fry them).

4. Bake blintzes on a baking pan in a 350° oven for about 10 minutes, until piping hot, or fry on both sides in butter until golden brown. Serve with sugar and sour cream and/or strawberry jam.

Savory Mountain Cake

SUBMITTED BY JUNE BURNS, APACHE JUNCTION, ARIZONA

For a special breakfast (great for Father's Day) or brunch, try this delicious new take on good ole biscuits and gravy.

Servings: 8

1 1/2 Tbs. butter

1 1/2 cups finely chopped onions

1/2 tsp. marjoram

1/2 tsp. salt

1/2 tsp. black pepper

3 cups flour

1/3 cup cornstarch

3 Tbs. baking powder

1 heaping tsp. salt

1/4 cup oil

1 1/2 cups milk

1 egg, beaten

3/4 cup sour cream

2 tsp. poppy seeds

1/4 tsp. paprika

1 recipe Sausage Gravy
   (see page 208)

1. Heat oven to 450°. Grease a 9-inch round pan. Melt the butter in a skillet over medium heat, and cook the onions until browned, about 10 minutes. Add marjoram and the ½ teaspoon each salt and pepper; cook 1 minute more, and then set aside.

(recipe continued on next page)

2. In a mixing bowl, whisk together the flour, cornstarch, baking powder, and 1 heaping teaspoon of salt. Stir in the oil, and then the milk, mixing only enough to combine (a few small lumps are okay—overmixing will make the cake less tender). Spread this dough into the greased round pan.

3. Beat together the egg and sour cream. Spread this mixture evenly over the dough. Spoon the onion mixture onto the cake, and top by sprinkling on the poppy seeds and paprika.

4. Bake at 450° until a toothpick comes out clean from the center, about 30 minutes. Cool to room temperature before turning from the pan. Serve with Sausage Gravy.

Tough Biscuits!

Dry biscuits can be caused by handling the dough too much or from baking at too low an oven temperature.

His house was perfect, whether you liked food, or sleep, or work, or story-telling, or singing, or just sitting and thinking, or, best, a pleasant mixture of them all.

J. R. R. Tolkien

Sausage Gravy

SUBMITTED BY JUNE BURNS, APACHE JUNCTION, ARIZONA

This stick-to-your-ribs gravy is custom-made for Savory Mountain Cake (page 206) and works well for any other biscuits that yearn for something to sop up.

Servings: 8
½ pound pork sausage
4 Tbs. butter
1 small onion, chopped
½ tsp. paprika
1 tsp. marjoram
2 tsp. chopped garlic (about 2 cloves)
2 tsp. salt
½ tsp. black pepper
1 cup flour
5 cups milk
1 cup chopped mushrooms, crisp-sautéed in butter
½ cup chopped tomato
Dash Tabasco

1. In a heavy-bottomed pot over medium heat, cook together the sausage and butter until lightly browned, about 10 minutes. Add the onion, paprika, marjoram, garlic, salt, and pepper. Cook 5 minutes more, until onions are translucent. Stir in flour and mix until it becomes a paste.

(recipe continued on next page)

2. Gradually stir in the milk, 1 cup at a time, allowing the mixture to thicken before adding more. You might find a whisk helpful for breaking up lumps. Lower heat to very low and simmer, covered, for 1 hour.

3. Stir in the mushrooms, tomato, and Tabasco sauce. Taste for seasoning before serving with Savory Mountain Cake or other biscuits.

.... & ....

Part of the secret of success in life is to eat what you like and let the food fight it out inside.

Mark Twain

Thickening with Roux

Velvety smooth sauces, soups, and gravies are often thickened by adding flour that's been cooked in butter or oil. The mixture, called roux, consists of equal parts flour and fat. Cooked slightly, "blond" roux is perfect for light sauces and for white or cream soups. Cooked longer, "brown" roux is the preferred thickener for New Orleans's famed Cajun *etouffée* and other stews. Uncooked, this mixture is called *beurre manié* and has a slightly starchy flavor that works well in only a few dishes.

Add cooled roux to hot liquid or hot roux to cold liquid. Start by adding a small amount of liquid to the roux and cooking until it thickens greatly, then add that mixture back to the rest of the liquid. This method prevents lumps, which sometimes form when roux is added directly to the whole volume of liquid at once.

Grandma Gertrude's Apple Fritters

SUBMITTED BY LYNDA FOLEY, NORTHRIDGE, CALIFORNIA

*During my only visit to my grandmother's home, she made my sisters
and me apple fritters. Whenever I make her delicious apple fritter
rings, I remember that wonderful visit with my grandmother.*

Servings: About 20 fritters

1 cup flour
1½ tsp. baking powder
½ tsp. salt
2 Tbs. sugar
¾ cup milk
1 egg, separated

5 tart apples (such as Granny Smiths),
    pared and cored
Cinnamon, for sprinkling each ring
Vegetable oil or shortening
1 cup powdered sugar

1. Sift together flour, baking powder, and salt. Mix in sugar. In a separate bowl, beat together the milk and egg yolk, and set aside. In another small bowl, beat the egg white until very stiff, and set aside.

2. Stir milk/yolk mixture into dry ingredients, blending well. Fold egg white into batter mixture.

3. Cut pared and cored apples into crosswise rings ¼-inch thick each.

4. Lightly sprinkle each apple ring with cinnamon, and then dip each ring into the batter. Carefully place in deep hot oil (around 350°) and fry until light brown. Drain on several layers of paper towels.

5. Smother generously with powdered sugar and serve warm.

There is more hunger for love and appreciation in the world than for bread.

Mother Teresa

A Cookbook Treasury

By Carol Crigger, Spokane, Washington

Marie Gandré on her wedding day in 1912

The cookbook is in poor condition, bearing the scars of age and use. It's about the size of a paperback and a plain black cloth covers the spine. The pages are yellowed and brittle, some spotted with cooking splatters. Each page is filled with the same spiky handwriting, written in the same black ink. The inside cover reads:

Miss Marie Gandré/January, 1907/
Sheboygan, Wis/Tested Receipts

Miss Marie Gandré is my grandmother, and when she wrote that she was nineteen. She immigrated to the United States from Germany at age three. She married late, and I didn't know her until she was more than sixty years old.

For the most part, there are no instructions in her cookbook. Maybe she was conserving space; maybe she figured that since she already knew how to cook, no further instruction was necessary. Little notes append many of the recipes: "Better with more salt." "Try adding maple flavor." "Omit celery leaves next time." I cook like that, too, and make similar notes. I must have learned it from her, watching as she made raised doughnuts and fried them in a cast-iron pot on a wood-fired stove.

Toward the back of my grandmother's cookbook are recipes she acquired later, with notes citing the donor. Some are names I recognize from when she and my grandfather lived in Washington, some from when they lived in Montana, and the latest neighbors I knew in Idaho.

A "receipt" for banana bread is on one of the book's earliest pages. How often, I wonder, were bananas available to an Idaho farmwife? How much did they cost? What a treat this loaf must have been, baked, buttered, and served up with pride at quilting bees and Grange charity drives. I know it was a frequent treat for Miss Marie's grandchildren.

Whole Wheat Bread

SUBMITTED BY AMY MAIDA WADSWORTH, SALT LAKE CITY, UTAH

My mother makes this dense bread with just the right amount of sweetness every Christmas and takes a loaf to each of her neighbors. They look forward to this simple gift as much as my children look forward to opening their packages under the tree. I love it warm with peanut butter and strawberry jam.

Amy Wadsworth, her mom, and her mom's special bread

Yield: 2 loaves

2 to 3 Tbs. yeast	1 cup hot water
4 cups warm water	1 cup brown sugar
1 Tbs. salt	6 Tbs. shortening
4 cups white flour	10 cups whole wheat flour

1. Soften yeast in 1 cup of warm water (110°).

2. Mix 3 cups warm water, salt, dissolved yeast, and 4 cups white flour until smooth. Let sit in a warm place for about 1 hour.

3. Combine 1 cup hot water, brown sugar, and shortening. Add to first mixture, and mix well. Add wheat flour and mix well.

4. Form into 2 loaves and bake at 350° for 35 minutes.

····🐚····

Friendship is the bread of the heart.

Mary Russell Mitford

Super Easy Cinnamon Rolls

SUBMITTED BY LINDA PILLING, SPIRITWOOD, SASKATCHEWAN, CANADA

These breakfast rolls are so good, they are addictive! My youngest sister loves them, and often when we get together, I try to surprise her by having some with me and popping them out from the most unexpected places—a purse, a suitcase, a pocket. This never fails to bring laughter, followed by a big hug.

Servings: 16

Rolls:
3 cups all-purpose flour
¼ tsp. salt
3½ tsp. baking powder
½ cup white sugar
½ cup milk
2 eggs, beaten
½ cup melted butter or margarine

Filling and Topping:
½ cup white sugar
1 tsp. cinnamon
½ cup melted butter or margarine,
   divided
½ cup packed light brown sugar
¼ cup chopped walnuts

1. Preheat oven to 375°. Combine flour, salt, baking powder, and ½ cup sugar in bowl. Combine milk, eggs, and ½ cup melted butter. Add milk mixture to flour mixture and mix well.

2. Knead dough on a lightly floured surface until smooth, about 5 minutes. Roll into a ½-inch thick rectangle. Combine ½ cup sugar, cinnamon, and ¼ cup melted butter in a bowl. Spread the cinnamon mixture over dough and roll jellyroll-style, as for cinnamon buns. Cut into 16 pieces.

3. Combine the brown sugar, walnuts, and remaining ¼ cup melted butter. Distribute brown sugar mixture into 16 greased cups of medium muffin tins. Bake for 25 to 30 minutes, or until rolls are light golden brown. Cool slightly before unmolding and serving brown-sugar-side up.

A Swiss Family Tradition

By Susan Tiberghien, Switzerland

In my mother's recipe box is a well-fingered card spattered with sugar and love. It is titled *Gaga's Christmas Stollen*. Gaga was my mother's mother. At sixteen, she sailed alone to America from Switzerland. She married a German immigrant and had one daughter. Widowed young, she moved from Washington to Philadelphia to New York City, and came to live with us when she was dying, her life compressed into less than half a century.

Once a year, just before Christmas, Mother would take out the recipe card with the list of ingredients running down both sides. As the loaf rose overnight, the scent would fill the house.

"It smells like Gaga," I used to say.

Thirty years ago, I sailed to Europe to live with my French husband. I brought parts of my childhood with me—including Gaga's stollen recipe, copied onto a card and placed in a red-and-white box like my mom's. Today, the recipe box is filled tight with recipes gathered from the places we've lived. Only Gaga's recipe card is as well fingered and spattered as those in my mother's box.

Every year at Christmas, we have a stollen night. My children gather around the kitchen table, helping to stir in the ingredients. Each year we make more loaves, doubling the recipe, tripling, up to twenty loaves. We sprinkle them with sugar and cinnamon, and during the night as they rise, the scent of Gaga fills our home. I close my eyes and know she's there.

(recipe appears on next page)

A small gift will do if your heart is big enough.

Anonymous

Gaga's Christmas Stollen

SUBMITTED BY SUSAN TIBERGHIEN, SWITZERLAND

Now that we live in Switzerland, where stollen is the traditional German-Swiss Christmas cake, our Gaga's stollen is still the best. Each Christmas, I take out the same love-spattered recipe and make this cherished tradition.

Servings: 1 large or 4 small loaves

2 cups milk
1 cup sugar
2 tsp. salt
1½ cups butter
2 cakes yeast
8 cups flour
4 eggs
2 cups raisins

2 cups slivered almonds
1 cup chopped candied fruit (diced lemon and orange peel)
2 tsp. almond extract
2 ounces brandy
Melted butter (to drizzle on top)
Sugar (to sprinkle on top)
Cinnamon (to sprinkle on top)

1. Heat oven to 350°. Scald milk. Mix together scalded milk, sugar, salt, and butter. Cool.

2. Crumble in yeast, and then add 2 cups of the flour and mix. Let rise 2 hours.

3. Add the rest of the flour, and then the eggs, raisins, almonds, candied fruit, almond extract, and brandy.

4. Knead well and form either 1 very large loaf or 4 bread-size loaves. Brush loaves with melted butter and sprinkle with sugar and cinnamon. Let rise 12 hours.

5. Bake in moderate (350°) oven for 1 hour.

Banana Nut Bread

For fun, you can make this recipe into banana-nut cupcakes or minimuffins by baking it for half the time in muffin tins. It freezes well.—J.W.

Yield: 1 loaf, about 10 to 12 servings

1¼ cups all-purpose flour
1 tsp. baking soda
¼ tsp. baking powder
½ tsp. cinnamon
½ tsp. salt
1 cup sugar
2 large eggs

½ cup oil
3 medium overripe bananas, mashed
   (1¼ cups)
1 tsp. vanilla extract
¾ cup coarsely chopped walnuts,
   toasted lightly in a dry pan until
   fragrant

1. Heat oven to 350°. Butter a 9- × 5-inch loaf pan. In a mixing bowl, whisk together the flour, baking soda, baking powder, cinnamon, and salt.

2. In a separate bowl, whisk together the sugar, eggs, and oil; whip vigorously until creamy and light in color, about 5 minutes. Add mashed bananas and vanilla extract to the egg mixture.

3. Add about one-third of the flour mixture at a time (that is, in 3 portions: one third, then one-third, then the final one-third) to the egg mixture. Mix only enough to incorporate the ingredients, since overmixing will toughen the batter. Stir in the nuts, and pour batter into prepared pan.

4. Bake in the center of the oven until the top is springy and a toothpick inserted in the center comes out clean, about 50 to 60 minutes. Allow to cool for 10 minutes; transfer to a rack to cool completely before slicing.

····ʂ····

Whose bread I eat, his song I sing.

German Proverb

chapter seven

Stuff to Save Room For

Pies, Cakes, and Cobblers

Audrey's Apple Pie

By Jody W. Weatherstone, Warwick, New York

My daughter and I lug our sacks of just-picked apples into the house and dump them on the counter. Mine holds a good twenty pounds of Greenings, Pippins, Macouns, and Winesaps; Audrey's holds three perfect Macintoshes (a mommy, a daddy, and a baby). I need to occupy her if I am to get anything done, so I put her to work at the sink washing apples, even though they will be peeled later. Next, I remove my made-the-night-before pie crust from the fridge (I'm nothing if not organized) to let it soften slightly in its wax paper wrapping.

Audrey is already yelling for something else to do, so I scramble to set out the marble slab, a large and a small rolling pin, and bowls of flour for dusting. Squealing and bouncing around, she sings a happy little pie song. I cut off a lump of dough for her to mold into shapes.

I begin peeling and coring the mismatched apples, some with golden juicy flesh, some crisp and white, trying with each to make one long curl of skin. I succeed with two out of eight. Audrey seizes these springy strands and nibbles away. (Yes, they were washed.)

The thick, chunky wedges fall into the yellow ceramic bowl until I have seven cups' worth. Next, I measure, and Audrey adds sugar and flour. Then she shakes in unmeasured and generous amounts of cinnamon and nutmeg, *mmm*-ing and licking her fingers all the while. This kid would eat cinnamon with a spoon straight from the jar if allowed. Stirring, we knock some of the apples out onto the floor. Oh well, pick them up, blow on them, and toss them back into the bowl.

The pastry has softened up, so Audrey throws flour onto the marble and pounds the dough with her sticky little fists. I coax her into returning to her decorative shapes, giving her a couple of leaf-shaped cookie cutters, and I start rolling out the bottom crust.

By this time she has succeeded in flouring the entire counter, her face and hair, the floor, and the cat. This is my fault. I tried to teach her how to dust the board when she was just two, and she's been practicing for over a year now. But since I am succeeding in getting this crust formed, I don't interfere. Quickly and gently, I roll it back onto the pin and lay it over the pie plate. I press it into place, stick it in the fridge, and begin on the top crust.

Now, Audrey is in on the action, child-sized rolling pin in hand. Together, we manage to produce a lumpy but acceptable top crust.

I retrieve the chilled plate from the humming fridge, and as I hold the bowl, my assistant scoops in the apples. The top crust is draped over the apples, and the edges are folded under and pinched closed. Our dual sets of fingers—large and deft, small and clumsy—form odd-shaped crimps all around. This pie would never win a beauty contest, but no one would mistake it for store-bought either. We lay on my daughter's squiggly, floury shapes and leaves and little round berries, dampening them with water to make them stick. A couple of gashes in the crust, a sprinkling of sugar by Audrey's abundant measure, and it is into the oven.

Is it done yet? Is it done yet? Is it done yet? Is it done yet?

Horrors! We have no ice cream. We page Dad. It is an emergency. *Pick up a pint of vanilla ice cream on your way home. Hurry!*

The fragrance fills the kitchen, warm, soothing, familiar. Butter blended with autumn fresh apples and a three-year-old girl's exuberance. 🍂

Basic Pie Crust

Flaky pie dough makes a pie memorable. The flakiness comes from bits of butter hidden in the dough, so don't overmix this wonderful, simple, all-purpose crust.—J.W.

**Yield: 1 double-crust 9-inch pie or
2 single-crust 9-inch shells**

*2 cups flour (pastry flour is best, but
you can use all-purpose)*

½ tsp. salt

*6 ounces (1½ sticks) unsalted butter,
cold, cut into pea-sized pieces*

¼ cup very cold water

1. Sift flour and salt together over a bowl containing the diced butter. Using your hands, break up the butter into the flour until the flour assumes the color of the butter. There should still be some nuggets of unmixed butter.

2. Sprinkle in most of the water, and work quickly with your hands until dough clumps together. Do not overmix. Separate dough into 2 balls, wrap separately, and refrigerate for at least 30 minutes before rolling.

Secrets to Blue-Ribbon Pie Crust

Use lard or butter (fat) rather than a vegetable-based shortening. Chill the fat (or shortening), and chop it into the flour as quickly as possible, using your hands or a pastry blender, large fork, or two knives. Toss the fat-flour mixture just enough to coat the small bits of fat with flour; the mixture should be the consistency of coarse bread crumbs. Use very cold water, and add it one tablespoon at a time, mixing the water into the dough with your hands. Chill the dough before mixing. Keep the rolling surface lightly dusted with flour. Always roll from the center outward, waiting until the circle is almost the size of the pie pan before rolling the outer edges.

Birthday Cherry Pie, Oh My!

SUBMITTED BY KATHY S. RYGG, BROOMFIELD, COLORADO

My family celebrated birthdays with pie, rather than cake. This posed a bit of a problem for me, because I didn't like the traditional flaky pie crust. So, one year my mother made me a cream-cheese pie with cherry filling on top and a graham cracker crust. To this day, no birthday of mine is complete without it!

Servings: 8 (one 9-inch pie)

1 graham cracker crust recipe (see Graham Cracker Crust on page 231), or store-bought

1 package (8 ounces) cream cheese, softened

1 can (14 ounces) unsweetened condensed milk

1/3 cup lemon juice

1 tsp. vanilla extract

1 can cherry pie filling

1. Prebake the pie shell according to package directions, or by lining the shell with waxed paper, filling it with dried beans or pie beads, and baking until golden, 10–15 minutes.

2. Blend the softened cream cheese and milk in a mixer. Add the lemon juice and blend. Add the vanilla and blend for several more minutes. Pour into the cooled graham cracker crust. Cover with plastic wrap and chill overnight.

3. The next day, pour the cherry pie filling on top and chill until served.

···· § ····

Cherry cobbler is shortcake for the soul.

Edna Ferber

Jelly Pies for Grandpa

By Deborah Gilchrist, Mount Clemens, Michigan

I loved pie-baking days at Grandma's. I'd stand next to her on a big chair, with one of her flowery aprons tucked and tied ceremoniously in place. While she measured and mixed, transforming the gooey mess into a smooth, round ball of dough and then into a perfectly symmetrical work of art, I'd watch in awe. When she began filling, covering, and trimming, my excitement would rise. As the scraps of dough fell away from Grandma's deft hands, I knew the real fun was about to commence.

Eagerly, I would gather the scraps together. Soon, I was rolling and shaping, until I had a crust large enough to fill the bottom of my petite pie tin. Of course, I wasn't as accomplished as Grandma, but after several tries, I was finally happy with my product. I held it up eagerly for Grandma's inspection. "All set?" she'd say.

Then came the most important part: choosing the filling. Now, jelly pie is a dessert befitting kings, and it had to be just right. Grandma would place the choices before me; inevitably, I would choose strawberry. I'd spread a few spoonfuls of the smooth, dark jam evenly across the bottom of the crust, and then Grandma would slide it into the oven.

After what was surely hours, she'd open the oven door, and while I danced from foot to foot in anticipation, she'd slowly withdraw my creation. Set on the counter to cool next to its bigger sisters in their fancy, fluted glass pie plates, my humble jam and pastry concoction awaited the one and only person privileged enough to indulge in such a confection—Grandpa. The fanfare he made when I placed my offerings on the table always made me feel like there was no greater delight on Earth.

(recipe appears on next page)

Heritage Apple Pie

SUBMITTED BY DEBORAH GILCHRIST, MOUNT CLEMENS, MICHIGAN

At nearly eighty years of age, my grandma still makes the best pies I've ever eaten (though I'd venture to say that mine are second best!). Over the years, I've garnered a collection of pie tins much like Grandma's. The small ones are still perfect for little hands to make jelly pies.

Servings: 8 (one 9-inch pie)

1 double-crust pie dough (see Basic Pie
   Crust on page 220), or store-bought
1 tsp. cinnamon
½ cup sugar

Pinch salt
8–10 medium-sized baking apples,
   peeled and sliced (about 6–8 cups)
2 Tbs. flour

1. Heat oven to 350°. In a large bowl, sprinkle cinnamon, sugar, and salt over apples. Fold gently to mix. Set aside.

2. With a lightly floured wooden rolling pin, roll half of the dough into approximately a 12-inch circle, about ⅛-inch thick. Carefully fold dough over the rolling pin for easy transfer and position in a 9-inch pie plate.

3. Fill with apple mixture, mounding slightly in the center. Sprinkle apples with flour. Repeat rolling with second half of the dough and place carefully on top of apples.

4. Using your fingers or a pastry brush, dip in water and lightly brush the edge of the crust and, between the two layers, press the top layer down to seal as you go. Trim with a sharp knife; set aside scraps of dough. Flute the edge of the pie crust by lifting and pinching between your thumb and first 2 fingers, moving around the pie in this manner. Cut a small hole in the top.

5. Bake for 45 minutes, until filling is bubbly and crust is golden brown. Cool on rack. Serve warm with vanilla ice cream.

Apple Walnut Upside-Down Pie

The baker who taught me how to make these incredible pies, whom I remember only as Kevin, had a broad smile, which would get even broader when he talked of how good this pie tastes with cinnamon-flavored ice cream.—J.W.

Servings: 8 (one 9-inch pie)

4 ounces (1 stick) unsalted butter

1 cup light brown sugar

1 cup toasted walnut pieces, roughly chopped

Pinch of salt (for both caramel and filling)

1 double-crust pie dough (see Basic Pie Crust on page 220),
   or store-bought

8 or 9 Granny Smith apples, peeled, cored, and diced into
   1-inch pieces.

½ cup sugar (give or take, depending on sweetness of apples)

¼ cup flour

1½ tsp. ground cinnamon

½ tsp. ground allspice

¼ tsp. ground cloves

1. Make the topping: Melt 1 stick of butter (4 ounces) and mix in 1 cup brown sugar in a heavy-bottomed skillet over medium-high heat, until smooth and bubbling. Cook 5 minutes. Stir in walnuts and a pinch of salt. Remove from heat.

2. Spread walnut mixture into bottom of 9-inch pie pan.

(recipe continued on next page)

3. Heat oven to 375°. Roll out bottom crust very thin (¼ inch) and drape over caramel/walnut-lined pie pan.

4. In a separate bowl, mix the apple slices, sugar, flour, spices, and a pinch of salt. Fill the pie with the apple mixture, mounding somewhat in the center.

5. Roll out dough for the top crust (¼ inch). Brush rim of bottom crust with a little water to seal the crusts together, and cover the pie loosely with the top layer of dough. Crimp the edges. Make several vents, using a fork or the tip of a knife.

6. Bake for 1 hour, until filling is bubbling. Cool and then reheat quickly in a hot oven before inverting and unmolding. Serve with cinnamon ice cream. (If commercially made cinnamon ice cream is unavailable, temper 1 pint of vanilla ice cream and then work 1 teaspoon of ground cinnamon into it with a wooden spoon. Refreeze for at least 1 hour before serving.)

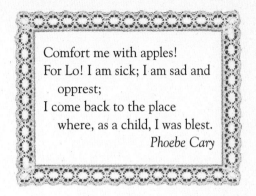

Comfort me with apples!
For Lo! I am sick; I am sad and
   opprest;
I come back to the place
   where, as a child, I was blest.
Phoebe Cary

To Market, to Market, to Buy a Fine Apple

When it comes to cooking, not all apples are created equal. Ask your fruit vendor for "baking apples," if you're making a pie or cake. Some wonderful eating apples, like McIntosh and Red Delicious, turn to mush when you bake them. Apples that seem mealy when raw, such as Rome or Cortland apples, are especially juicy and silky when baked or stewed. Granny Smiths and Golden Delicious are versatile and good raw or cooked.

Oma's Zuke Surprise

By Garnet Hunt White, Doniphan, Missouri

My mother said she knew 100 ways to fix zucchini—and no doubt she used every one the first year we grew our own and made the mistake of planting two whole rows of them in our garden. That is also the year Mother started taking her special "apple" pies to friends and to every social event and church meeting she had the opportunity to attend. Everyone raved about her delicious apple pies. Mother smiled sweetly and said, "Thank you." My father and I also loved them.

One day, my father said, "Oma, set aside some of those pie apples. I'd like to have a raw one now and then."

Mother grinned slyly but said nothing. Father looked at the empty fruit bowl and then back at Mother, who continued to grin not so innocently.

Sensing something amiss, he said, "Is there something funny about the apples?"

Mother laughed out loud then and confessed, "Those 'apple' pies you've been enjoying all these weeks . . . well, those were zucchini pies."

(recipe appears on next page)

Cooking is like love. It should be entered into with abandon or not at all.

Harriet Van Horne

Zucchini "Apple" Pie

SUBMITTED BY GARNET HUNT WHITE, DONIPHAN, MISSOURI

My mother's faux apple pies were such a hit with friends and neighbors that, once she fessed up to her clever substitute, they all asked for the recipe. Now, the whole town makes these moist, sweet, and healthy vegetable "fruit" pies.

Servings: 8 (one 9-inch pie)

1 double-crust pie dough (see Basic Pie Crust on page 220), or store-bought
4 cups sliced zucchini
1¼ cups of sugar
1½ teaspoons cream of tartar
1½ teaspoons cinnamon

3 Tbs. flour
Pinch of nutmeg
2 Tbs. lemon juice
Dash of salt
1 Tbs. butter

1. Heat oven to 400°. Roll out a top and a bottom pie crust and set aside.

2. Boil zucchini until tender; drain well. Combine sugar, cream of tartar, cinnamon, flour, and nutmeg in a bowl. Add cooked zucchini, lemon juice, and dash of salt to the mixture, and toss to coat. It may be runny, but that will not hurt it.

3. Transfer this filling to a 9-inch crust and dot with butter. Add a top crust, cut a vent in the top, and bake for 40 minutes or until golden brown. Cool completely before slicing.

···· ❧ ····

A typical mother, seeing there are only four pieces of pie left for five people, promptly announces she never did care for pie.

Anonymous

Amazing Coconut Custard Pie

SUBMITTED BY DIXIE R. CLIFFORD, OREM, UTAH

Servings: 8 (one 9-inch pie)

2 cups milk

¾ cup sugar

½ cup biscuit mix (such as Bisquick)

4 eggs

¼ cup unsalted butter

1½ tsp. vanilla extract

1 cup coconut

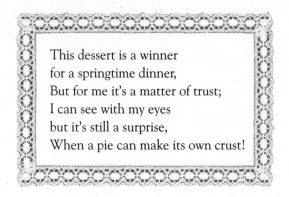

This dessert is a winner
for a springtime dinner,
But for me it's a matter of trust;
I can see with my eyes
but it's still a surprise,
When a pie can make its own crust!

1. Heat oven to 350°. Put milk, sugar, biscuit mix, eggs, butter, and vanilla in blender. Blend 3 minutes on medium speed.

2. Pour into a buttered 9-inch glass pie pan. Let stand 5 minutes and sprinkle coconut on top.

3. Bake for 40 minutes.

···· &ยง ····

Because [our children] had had the privilege of growing up where they'd raised a lot of food, they were never hungry. They could share their food with people. And so, you share your lives with people.

Ella Baker

Andersen's Heavenly Light Pumpkin Pie

SUBMITTED BY LIZ J. ANDERSEN, EUGENE OREGON

My grandmother, Pauline Andersen, inherited this recipe from her mother. My mom, Jean, added some spices, and my sister, Kristine, made it safe for the lactose-intolerant. Every Thanksgiving and Christmas, we make this traditional family dessert, and remember with laughter the way Grandma would slice up the pie into equal sections and encourage us to take a generous serving of ice cream with it, despite the tremendous feast we'd just consumed. Now, our family would like to pass on this special recipe, which is lighter than most pumpkin pies, for others to enjoy.

Servings: 8 (one 9-inch pie)

3 eggs

1 cup pumpkin or butternut squash (Grandmother used canned; we use steamed)

1 cup sugar

2 heaping Tbs. flour

2 tsp. cinnamon

¼ tsp. salt

½ tsp. ground ginger

¼ tsp. ground nutmeg

¼ tsp. ground cloves

¾ cup milk

1 single-crust pie dough (see Basic Pie Crust on page 220), or store-bought

1. Do *not* preheat oven. Separate eggs, and set aside egg whites. Blend together pumpkin, sugar, egg yolks, flour, cinnamon, salt, ginger, nutmeg, and cloves. Stir in milk by hand.

2. Beat egg whites until stiff but not dry. Fold egg whites into pumpkin mixture. Pour mixture into pie shell.

3. Place in oven and set for 350°. Bake for 1 hour, or until browned on top. Top may crack, but that's okay. Best served warm!

Grandma Gypsy's Lemon Meringue Pie

SUBMITTED BY LINDA S. CLARE, EUGENE, OREGON

To learn my grandma's pie-making secrets, I had to join her in her kitchen at 4:00 A.M. The secrets shared, about pie and life, were well worth the early rising.

Servings: 8 (one 9-inch pie)

1 single-crust pie dough (see Basic Pie Crust on page 220), or store-bought

3 eggs, separated

1/4 tsp. cream of tartar

1 1/2 cups sugar, plus 6 Tbs.

1/2 tsp. vanilla extract

1/3 cup, plus 1 Tbs. cornstarch

1 1/2 cups water

3 Tbs. butter or margarine

2 tsp. grated lemon peel

1/2 cup lemon juice

1. Prebake the pie shell according to package, or by lining the shell with waxed paper, filling it with dried beans, baking until golden, 10–15 minutes.

2. Heat oven to 400°. Beat egg whites and cream of tartar until foamy. Beat in 6 tablespoons sugar, 1 tablespoon at a time; continue beating until stiff and glossy. Do not underbeat. Beat in vanilla and set aside in refrigerator.

3. Mix sugar and cornstarch in medium saucepan. Blend egg yolks and water; gradually stir into sugar mixture. Cook over medium heat, stirring constantly, until mixture thickens and boils. Boil and stir 1 minute. Remove from heat; stir in butter, lemon peel, and lemon juice. Immediately pour lemon filling into baked pie shell.

4. Top the hot filling with meringue using a spoon or a pastry bag, forming a mound in the center. Seal meringue to edge of crust to prevent weeping.

5. Bake about 10 minutes, or until meringue tips are a delicate brown. Cool away from draft.

Graham Cracker Pie Crust

Perfect for meringue pies, cream pies, pudding pies, and many other no-bake desserts, this multipurpose crust can be made and baked in advance. Once cooked, it keeps for up to two weeks at room temperature or one month in the freezer. Isn't it comforting to know you'll always be minutes away from an easy pie?—J.W.

Servings: 8 (one 9-inch pie crust)

1 1/4 cups graham cracker crumbs
  (about a dozen crackers)

1/4 cup granulated sugar
1/3 cup unsalted butter, melted

1. Heat oven to 350°. In a small bowl, mix the graham cracker crumbs, sugar, and butter until well combined. Press the mixture into a 9-inch pie pan, making sure to go all the way up the sides of the pan.

2. Bake on middle rack for about 8 minutes. Cool to room temperature on a rack.

Coffee Cake

BY JEWELL JOHNSON, FOUNTAIN HILLS, ARIZONA

"What's this crunchy brown stuff at the bottom of the cake?" I asked our son.

Bryan had baked his first cake, and I was eating a piece.

"I think it's coffee," he said.

Bryan had found a recipe in an old cookbook that called for coffee. The writer apparently had assumed that every cook would know she meant liquid coffee—not coffee grounds!

Now, when my son grabs a recipe book, I hover nearby. And I never assume that young cooks know how to read between the lines.

Sweet Potato Pie

SUBMITTED BY JUNE BURNS, APACHE JUNCTION, ARIZONA

Loaded with Southern charm, this rich and creamy
pie is an all-time favorite anywhere, anytime.

Servings: 8

1 single-crust pie dough (see page 220), or store-bought

2 cups mashed sweet potatoes

4 eggs

2 Tbs. melted butter

3/4 cup sugar

1 1/2 cups cream

1/4 cup chopped walnuts, plus 4 walnut halves for garnish

1/3 cup apricot preserves

1/2 tsp. salt

3/4 tsp. cinnamon

1/2 tsp. ginger

1/2 tsp. nutmeg

1/8 tsp. cloves

1. Prebake the pie shell according to package directions, or by lining the shell with waxed paper, filling it with dried beans or pie beads, and baking until golden, 10–15 minutes.

2. Heat oven to 350°. In a large mixing bowl, whisk together the mashed sweet potatoes, eggs, melted butter, sugar, cream, chopped walnuts, apricot preserves, salt, cinnamon, ginger, nutmeg, and cloves. Pour into the prebaked pie shell.

3. Bake 30 minutes. Arrange the 4 walnut halves on top, and bake 10 minutes more. Cool before slicing.

Welcome is the best dish.

Proverb

Chocolate Peanut Butter Pie

SUBMITTED BY JUNE BURNS, APACHE JUNCTION, ARIZONA

The perfect dessert when you want to be a little bit naughty and oh so nice.

Servings: 16 (two 9-inch pies)

2 regular or chocolate graham cracker crusts,
*   (see page 231), or store-bought*
1 package (8 ounces) cream cheese, softened
*   and brought to room temperature*
1 cup peanut butter
1 cup sugar
1½ cups heavy cream, whipped to soft peaks
1 cup heavy cream, heated just to a boil
12 ounces (1 package) semisweet chocolate chips

1. Prebake the pie shell according to package directions, or by lining the shell with waxed paper, filling it with dried beans or pie beads, and baking until golden, 10–15 minutes.

2. Mix together the soft cream cheese, peanut butter, sugar, and whipped cream. Spread evenly into 2 graham cracker crusts. Chill in the refrigerator for 4 hours.

3. Combine the boiling hot cream with the chocolate chips. Whisk until smooth. Spread this mixture over the tops of both pies. Refrigerate for 2 more hours before serving.

Whip It Good . . .

If the whipping cream or egg whites pull up with the whisk and then flop back, it has reached the soft-peak stage. If the whipped substance forms points that stand straight up, it's gone to stiff peaks. Whipping cream past stiff peaks leads to butter. Overwhipping egg whites leads to a "weeping" watery mess. Once cream begins to butter and whites to weep, there's no turning back.

The surest way to whip cream or egg whites to just the right point is in a cold steel or glass bowl with a thin-wired balloon-shaped whisk. For large amounts, you can use an electric mixer, but watch it like a hawk.

Susie's Breakfast Hut

SUBMITTED BY MARY BRYANT, NASHVILLE, TENNESSEE

Every community has its early-morning place where the locals gather for coffee and conversation. In Westcliffe, Colorado, folks congregate at Susie's Breakfast Hut.

Susie serves fresh homemade pies, bread, biscuits, and muffins, made right there, in her little café. She gets to work sometime in the middle of the night to start her daily baking, and opens the doors for breakfast at 5:30 A.M.

The Wet Mountain Valley is nearly totally dependent on agriculture. The early-morning clientele is mostly farmers and mechanics, and retired farmers and retired mechanics. In this community, friends and neighbors are dependent on one another, and the barter system is alive and well. Over breakfast at Susie's, these hardworking people talk about the goings-on and the ups and downs of daily life. Yet, the conversation is always lively, and there's always something new to discuss.

As the regulars trade stories and laughter, advice and opinions, Susie fries up their eggs and bacon, refills their coffee cups, and serves up a steady stream of fresh baked goodies—smiling and humming all the while.

(recipe appears on next page)

Mary's Peach Pie

SUBMITTED BY MARY BRYANT, NASHVILLE, TENNESSEE

Susie, of Susie's Breakfast Hut, and I have often discussed the gentle and almost-lost art of pie making. We seem to have learned our techniques from the same grandmother, though our family trees don't bear this out. I'm sure the Hut's regulars would love my peach pie as much as they love Susie's.

Servings: 8 (one 9-inch pie)

4 large, ripe peaches, peeled and sliced (about 3 cups)

Juice of ½ lemon

½ cup plus 1 Tbs. sugar, divided

Pinch of salt

1 Tbs. flour

½ tsp. cinnamon

1 Tbs. butter

1 double-crust pie dough (see page 220) or store-bought

1. Heat oven to 425°. In a large bowl, mix together the peaches, lemon juice, ½ cup sugar, salt, and flour.

2. In a separate bowl, combine one tablespoon sugar and cinnamon.

3. Roll out bottom crust and place into 9-inch pie plate. Add peach filling, and dot with several small pieces of butter. Roll out top crust and cut into ¾-inch strips. Weave strips over pie into a lattice top. Crimp crusts together. Sprinkle top with cinnamon sugar.

4. Bake at 425° for 15 minutes. Lower oven to 325°, and bake for 45 minutes longer, until filling appears waxy and bubbly. Cool before cutting.

···· § ····

Money brings you food, but not appetite; medicine, but not health; acquaintances, but not friends.

Henrik Ibsen

Chess Pie

SUBMITTED BY JANE PARKS-MCKAY, SANTA CRUZ, CALIFORNIA

Raised by parents who hailed from North Carolina, I was born in Atlanta and spent a good part of my childhood in the South. Now that I'm a Yankee in California, I am amazed that hardly anyone "out West" has heard of Chess Pie. I've seen a few variations, but this one, handed down through our family, is easy and inexpensive to make, and it's truly the best I've tasted. Even those Yankees out here ask for seconds and thirds.

Servings: 8 (one 9-inch pie)

1 double-crust pie dough (see page 220), or store-bought
1 cup brown sugar
½ cup white sugar
1 tsp. flour
2 eggs unbeaten
1 tsp. vanilla extract
½ eggshell of milk
½ cup melted butter
Heavy whipping cream

1. Heat oven to 325°. Line a 9-inch pie dish with the bottom crust; set aside.

2. Mix together the brown and white sugar and flour. Break the 2 eggs into mixture; add milk and vanilla. Melt butter and pour in last. Transfer mixture to the prepared pie shell.

3. Bake about 30 to 45 minutes. (It is better to cook this pie slowly.) When done, the pie will look puffy and yellow. When cooled, it falls into a rich jelly-like consistency.

4. Before serving, blend real whipping cream. No need to add vanilla or sugar, as the pie is the star. Dollop whipped cream on each serving.

···· ❦ ····

Warm food, warm friendships.
Czech Proverb

Apple Crumble

SUBMITTED BY JENNY AARTS, ANNANDALE, AUSTRALIA

As a newlywed, making Apple Crumble was a great way of putting a soul-soothing finish to a low-budget dinner. As my children were growing up, this dessert was a family favorite. Now, I bake it as a special treat for my four grandchildren.

Servings: 8

6 Granny Smith or other cooking apples, peeled, cored, and sliced

²/₃ cup sugar, divided

4 Tbs. butter, chopped

1 cup self-rising flour

¹/₂ cup unsalted almonds, chopped finely in a food processor or by hand

1 recipe Vanilla Custard Sauce (page 239) or whipped cream

Fresh mint sprigs

1. Heat oven to 350°. Stew apples in a heavy pan with enough water to get them started (about ½ cup). When they begin to cook down to a pulp, add ¹/₃ cup sugar and leave them on the heat until the sugar has dissolved and they can be broken up easily with a fork. They should be moist, not too runny, and not dried out. Mash with a potato masher and tip the purée into a small baking dish (such as an 8-inch square).

2. Make a crumble topping by rubbing the butter into the flour with your hands until it is mostly distributed, then mixing in the remaining ¹/₃ cup sugar and the finely chopped almonds. Sprinkle the crumble topping over the hot apples and bake for 45 minutes, until top browns lightly.

3. Cool to room temperature before serving with whipped cream or Vanilla Custard Sauce and sprigs of fresh mint.

Peach Cobbler

SUBMITTED BY KIMBERLY SKOPITZ, MARIETTA, GEORGIA

My mother claims that the first solid food I ate was Peach Cobbler. My fashionably slim mom disliked cooking, and Peach Cobbler was a welcome exception to the low-calorie, microwave food we typically ate. On snowy days, Mom would take to the kitchen long enough to bake a pan of Peach Cobbler. Now that I live in Georgia, where peaches are as easy to come by as snowy days are not, I still enjoy this comfy concoction on cool wintry days.

Servings: 12

6 to 8 large peaches, cut into thin slices
   (about 8 cups)
¹/₃ cup light brown sugar
1 Tbs. lemon juice
2 tsp. vanilla extract
1 scant tsp. cornstarch
¼ tsp. nutmeg

1½ tsp. ground cinnamon, divided
1 cup all-purpose flour
2 tsp. sugar
½ tsp. baking powder
½ tsp. salt
¾ cup heavy cream

1. Heat oven to 425°. Butter a 2-quart casserole. Combine peaches, brown sugar, lemon juice, vanilla extract, cornstarch, nutmeg, and ½ teaspoon cinnamon in a small bowl. Transfer peaches (along with juices in the bowl) to a 9- × 13-inch baking dish and bake for 10 minutes.

2. While peaches are baking, whisk together flour, sugar, 1 teaspoon cinnamon, baking powder, and salt in a medium bowl. Add cream slowly, while constantly stirring biscuit mixture with spoon. Once combined, beat gently just until batter is smooth. Put spoonfuls of batter on top of hot peach mixture, creating a dumpling effect.

3. Bake until biscuits are golden brown, about 20 minutes. It's a good idea to start checking at about 15 minutes, though.

Vanilla Custard Sauce for Desserts

This smooth, velvety sauce is the perfect accompaniment to fruit crisps, pies, and any cobbler-type dessert such as Apple Crumble or Peach Cobbler.—J.W.

Servings: 8

6 large egg yolks

½ cup sugar

2 cups milk

1 tsp. vanilla extract

1. Fill a large mixing bowl with ice water. In a separate bowl, whisk together yolks and sugar.

2. In a heavy saucepan, heat milk almost to the boiling point. Whisk the hot milk into the yolk mixture, starting slowly and then adding it in a steady stream. Transfer the mixture back into the saucepan and cook, stirring constantly and vigorously with a wooden spoon, until it thickens but does not yet boil (about 5 minutes; 150° on an instant-read thermometer). Remove from heat, and stir in the vanilla.

3. Place the pot directly into the ice-water bath and stir until custard sauce is cool. Will keep refrigerated for 1 week.

Older women are like day-old strudels—the crust may not be so lovely, but the filling has come at last into its own.

Robert Farrar Capon

Blueberry Love Across the Miles

By Loretta Kemsley, Sylmar, California

The postman always carried Grandma's package up the long driveway to the front door, wheezing and grunting. His moans were the signal for us kids come running, slamming through the screen door in an effort to be first. Only then did his smile give away the charade.

Mom let us kids take turns snipping the twine and tearing away the brown paper wrapping. We never knew what we'd find inside: hand-knit sweaters, crocheted doilies, or embroidered pillowcases, dried venison, wild rice, or blueberries. When it was my turn, I always prayed for blueberries.

Grandma lived in a town too small for indoor plumbing: Bena, Minnesota, land of 10,000 lakes. She fished off the pier at the other end of town, a mere three-minute walk. To please us California kids, she added coloring to the white store-bought butter, the only brand available. She shot a buck for meat every winter, and she harvested the wild rice and blueberries herself.

Although I loved the wild rice, it was the blueberries I treasured. Mom had to hide them quick, or they'd be gone before day's end. The wait was always worth it, even when she froze the berries for later use. Sometimes we ate them fresh; other times Mom would bake blueberry pies, letting us help if we had the notion. If not, they'd be waiting when we returned from school, still warm from the oven. She cooled them on the windowsill where the lilacs bloomed, the two fragrances competing for our attention. The blueberries rarely lost.

The neighborhood agreed: Mom was the best cook in the world. Our house was often a gathering place for community dinners. But the blueberry pies were just for family. "I don't have enough to go around," Mom would lament, although I think she was secretly pleased, as we were, to keep this treat special.

Blueberry and Pear Crisp

Serve this fruity treat warm or at room temperature with Vanilla Custard Sauce or fresh whipped cream and sprigs of fresh mint.—J.W.

Servings: 8

8 or 9 Bosc or other firm pears, cored
   and cut into 1-inch cubes
2 cups blueberries, washed
3 Tbs. sugar
1/4 tsp. ground cloves
1/2 tsp. ground cinnamon
Juice of 1/2 lemon

1 cup, plus 2 Tbs. all-purpose flour
1 cup almonds, roughly chopped
1/8 tsp. salt
1 cup light brown sugar
4 ounces (1 stick) unsalted butter, cold,
   cut into pea-sized pieces

1. Heat oven to 350°. Toss the pears and blueberries with granulated sugar, spices, lemon juice, and 2 tablespoons flour. Spoon into a 6- × 10-inch baking dish. Toast almonds lightly in moderate oven. Cool.

2. Using your hands, rub together 1 cup flour, salt, brown sugar, and butter until mixture clumps. Add toasted nuts and cover the fruit evenly with this topping.

3. Bake on bottom shelf of oven for 1 hour, until fruit is bubbling and topping is crisp. Cool partially or completely before serving in bowls with Vanilla Custard Sauce (page 239), whipped cream, or ice cream.

In time of test, family is best.

Burmese Proverb

Great-Grandma Minnie's Crumb Cake

SUBMITTED BY KATE EPSTEIN, WHITMAN, MASSACHUSETTS

My great-grandmother created this cake as an easy, one-bowl cake, and it's the first cake I ever made by myself. (Or at least, at ten years old, I thought I'd made it by myself. Mom was hovering near, and I think she took it out of the oven.) There's a mystery about it: Sometimes the crumbs stay on top, forming a sweet crunchy crust, and sometimes they fall in, distributing through the cake and making it even sweeter throughout. No one knows what causes the difference. I like it both ways. It can be mixed by hand or with a mixer.

Great-Grandma Minnie
and her family

Servings: 16

2 cups sifted cake flour	2 tsp. baking powder
1 scant cup sugar	2 eggs, beaten
4 ounces (1 stick) butter	½ cup milk
1 tsp. cinnamon	1 tsp. vanilla extract

1. Heat oven to 350°. Grease an 8-inch square baking pan. Sift flour and sugar together into a mixing bowl. Cut in the butter with a tool or by breaking it into the flour with your hands until the flour clumps and has assumed the color of the butter. Set aside ½ cup of the flour-butter-sugar mixture for the crumb topping and add the cinnamon to it. Add baking powder to the flour mixture in the bowl, and mix well.

2. Add eggs one at a time, beating all the while with a wooden spoon. Gradually add the milk and vanilla until incorporated, beating only as much as necessary to combine the ingredients. Pour into the prepared baking pan. Top with the crumbs.

3. Bake for about 30 minutes, until a toothpick comes out clean.

Lemon-Lover Pudding Cake

SUBMITTED BY JEWELL JOHNSON, FOUNTAIN HILLS, ARIZONA

Since childhood, I've loved the piquant taste of lemon. It started with my mother, who baked lemon pies—my father's favorite—made with freshly squeezed lemons and a thin, flaky crust. Today, a whiff of lemon evokes images of Mom bending over the kitchen table, rolling out pie crust as the pie filling bubbled on the stove. This crustless lemon curd cake is my contribution to our family's lemon delicacy legacy. With a custardy but sliceable consistency and a handsome cakelike top, it makes an excellent hot-weather dessert for casual or formal dining.

Servings: 12

½ cup flour
2 cups sugar
2 tsp. grated lemon rind
½ cup lemon juice

3 egg yolks, beaten
2 cups milk
3 egg whites, beaten just until stiff
     peaks form

1. Heat oven to 350°. Lightly butter a 10-inch cake pan or casserole dish, and prepare a water bath. In a large mixing bowl, whisk together flour and sugar. Stir in lemon rind, lemon juice, egg yolks, and milk. Fold in egg whites.

2. Pour into prepared pan.

3. Set in hot water bath. Water should come 1 inch up sides of the cake pan. Bake 50 minutes, until cake jiggles like gelatin (but don't shake it too hard!). Cool completely, and chill before serving.

A messy kitchen is a happy kitchen, and this kitchen is delirious.

Anonymous

Beulah Calvert's Gingerbread

SUBMITTED BY CAROL ANN ROUND, GROVE, OKLAHOMA

Of all the wonderful aromas wafting from my grandmother's kitchen, one of my absolute favorites was her gingerbread. And it was even yummier to eat than it was to smell! When I make this dessert, the scent of gingerbread lingers in my house for a while, filling me with a warm glow, just like a hug from Grandma.

Servings: 16

½ cup boiling water
½ cup shortening
½ cup brown sugar
½ cup light molasses
1 egg, beaten
1½ cups flour

½ tsp. salt
½ tsp. baking powder
½ tsp. baking soda
1 tsp. ginger
¾ tsp. cinnamon

1. Heat oven to 350°. Line a greased 8-inch square baking pan with waxed paper.

2. In a mixing bowl, pour boiling water over shortening; add sugar, molasses, and egg; beat well. Sift together the flour, salt, baking powder, baking soda, ginger, and cinnamon. Add sifted dry ingredients to shortening mixture; beat until smooth.

3. Bake in center of oven for 35 minutes, until a toothpick inserted into the center comes out clean. Cool in pan. Serve with a dollop of whipped cream, if desired.

···· ❦ ····

We should lay in store of food, but never of pleasures;
these should be gathered day by day.

Ninon de Lenclos (1665)

Fresh Apple Cake

SUBMITTED BY VALERIE HOHENBERGER, CONWAY, ARKANSAS

The following recipe came from my mother-in-law, Mary Bernice Fisher. Before I'd had the chance to meet her and before my wedding, she'd sent this recipe to me with a note stating that it was one of her son's favorite cakes and to get him to help me stir it. One time, after baking this cake, my husband and I went for a drive while it was cooling. Upon entering the house, we discovered that our dog had eaten the whole cake! So, I guess you can say this cake comforts man and beast!

Servings: 12

1½ cups oil
1½ cups sugar
½ cup brown sugar
3 eggs
3 cups flour
2 tsp. cinnamon

1 tsp. baking soda
½ tsp. nutmeg
½ tsp. salt
3½ cups apples, peeled and diced
1 cup chopped walnuts
2 tsp. vanilla extract

1. Heat oven to 325°. Butter and lightly flour a 10-inch tube pan (bundt) or cake pan. Combine oil and sugars; add eggs. Sift or whisk together flour, cinnamon, baking soda, nutmeg, and salt.

2. Fold in apples, nuts, and vanilla. Batter will be very stiff. Transfer to prepared baking pan.

3. Bake for 90 minutes or until toothpick inserted into cake comes out dry. Allow to cool slightly before turning out of pan to cool completely. Top with your favorite caramel icing or keep it plain. This also makes a great layer cake or sheet cake.

Gathering of the Clan

By Ellyn L. Geisel, Pueblo, Colorado

There's nothing like a good funeral, or so we say in my family. We gather to mourn, and then to reminisce and eat. With so many of us living thousands of miles from ancestral soil, our funerals have become our unplanned reunions. Unlike a planned get-together, where factions and frictions are often displayed, we're all on our best behavior.

It is to our funerals that we bring our greatest compassion, our fondest memories, and our finest recipes. One aunt will bring her famous crab casserole, another her prized strudel. Abundant with familiarity and tradition, these specialties comfort the bereaved as we celebrate the life of the departed. From the fresh ingredients and hands-on preparation to the presentation, each dish honors the memory of our departed loved one.

Nurturing the spirit and feeding the spirit are often one and the same. At least, that's what we say in my family.

(recipe appears on next page)

No one who cooks, cooks alone. Even at her most solitary, a cook in the kitchen is surrounded by generations of cooks past.

Laurie Colwin

Chocolate Comfort Pound Cake

SUBMITTED BY ELLYN L. GEISEL, PUEBLO, COLORADO

In my family's tradition of serving comfort foods to the bereaved, I bake this cake for friends when I learn of a loved one's death. It is my attempt to bring consolation to a family in their time of sorrow.

Servings: 15

1 cup butter, softened
½ cup vegetable
   shortening
3 cups sugar
5 eggs beaten
3 cups flour

½ tsp. baking powder
½ tsp. salt
5 Tbs. unsweetened
   cocoa powder
1 cup buttermilk
1 Tbs. vanilla extract

1. Heat oven to 325°. Grease and flour a 10-inch tube pan or two 6-cup loaf pans.

2. Cream butter, shortening, and sugar until fluffy. Add eggs in several small additions. Set aside.

3. Sift together the flour, baking powder, salt, and cocoa.

4. Alternating with buttermilk and vanilla, add dry mixture to creamed mixture, mixing well with each addition. Pour batter into prepared tube pan.

5. Bake for 60 to 90 minutes, until a wooden pick or cake tester comes out clean. Allow cake to cool and settle for 20 minutes before removing from pan. Freezes well.

Dutch Treat?

Cocoa that is "Dutch processed" has been treated with alkali to create a predictably robust chocolate flavor, which many bakers prefer. It also yields baked goods with an especially dark, rich color. Cocoa powder that is not Dutch-processed usually produces a reddish-colored baked good with a fruitier flavor. Results with this type of cocoa are less predictable, but sometimes that is half the fun.

Cherub Pound Cake

SUBMITTED BY LISA KAUFMAN, TONEY, ALASKA

*My early childhood memories of making this moist cake at
my mother's elbow are sweet and rich . . . like butter.*

Servings: 12

2 sticks softened butter or margarine
½ cup vegetable shortening
3 cups sugar
5 eggs, room temperature

3 cups cake flour, such as Swan's
　Down (not self-rising)
Pinch of salt
1 cup milk
2 tsp. vanilla extract

1. Grease and flour a 10½-inch fluted tube pan. Cream together the butter, shortening, and sugar. Add eggs one at a time.

2. Sift the flour and salt together twice. Alternately add spoonfuls of flour and portions of the milk to the batter until all is used. Begin this step with the flour and end with the milk. Add the vanilla and mix well.

3. Pour batter into the prepared cake pan. Start cake in a cold oven, and bake for 1 hour and 45 minutes at 350°. Do not open the oven door during baking. Cool completely in the pan.

···· ❦ ····

Stressed spelled backward is desserts.
Anonymous

New York Cheesecake

This dessert is so decadently rich you can serve sixteen people with it—and maybe sixteen years for contributing to the culinary delinquency of your exceedingly happy guests.—J.W.

Servings: 16

1 package (5 ounces) shortbread cook-
    ies (such as Lorna Doone)
2½ cups sugar, divided
2 Tbs. zest from lemons and limes
4 Tbs. (½ stick) butter, melted
Pinch salt
3½ pounds cream cheese, softened to
    room temperature

¼ cup flour
¼ cup lemon juice
2 Tbs. vanilla extract
3 Tbs. Triple Sec or other citrus liqueur
    (such as Grand Marnier)
7 ounces fresh cream
5 whole eggs, beaten
6 yolks, beaten

1. Heat oven (for crust) to 325°. In a mixer or food processor, crush cookies; add ¼ cup sugar and zest. Gradually add melted butter and salt. Pat mixture into a 9½-inch springform pan. Bake for 15 minutes. Cool.

2. Mash cream cheese until smooth. Combine the remaining sugar and flour; add to cream cheese. Add lemon, vanilla, Triple Sec, and cream. Mix until smooth. Add eggs and yolks. Scrape down sides of bowl and mix until smooth. Transfer mixture into prepared crust.

3. Heat oven (for cake) to 275°. Wrap the springform in foil. Create a water bath by filling a pan with enough water to submerge about two-thirds of your springform. Bake for about 1 hour. Turn off oven, and leave cake undisturbed in oven for another hour. Chill before serving.

Texas Brownie Sheet Cake

SUBMITTED BY AMY MAIDA WADSWORTH, SALT LAKE CITY, UTAH

I grew up in an old house on Maple Mountain in Utah. One winter, we had a particularly heavy snowfall and couldn't go to school or make our way down the dirt road to town. While we were snowbound, herds of deer came into our yard to forage for food. Huddled in our cozy home, my parents, brother, sister, and I nibbled on fresh-baked Texas Brownie Sheet Cake as we watched the deer from the windows. Since then, I think of family togetherness every time I smell this wonderful cake baking.

Servings: 24

1 cup water	2 cups flour	½ cup buttermilk
4 Tbs. cocoa	1 tsp. baking soda	1 tsp. vanilla extract
1 cup margarine	½ tsp. salt	
2 cups sugar	2 eggs	

1. Heat oven to 350°. Grease and flour a 9- × 13-inch baking dish. In a small saucepan, gradually stir water into cocoa powder to form a paste. Add margarine, and heat until margarine is melted and mixture is smooth. In a large bowl, combine the sugar, flour, baking soda, and salt.

2. Combine the flour mixture and chocolate mixture until smooth (a whisk works best for this). Add the eggs, buttermilk, and vanilla. Mix until smooth; then pour into prepared pan.

3. Bake for 25 to 35 minutes, until toothpick comes out clean when poked in the center. Cool before cutting into 24 squares.

···· ❦ ····

One cannot think well, love well, sleep well, if one has not dined well.

Virginia Woolf

Flourless, Flawless, Fabulous Chocolate Cake

Luxury incarnate, this voluptuous chocolate cake is a vehicle for fine chocolate, so use the best you can get. Chocolate is high in heart-healthy antioxidants.—J.W.

Servings: 12

8 large eggs
1 pound semisweet chocolate

8 ounces (2 sticks) unsalted butter, cut into pieces the size of a hazelnut
¼ cup strong coffee (optional)

1. Heat oven to 325°. Grease an 8- or 9-inch springform pan, and line the bottom with waxed paper. Wrap the outside of the pan in foil to prevent leaks. Prepare a pot of boiling water.

2. Using a handheld or standing electric mixer, beat the eggs until double in volume (about 1 quart), about 5 minutes. Melt the chocolate, butter, and coffee in a double boiler or microwave until very smooth, stirring occasionally. Fold in the whipped eggs in three additions, mixing only enough as is necessary to incorporate them. Pour into prepared springform pan.

3. Place springform into a deep roasting pan, and place on the lower-middle rack of the oven. Pour enough boiling water into the roasting pan to come about halfway up on the sides of the cake. Bake about 25 minutes, until the cake rises slightly, has a thin, wispy crust, and reads 140° on an instant-read thermometer inserted in the center.

4. Transfer springform to a wire rack and cool to room temperature. Refrigerate overnight. Warm sides of springform with a hot, wet towel to loosen; then pop open. Cut with a hot, wet knife, and serve dusted with confectioners' sugar and/or cocoa powder.

Gift Box of Memories

BY CARRIE P. JONES, SNOHOMISH, WASHINGTON

Each Christmas season during the 1950s, the mailman making rural deliveries would bring us a very special box. Oh, how we two youngest children eagerly awaited its arrival! The person sending this gift box was our wonderful Aunt Prussia.

The season began with a letter from Auntie telling us when to expect the package, and the days would literally crawl by as we waited for its arrival. Each day after school, we'd hurry home to check the mailbox. On Saturdays, we repeatedly rode our bikes down our country lane, hoping the mail carrier had left the parcel beneath the mailbox. The row of mailboxes stood like a band of sentinels, standing guard for our special delivery, as the two of us circled the perimeter like scouts.

Eventually the much-anticipated package would arrive, and my brother and I would ride our bikes home as fast as our legs could pedal and then dash back on foot to retrieve the box. Some years we could barely carry it. Sheer determination and adrenaline carried us down the quarter mile gravel road, our small arms struggling to keep a grip on the box. Then, we'd lie in wait for Dad to come home, so we could open it. As soon as we saw him coming, we'd rush to the car to escort him quickly into the house. Dad would take his pocketknife out of his overalls, snip the string, and watch with an amused smile as we dove in.

Our mother had passed away when we were small, and our lives didn't have much sparkle in those days. The arrival of our aunt's gift

My brother with Uncle Roy and Aunt Prussia at the beach

box was always a joyful exception. Aunt Prussia's gifts were always wrapped in cheerful paper and tied with pretty bows. As we carefully removed each present and placed it under our Christmas tree, an instant merriment filled our home.

My uncle was a pharmacist, and during the year, my aunt would put away items he brought home from the drugstore to later fill our Christmas box. These gifts were never grand or expensive—paper dolls, crayons, and a handmade dress for me—but they always brought immense joy. To us, the Christmas box meant love.

After Uncle Roy passed away, Auntie continued to send those tokens of love, never failing us. Once when I was visiting her as an adult, she showed me a file of thank-you notes, each labeled with the year and our ages. She'd kept those smudged, oft-erased messages with her most valued documents.

As my siblings and I matured, we came to know and appreciate Aunt Prussia's love not only by those Christmas boxes, but in many other ways as well. By her example, she taught us to value faith and family. She instilled in us a love of nature by taking us on picnics to the beach and mountains. Her picnics, like her Christmas gifts, were never fancy, but always memorable.

Auntie used to say, "It doesn't matter if it's just a can of pork and beans, as long as it's shared with family or friends."

Our beloved aunt Prussia has been gone now for more than a decade. When my sister uses Auntie's picnic tablecloth for family outings, it reminds us of her wise words and her kind deeds. Country markets rekindle memories of driving with Auntie in her brightly colored Ford Fiesta and stopping at produce stands to buy fruit and vegetables. Produce was treated like sweets at a candy store. She served whatever was in season, gathered at those stands: sliced beefsteak tomatoes, green beans we helped her snap, baked squash, tossed salad.

Turkey roasting reminds me of summer visits at Auntie Prussia's home, of sitting around the harvest table on her screened-in porch. Turkey wasn't just for holidays, either. It was for any time the gathering was too large for a chicken, a tradition we continue today. As the cooking aromas permeated the small house, we would happily chatter away the afternoon, sharing our dreams with our aunt and being steered by her gentle hand toward worthy goals.

I delight in remembering Aunt Prussia's pecan pie, served with a dollop of fresh whipping cream on top. She had received the recipe at her bridal shower in 1939. Thirty-four years later, she gave me a handwritten copy as a gift at my bridal shower.

Aunt Prussia was also mindful of those in her community, particularly those who had no family nearby. During the one year I lived with her, on Saturdays the two of us would mix up a large dish of what is labeled in my recipe file as simply "Auntie's Casserole." Then, she'd invite neighbors and friends over for a Sunday "supper" of casserole, salad, and her famous pecan pie.

My brother, who helped carry those boxes of our youth, now has children of his own. Although they are too young to have known Auntie Prussia while she was still alive, she lives on through our memories and stories. Now, each holiday season, I find myself sending a letter to my brother's family, telling them their Christmas box is on the way. Just like those parcels of long ago, mine, too, are filled with simple gifts, cheerfully wrapped, tied with pretty bows, and sent with a great deal of love.

Aunt Prussia's Pecan Pie

SUBMITTED BY CARRIE P. JONES, SNOHOMISH, WASHINGTON

The richness of this divine pie always reminds me of my wonderful Aunt Prussia. We often enjoyed her pecan pie on the sun porch, on picnics, and at holidays.

Servings: 8

3 eggs
¾ cup sugar
1 cup Karo white syrup
½ tsp. salt
1 cup pecans

2 Tbs. cornstarch or flour
1 tsp. vanilla extract
1 single-crust pie dough (see Basic Pie Crust on page 220) or store bought

1. Heat oven to 325°. Beat eggs slightly. Add sugar, syrup, salt, nuts, flour or cornstarch, and vanilla.

2. Pour into unbaked pie shell and bake 50 minutes in middle of oven. The pecans float to the top, forming a crust. Serve with a dollop of whipping cream.

....

Mother's words of wisdom: "Answer me! Don't talk with food in your mouth!"

Erma Bombeck

Aunt Bonnie's Chocolate Pudding Cake

SUBMITTED BY ANN KIRK SHOREY, SUTHERLIN, OREGON

In 1989, my husband was hospitalized with terminal cancer. One night after returning to an empty house, I was too distraught to sleep. I needed something familiar, something comforting—Aunt Bonnie's Chocolate Pudding Cake! Setting to work, I assembled the ingredients and before long, I popped the covered casserole dish into the oven. Later, as I took slow bites of the warm pudding, my jangled nerves were soothed, and I felt as though my aunt had reached through time to give me a reassuring hug.

Servings: 8

1 cup sugar, divided
1½ cups water
16 large marshmallows
2 Tbs. softened butter
1 cup flour
½ tsp. salt

1 tsp. baking powder
3 Tbs. cocoa powder
½ cup milk
½ cup chopped walnuts
1 tsp. vanilla extract

1. Heat oven to 350°. Combine ½ cup sugar, 1½ cups water, and the marshmallows in a 6-cup microwave-safe casserole dish. Microwave until marshmallows dissolve, about 3 minutes. Set aside.

2. In a large mixing bowl, make a batter by combining butter, remaining ½ cup sugar, flour, salt, baking powder, cocoa powder, milk, walnuts, and vanilla. Drop batter by spoonfuls into marshmallow syrup. Cover dish tightly with foil.

3. Bake 45 minutes. Batter rises to the top during baking, leaving a thick marshmallow-chocolate sauce at the bottom. Serve generous scoops of pudding smothered in sauce, either warm or cold, with ice cream or whipped cream.

Mango Cake

SUBMITTED BY DEBORAH MILLER ROTHSCHILD, HOUSTON, TEXAS

When we lived abroad in Africa and my family craved anything with apples—which, of course, are impossible to find in the sub-Sahara—I created this almost-like-home dessert. Now that we're all stateside, they crave Mango Cake!

Servings: 10

1¼ cups cooking oil

2 cups sugar

2 eggs

2 to 3 tsp. vanilla extract

3 cups flour

1 tsp. salt

1½ tsp. baking soda

2 tsp. cinnamon

3 cups peeled and chopped mango

1 cup chopped walnuts or pecans
   (optional)

1. Preheat oven to 350°. Butter and lightly flour a 10-inch tube pan or cake pan. Mix oil and sugar together. Add eggs and vanilla.

2. In a separate bowl, sift or whisk together flour, salt, baking soda, and cinnamon. Stir these dry ingredients into sugar mixture. Batter will be stiff. Fold in mango and pecans. Transfer batter to prepared pan.

3. Bake for 1 hour or until medium golden brown.

The seat of the greatest patriotic loyalties is in the stomach. Long after giving up all attachment to the land of his birth, the naturalized American citizen holds fast to the food of his parents.

Vicki Baum

I'll Gladly Pay You Tuesday for a
Spicy Cupcake Today!

By Lee Kirk, Eugene, Oregon

When I was growing up in Portland, Oregon, dairies brought orders of milk, butter, cream, and even eggs to doorsteps. Neighborhood produce carts sold fresh seasonal fruits and vegetables. Ice cream wagons announced their presence with bells or music. But the one truck I awaited with the greatest eagerness was the Ann Palmer Bakery van.

The bakery truck always carried a small supply of individually packaged impulse items—including the zenith of my desire, spicy cupcakes. I'd try to save the required nickel during the week. Failing that, the appearance of the truck would result in some fast and furious negotiations with my mother to acquire the needed funds.

Sometimes the driver would pretend to have no idea what I wanted and make me describe the cupcake in detail. Other times he'd look at me in astonishment and say, "Oh, no, I think I'm all out of cupcakes today"—and then, "Well, I'll take a peek waaaaay back here." Of course, he'd always find one.

The cupcakes were dark, moist, full of raisins, and topped with a swirl of chocolate cream frosting. I had a ritual for eating them. First, I'd find a secluded spot, and then carefully peel off the paper skirt, so as not to pull off any chunks and spoil the cake's perfect symmetry. With my tongue, I'd remove any crumbs clinging to the paper and flatten the blob of chocolate frosting to cover the top of the cake. Next, I'd separate the top from the bottom and consume the lower portion in very small bites. Then came the ultimate finish: slowly and mindfully eating the top with its layer of frosting. Finger licking was the proper mode of cleanup.

Fifty-odd years later, I can still taste it.

(recipe appears on next page)

Old-Fashioned Spice Cupcakes

SUBMITTED BY LEE KIRK, EUGENE, OREGON

Many times over the years, I have tried to duplicate the taste and texture of Ann Palmer spicy cupcakes. Was the moistness from molasses or applesauce or both? What were the spices that gave it such a sharp, rich flavor: cinnamon, mace, ginger, nutmeg, cocoa? This recipe for old-fashioned spicy cupcakes comes very close . . . but it's still not quite That Cupcake.

Yield: 12 cupcakes

1 1/2 cups all-purpose flour
1/2 cup sugar
1 tsp. baking powder
1/8 tsp. baking soda
1/2 tsp. salt
1/2 tsp. cinnamon
1/4 tsp. ginger

1/8 tsp. nutmeg
1/4 cup soft shortening
1/2 cup milk (at room temperature)
1 egg
1/2 tsp. vanilla extract
3/4 cup seedless raisins or sultanas
1/4 cup dark molasses

1. Heat oven to 375°. Grease bottoms of muffin tins, or line them with paper cups.

2. In a large bowl, mix dry ingredients. Add shortening, milk, egg, vanilla, and raisins, and mix until well incorporated. Add molasses, and beat until well mixed. Pour into tins.

3. Bake for 15 minutes, or until toothpick inserted in center comes out clean. Frost if desired.

Good food is a celebration of life.

Sophia Loren

Kay's Carrot Cake

SUBMITTED BY MELISSA HART, EUGENE, OREGON

I'm not a cake-baker. In fact, this is the only one I've ever made and probably ever will make. If you, too, only ever make one cake in your entire life, let it be this one—simple and simply delicious!

Servings: 20

3 cups grated carrots (approximately 4 large carrots)

2 cups sugar

4 eggs

1½ cups canola oil

1 package (8 ounces) cream cheese, softened

2 cups flour

2 tsp. baking soda

1 tsp. salt

1 tsp. cinnamon

1 tsp. vanilla extract

1 cup chopped nuts

1. Heat oven to 350°. Grease and flour a 9- × 13-inch baking dish or pan. Beat together carrots, sugar, eggs, oil, and cream cheese.

2. In a separate bowl, sift or whisk together flour, baking soda, salt, and cinnamon. Stir into carrot mixture. Add vanilla and nuts, and mix well.

3. Pour batter into prepared pan. Bake for 55 minutes, until a toothpick inserted in the center comes out clean. Cool, and then frost with Cream Cheese Frosting.

A great step toward independence is
a good-humored stomach.

Seneca

Cream Cheese Frosting

SUBMITTED BY MELISSA HART, EUGENE, OREGON

When it comes to carrot cake, this frosting is a show-stopping topping!

Servings: enough for 1 cake
(see Kay's Carrot Cake on facing page)
¼ cup butter, softened to room temperature
8 ounces cream cheese, softened to room
    temperature
1-pound box powdered confectioners' sugar
2 Tbs. milk
1 tsp. vanilla extract

1. Cream together softened butter and cream cheese.

2. Sift powdered sugar into cream cheese mixture in a mixing bowl.

3. Add milk and vanilla. Beat until smooth.

.... § ....

Hospitality: a little fire, a little food, and an immense quiet.

Ralph Waldo Emerson

Vanillas of the World

The highest-quality vanilla beans and extracts come from Tahiti and Madagascar. Cheaper (and often watery) extracts come from Mexico. Major U.S. brands are not as finessed as most exotic imports but provide reliable vanilla flavor. For best results, don't skimp on vanilla.

Mom's Southern Cake

SUBMITTED BY EVELYN BRISBOIS, RIFTON, NEW YORK

This was my grandmother's recipe from 1935, passed on to me by my mom. It is wonderful, rich, and tasty. My mom told me that she remembers the farmers in town coming over at the end of a long day for some of Grandma's Southern Cake.

Servings: 12

6 eggs
3 sticks butter or margarine
1 box (16 ounces) confectioners' sugar
1 tsp. pure vanilla extract
4 cups flour
1 tsp. baking powder
¼ cup chopped pecans and walnut halves

Evelyn Brisbois, as a child, with her sister and mother

Mix the eggs, butter, sugar, and vanilla. Sift the flour and baking powder. Stir the egg mixture into the flour and blend. Grease and flour a tube-shaped pan and pour in the batter. Cover with pecan and walnut halves. Bake at 350° for 1 hour.

....

If a man will . . . count at the tips of his fingers how many things in his life truly give him enjoyment, invariably he will find food is the first one.

Lin Yutang

chapter eight

Indulgences

Cookies, Brownies, and Dessert Bars

Old Pizzelle, Full of Grace

By Christine Basham, Lexington Park, Maryland

When my great-grandmother, Rosalia Bruni, came to the United States, she brought a husband, two sons, and a pizzelle iron. Each of her crisp, licorice-flavored cookies had her initials, RB, impressed on its face. Likewise, the nine children she raised in suburban Pennsylvania were molded with her love and, just as deeply, with their Italian heritage.

Her daughter Elizabeth, my grandmother, found her own pizzelle iron at an Italian market in Philadelphia. While other children in their neighborhood enjoyed oatmeal cookies or brownies after school, my mother and her brothers grew up eating pizzelle, hot from the iron.

In the 1970s, Grandma Elizabeth's daughter, Christina, made rice krispy treats, chocolate chip cookies, and Buckeyes for her children. But when the holidays came around, she used her new electric, non-stick pizzelle iron. Fast, modern, and easy, it produced two cookies at a time. She'd make tins full of the cookies. I grew up thinking that everyone ate pizzelle—as much a part of our Christmas as a decorated tree and candy canes.

I married in college, and after graduation we moved to Thailand. For three years we had tropical Christmases, lush and green—no tree, no candy canes, and absolutely no pizzelle. Back in the States, I camped out at the pizzelle platter. These were some mysterious cookies. I didn't know how to make them myself, but I ate them every chance I got.

In 1996, my grandmother passed away. Mom and I spent Saturdays at Grandma Capannelli's house, cleaning out the closets and organizing the basement. It was my mother's job. My uncles couldn't bear to do it. We washed and polished and sorted, sent pictures to the family and divvied up my grandmother's things. She kept spare buttons in a plastic Chantilly dusting powder box. I took the box, and for weeks after her funeral I would open it just to smell my grandmother's perfume.

There in the basement, amongst the stacks of tomato-stained Tupperware she had used to take sauce to countless office parties, we found my grandmother's pizzelle iron. Heavy, well-seasoned, it was the only thing my grandmother left behind that I really wanted.

We called my mother's Aunt Ida for a recipe. Grandma had never liked observers in the kitchen, but Aunt Ida was willing to share.

I put the recipe aside until Christmas. The iron sat in my hall closet. I was a little intimidated. It looked so primitive. My mother couldn't

From left to right: the author's grandmother, great-grandmother, and great-aunt Jean Ramey

understand why I didn't just use her electric iron, if I wanted to make pizzelle so badly. But when the holidays came, I did it. I mixed my dough, rolled my little balls, and pressed.

My father and my four sons sat around the kitchen table while I cooked. As each cookie dropped from the iron, a hand would reach out and catch it. As the morning went on, I had five happy men behind me, but no stack of pizzelle. They just kept eating. My mother walked in and saw us—her husband and grandsons stuffed with the cookies that had fed her, her brothers, and her children, and her smart-mouth daughter, mumbling the Hail Mary as she learned on the pizzelle iron and carried on in the family tradition.

Grandma Capannelli's Pizzelle

SUBMITTED BY CHRISTINE BASHAM, LEXINGTON PARK, MARYLAND

I've become a bit of a pizzelle evangelist. I make them for my neighborhood cookie swap and for PTA lunches. I feel like I'm sharing my Italian ancestry. But the smell of those cookies and the weight of the iron in my hand mean a lot more to me than that. As I say the Hail Mary and lean on the iron, my grandmother is with me.

Servings: 6 dozen 5-inch cookies

¾ cup butter or margarine, melted
¾ cup sugar
6 eggs
3 Tbs. baking powder
Pinch salt
1 tsp. vanilla extract
4 cups flour
Anise seeds or flavoring

Mix into a soft dough. Pinch off balls and press onto the hot iron. Say a Hail Mary before flipping the iron and again as the second side cooks.

···· ❦ ····

Cooking is at once child's play and adult joy.
And cooking done with care is an act of love.

Craig Claiborne

Hello Dollys (Coconut-Chocolate Nut Bars)

SUBMITTED BY HARRISON KELLY, BARTLETT, TENNESSEE

Graham cracker squares covered with chocolate, coconut, peanut butter—and love. My mom's Hello Dollys were simply unbeatable. When I was a college freshman living in a dorm 500 miles from home, they were the only thing I wanted for my eighteenth birthday. My mom couldn't send or bring any to me, so I borrowed my coach's kitchen, and while I was baking my mom's famous cookies, I talked with her on the phone. As the sweet aroma of Hello Dollys filled the kitchen, all the sweet memories of my childhood filled my heart.

Yield: 60 small (or 30 large) squares

2 cups crumbled graham crackers

½ cup (1 stick) butter, softened to room temperature

1 package (12 ounces) chocolate chips

1 package (10 ounces) peanut butter chips

1 cup roughly chopped pecans

1 bag (7 ounces) sweet shredded coconut

1 can (14 ounces) sweetened condensed milk

1. Heat oven to 350°. Combine graham cracker crumbs and soft butter, and mix well. Spread this mixture into a 13- × 9- × 2-inch baking dish, pressing it flat with your hands so it comes very slightly up the sides of the pan.

2. Add the chocolate chips to form a layer; then add a layer of peanut butter chips, and then the pecans. Top with a layer of coconut. Pour the sweetened condensed milk evenly over the top.

3. Bake 20 to 25 minutes, until the coconut begins to lightly brown on top. Chill thoroughly before cutting into bars.

Toll House Cookies

Ruth Wakefield invented the classic "toll house" cookies that we love today quite by accident, while trying to make chocolate-flavored cookie dough. The cookies are named for the Toll House Inn, which she and her husband owned in the 1930s. Nestlé later bought the recipe from Mrs. Wakefield and kept the "toll house" name and deliciousness.—J.W.

Yield: 1 dozen cookies

2½ cups all-purpose flour
1 tsp. baking soda
1 tsp. salt
1 cup (2 sticks) unsalted butter, softened
¾ cup sugar

¾ cup (packed) light brown sugar
1 tsp. vanilla extract
2 large eggs
2 cups (12-ounce package) semisweet chocolate chips

1. Heat oven to 375°. In a mixing bowl, whisk together flour, baking soda, and salt. In a separate bowl, cream together the butter, granulated sugar, brown sugar, and vanilla, using a wooden spoon. Add the eggs one at a time, mixing until incorporated before adding the next one.

2. Add the flour in three additions, mixing just enough to incorporate after each addition. Stir in the chocolate chips. Drop the dough in tablespoon-sized drops onto ungreased baking sheets.

3. Bake until golden, about 10 minutes. Cool the pans for a few minutes before transferring the cookies to a wire rack to cool completely.

C is for cookie, it's good enough for me; oh cookie cookie cookie starts with C.

Cookie Monster (Sesame Street character)

Ranger Joes (Oatmeal-Coconut Cookies)

SUBMITTED BY MARY JANE NORDGREN, FOREST GROVE, OREGON

We welcome newcomers to our family with these delightful morsels.

Yield: 4 dozen large cookies

1 cup shortening

1 cup white sugar

1 cup brown sugar

2 eggs

1 tsp. vanilla extract

2 cups flour

½ tsp. salt

½ tsp. baking powder

1 tsp. baking soda

2 cups quick oats

1 cup shredded coconut

1. Heat oven to 350°. Cream together the shortening and sugars. Gradually add eggs and vanilla.

2. In a separate bowl, sift or whisk together the flour, salt, baking powder, and baking soda. Add to sugar mixture, and mix. Then add oats and coconut, and mix.

3. Shape into walnut-sized balls and drop by the tablespoonful onto lightly greased cookie sheets. Bake approximately 15 to 20 minutes or until light brown.

···· ς ····

One of the secrets of a happy life is
continuous small treats.

Iris Murdoch

Sugar Cookies

SUBMITTED BY ANGELA ENOCHS PAULEY, MADISON HEIGHTS, UTAH

One of our family traditions is to make Christmas sugar cookies and then to decorate them in creative ways. It wasn't unusual to find a pink and purple Christmas tree cookie at our house. My mom still talks about the time we were making Christmas cookies, when I was about four years old, and I said, "Know what, Mom? We're making memories." And we were.

Yield: 6 dozen cookies

2½ cups flour

1 tsp. baking powder

½ tsp. salt

1 cup shortening

1½ cups sugar

2 eggs, well beaten

1½ tsp. vanilla extract

1. Heat oven to 400°. Lightly grease 2 cookie sheets. In a mixing bowl, sift or whisk together flour, baking powder, and salt. Cream together the shortening and sugar.

2. Gradually add the eggs and vanilla until evenly combined. Add flour mixture to shortening mixture in two or three additions, mixing only enough to incorporate between additions. Chill about 15 minutes.

3. On a well-floured surface, roll dough out as thin as possible. Cut with cookie cutter. Sprinkle tops of cookies with sugar, then transfer to prepared cookie sheets, spacing at least 2 inches apart.

4. Bake in small batches for about 6 to 8 minutes.

Blessed is the holiday which engages the whole world in a conspiracy of love.

Hamilton Wright Mablie (referring to Christmas)

Lacy Pecan Cookies

SUBMITTED BY GINNIE SIENA BIVONA, DALLAS, TEXAS

These elegant thin wafers are deliciously crisp and sweet . . . and easy to make.
They're perfect for afternoon tea parties and after-school snacks.

Yield: 4 dozen cookies
2 eggs
1 1/3 cups firmly packed brown sugar
5 Tbs. all-purpose flour
1/8 tsp. salt
1/8 tsp. double-acting baking powder
1 tsp. real vanilla
1 cup chopped nuts (pecans or walnuts)

Ginnie Siena Bivona and her grandchildren

1. Heat oven to 375°. Grease and dust with flour 2 cookie sheets.

2. In a mixing bowl, beat the eggs until foamy and light. Whisk in the brown sugar, and mix well.

3. In a separate bowl, sift or whisk together the flour, salt, and baking powder. Combine the flour mixture into the egg mixture in two additions, beating only as much as necessary to incorporate the ingredients. Stir in the vanilla and nuts.

4. Drop batter by half-teaspoon onto the prepared cookie sheets, spacing well apart; these spread quite a bit. Bake about 8 minutes.

Half-Moon Cookies

SUBMITTED BY NETTIE BOZANICH, WINDSOR, ONTARIO, CANADA

I have vivid childhood memories of watching my mother bake for hours at a time. Placing myself in front of the oven window, I'd watch her creations bake and alert her with an excited shout when I thought they were done. The tasty morsels of her labors became food for my soul, and my absolute favorite soul food is Half-Moons. The recipe passed to my mother from my father's mother. I've always been more enamored of this cookie's unique taste than of its charming name. Actually, the shape isn't a half moon at all; it's a quarter moon. The misnomer just adds to the fun.

Yield: 4 dozen cookies

3 hard-boiled egg yolks
¼ pound butter
½ cup, plus 2 Tbs. sugar, divided
2 whole eggs
¼ tsp. ground cloves

1 lemon rind, grated
1½ cups flour (approximate), enough to make a medium dough (stiff, but moist enough to roll out without cracking)
1½ cups ground walnuts

1. Heat oven to 350°. In a bowl, mash the egg yolks into fine crumbs. Add butter, ½ cup sugar, 1 fresh whole egg, cloves, and lemon rind. Mix well. Start adding flour slowly until the dough becomes firm (hard enough that when you cut the cookies you can handle them).

2. Add 2 tablespoons sugar to ground walnuts. Set aside. In a separate bowl, beat 1 egg. Set aside. Split dough into three parts, work with one ball and put others in fridge, covered.

3. On a floured surface, roll out the dough to a ¼-inch thick. Using the edge of a drinking glass, cut out quarter-moon shapes. One by one, turn each cookie upside down and dip the top of the cookie first in the beaten egg and then in the walnut mixture. Arrange in pan Bake for about 15 minutes, until golden brown.

Mostly Oatmeal Cookies

SUBMITTED BY MICHAEL PAYDOS, BOSTON, MASSACHUSETTS

*These work best as larger cookies. Here's a secret: Keep about 1 inch
of space between the cookies and make sure there aren't too many
chips on the edges (they will melt and burn).*

Servings: about 3 dozen cookies

1 cup flour	2 eggs
1 tsp. baking soda	3 cups rolled oats
½ tsp. salt	1½ cups chocolate chips
1½ cups dark brown sugar	1 cup walnuts (or pecans)
1 cup butter, softened	½ cup white chocolate chips
2 tsp. vanilla extract	½ cup peanut butter chips

1. Heat oven to 375°. Line cookie sheets with butter and flour. Sift together
flour, baking soda, and salt; set aside. Combine the nuts and chips in a bowl.

2. With a mixer, cream together the sugar and butter at medium speed. Add
the vanilla, then the eggs (one at a time). Beat until thoroughly blended.

3. Reduce the mixer's speed to its lowest setting and add the flour mixture
slowly and evenly. Fold in the oats and remaining ingredients.

4. Place about 3 tablespoons of dough on the cookie sheet and pat down until it
is about ½-inch thick. Bake for 8–12 minutes (less time for gooier cookies, more
for crunchy). Cool on the pan for about 5 minutes, then place on a cooling rack.

The best way to feel at ease in the kitchen is
to learn at someone's knee . . . as a child.

Laurie Colwin

Applesauce Cookies

SUBMITTED BY JUNE BURNS, APACHE JUNCTION, ARIZONA

*These cakelike cookies are oh-so-moist and just the right amount of chewy,
thanks to the applesauce. The flavors of apple, raisins, currants,
spices, and coffee combine into a sweet-tart-spicy bit of heaven.*

Yield: 2 dozen cookies

4 ounces (1 stick) butter, soft

1 cup brown sugar

¼ cup cold coffee (liquid)

½ cup applesauce

1¾ cups flour

½ tsp. baking powder

¼ tsp. baking soda

½ tsp. salt

½ tsp. nutmeg

½ tsp. cinnamon

½ cup white raisins

½ cup dried currants

1. Heat oven to 425°. In a mixer, or by hand with a wooden spoon, cream together the butter and brown sugar. Gradually work in the cold coffee and applesauce. In a separate bowl, combine the flour, baking powder, baking soda, salt, nutmeg, and cinnamon; whisk vigorously, or sift together twice.

2. Mix the flour mixture into the butter mixture in two or three additions, mixing only enough to combine ingredients well. Stir in raisins and currants.

3. Drop by rounded tablespoons onto lightly buttered cookie sheets. Bake until lightly browned on the bottom, about 10 minutes. Cool before serving.

What's the difference between a boyfriend and
a husband? About thirty pounds.

Cindy Garner

When You Are Left Behind

By Susan Billings Mitchell, Taylorsville, Utah

It's hard to be the youngest; just ask four-year-old Christine. She was sitting at the breakfast table when her twin sisters Laurie and Carrie paraded in with new outfits and new hairdos for the first day of school. She watched as her big brothers Rob and Rick filled new book bags with notebooks, pens, glue, markers, and tissues. Even Daddy wore a new shirt and tie for this big day. He's a teacher. As everyone busied themselves with first-day-of-school preparations, Christine and Mommy drew pictures on paper bags that were then stuffed with school lunches.

Christy climbed onto the couch and leaned over its back to get a good look out the front window. Neighborhood children were lined up and waiting to climb on the school bus. They were smiling and laughing and enjoying themselves. She watched until the big door closed and the bus drove out of sight. How she longed to be one of the "big" ones. Just then Mother called to her from the kitchen.

"Christy," she said, "Do you realize that you are the oldest child in the house today?"

While Christy tried to process that, her mother went on. "I have a special job for you. Before the others get home, you need to bake cookies for the first day of school. What kind do you want to make?"

That was an easy question. Christy loved chocolate chip cookies more than anything. After washing her hands, Christy climbed onto a stool. Mother tied the aprons. Christy started counting (and tasting)

Susan Mitchell, center left, and the entire Mitchell family: (back, left to right) Carolee, Rick, Kathy, Ryan, Rob, Lauralee, (center right) Bob, (front, left to right) Becki, Christy, Debbie

chocolate chips. She dumped in ingredients, cracked the eggs, and got out the cookie sheets. Then she shaped giant-sized cookies onto one pan and tiny baby cookies onto another. She was the official taster, of course.

Fragrant chocolate chip cookies greeted schoolgoers when they returned. Over cookies and milk, Mother heard detailed reports of the first school day. It didn't take long, but results were priceless.

"You got to ride the school bus, but I got to make the cookies!" Christy said.

Everyone was pleased with that.

The next year, four-year-old Kathy couldn't wait for Christy and the others to get on the school bus. Now, she was the "oldest" one at home and had an important job to do. If you want to know what her job was, just read this little story again. Then, read it again for Debbie and then for Becki and finally for Ryan. Even then, you will not be at the end of our story.

You see, the first day of school is the one time it is legal to drop everything else to bake chocolate chip cookies, at our house, at least. We haven't missed since 1973. "First day of school cookies" have been mailed when students go away to college. Now preschool grandchildren often help with the tradition.

(recipe appears on next page)

First Day of School Cookies

SUBMITTED BY SUSAN BILLINGS MITCHELL, TAYLORSVILLE, UTAH

We have used the same wonderful recipe for chocolate chip cookies for thirty years. But be warned: If you try it, you may start a tradition of your own!

Servings: 2½ dozen

¾ cup butter or butter-flavored
    vegetable shortening
1¼ cups brown sugar
2 Tbs. milk
1 Tbs. vanilla extract
1 egg

1¾ cups flour
1 tsp. salt
¾ tsp. baking soda
1 cup chocolate chips
1 cup pecans

1. Heat oven to 375°. Combine shortening, brown sugar, milk, and vanilla in large bowl. Beat by hand or with an electric mixer at medium speed until creamy. Beat egg into mixture.

2. Combine flour, salt, and baking soda in a separate bowl. Add the dry mixture to the creamed mixture, and blend well. Stir in chocolate chips and nuts.

3. Drop by rounded tablespoons onto ungreased cookie sheets. Bake for 8 to 10 minutes. Remove immediately from cookie sheet and cool on rack.

....

He who distinguishes the true savor of his food can never
be a glutton; he who does not cannot be otherwise.

Henry David Thoreau

Nana Ann's Best Biscotti

SUBMITTED BY BARBARA BEAUDOIN, CHELMSFORD, MASSACHUSETTS

My ninety-two-year-old mother still loves to cook. The tasty dishes she makes for her family are amazing, especially considering that, as a young bride, she once placed an unopened can of soup in a saucepan and tried to heat it. Before then, she'd seen only soup made from scratch. She quickly acquired culinary skills that have pleased her loved ones for generations. Family celebrations always include a large tray of her assorted cookies and squares, like Nana's ever-popular biscotti.

Yield: 3 dozen cookies

6 eggs

1 cup shortening

1 1/3 cup sugar

1 tsp. vanilla extract and/or 1/2 tsp. almond extract

4 drops anise oil (optional)

3 cups flour

1 Tbs. baking powder

Pinch of salt

1/2 cup toasted almonds

1. Preheat oven to 350°. Lightly grease 11- × 17-inch cookie sheet. All ingredients should be at room temperature. In a large bowl, beat eggs at high speed, until tripled in volume and foamy.

(recipe continued on next page)

2. In another bowl, beat shortening and sugar at medium speed until creamy. Add beaten eggs; continue beating till well blended. Add vanilla and/or almond extract and anise oil.

3. Sift flour, baking powder, and salt and add to egg mixture. Fold in almonds. On lightly greased baking sheet, shape batter into 3 loaves (each loaf will be about 1½ inches wide and ½-inch thick). (It helps to lightly oil your hands—canola oil won't affect taste.)

4. Bake for about 20 minutes. Do not over-bake. Remove from oven, and cool slightly.

5. Cut into ½-inch slices. Return to oven and bake for 5 to 10 minutes, until lightly toasted. Flip slices over and toast again. Cool on rack.

Nana Ann as a young bride

When I write of hunger, I am really writing about love and the hunger for it, and warmth and the love of it . . . and it is all one.

M. F. K. Fisher

Nilly-Vanilly Wafers

SUBMITTED BY JUNE BURNS, APACHE JUNCTION, ARIZONA

You'll want to fill a whole cookie jar with these sweet and simple cookies. For best results, use high-quality vanilla from Tahiti or Madagascar, if you can get it.

Yield: 2 dozen cookies

6 Tbs. soft butter

1/2 cup sugar

1/2 egg, beaten (whisk egg lightly in bowl, divide contents in half, use only half)

1/4 tsp. vanilla extract

6 Tbs. flour

6 Tbs. cornstarch

1/8 tsp. cream of tartar

1. Heat oven to 350°. In a mixer on low speed, or by hand with a wooden spoon, cream together the soft butter and sugar. Gradually work in the egg and vanilla.

2. In a separate bowl, whisk or sift together the flour, cornstarch, and cream of tartar. Add the flour mixture to the butter mixture in two additions, mixing only enough to combine.

3. Roll the dough into teaspoon-sized balls, and line up on an ungreased baking sheet. Bake 15 minutes, or until the edges are slightly brown. Cool before removing from sheet with a spatula.

···· § ····

A balanced diet is a cookie in each hand.

Anonymous

Fudge Brownies

*Addictive? Yes. Essential to good mental health? Definitely.
Ask any college student, lovelorn single, or school kid.—J.W.*

Yield: 2 dozen brownies

4 ounces unsweetened baking chocolate
¾ cup butter or margarine
1½ cups sugar
3 eggs

1 tsp. vanilla extract
1 cup flour
1 cup chopped walnuts (optional)

1. Heat oven to 350° (325° if using a glass baking dish). Grease a 9- × 13-inch baking dish or pan. Melt chocolate and butter together in a pan or in the microwave (2 minutes on high), stirring until smooth and chocolate is just melted.

2. Stir sugar into chocolate until thoroughly mixed in. Mix in eggs and vanilla. Stir in the flour and nuts until combined. Transfer to prepared pan.

3. Bake 30 to 35 minutes, until a toothpick inserted in the middle comes out with fudgy crumbs. Cool in pan before transferring to a cutting board and cutting into squares. Remove the brownies from the pan either by dumping and flipping, or by halving the batch and lifting each half out with a spatula. You'll get much cleaner squares by cutting on a board, rather than in a pan, and it won't ruin your knives.

The Hotter the Bakeware, the Shorter the Baking Time

When baking in glass bakeware, oven temperature should be adjusted slightly lower than in other types of pans. Glass retains more heat, and the item continues to cook long after leaving the oven.

Blondies

*These chewy, butterscotch-flavored, chocolate-chunk
brownies taste great out of the icebox.—J.W.*

Yield: 36 small squares

1½ cups flour

½ tsp. baking powder

½ tsp. salt

6 ounces (1½ sticks) unsalted butter, at
    room temperature

Generous 1¾ cups brown sugar

2 tsp. vanilla extract

3 large eggs

6 ounces (about 1 cup) semisweet
    chocolate chunks or chips

1. Heat oven to 350°. Butter a 9-inch baking pan. In a medium bowl, whisk together the flour, baking powder, and salt.

2. Separately, combine the butter, brown sugar, and vanilla, and cream them together using an electric mixer or by hand, until light and fluffy (about 2 minutes). Gradually beat in the eggs one at a time, working each one in completely before adding the next. Scrape down the mixing bowl, and add the flour mixture, beating just long enough to mix together the wet and dry ingredients. Mix in the chocolate chunks.

3. Transfer the batter into the prepared baking pan, and smooth with a spatula. Bake until a toothpick inserted in the center comes out clean, about 30 to 35 minutes. Cool at room temperature at least 1 hour before cutting into squares. Will keep refrigerated for 1 week or in freezer for up to 6 weeks.

···· ❧ ····

Almost every person has something secret he likes to eat.

M. F. K. Fisher

Grandma's Molasses Cookies

SUBMITTED BY JUDITH LYNN GYDE, TOLEDO, OH

Although Grandma was diabetic, she always had homemade cookies on hand. Her friends really loved her molasses cookies and all of us enjoyed Grandma's sweet spirit.

Yield: 2 dozen cookies

1¼ cups soft butter

2 cups sugar

½ cup molasses

2 eggs

4 cups flour

3 tsp. baking soda

1½ cups ground cloves

1 tsp. ginger

2 tsp. cinnamon

¼ tsp. salt

Sugar

A four-generation shot from 1985—the author, second from right, with (from left) her daughter Beth, Grandma Beadle, her daughter Christina, and her mother, Helen Rofkar

1. Heat oven to 350°. Mix butter, sugar, molasses, and eggs with mixer until smooth.

2. Stir in by hand: flour, baking soda, cloves, ginger, cinnamon, and salt. Mix thoroughly. Refrigerate for an hour before baking.

3. Form into walnut-sized balls and roll the tops in sugar; slightly flatten when putting them on cookie sheet. Place 2 inches apart on a greased cookie sheet.

4. Bake for 10 to 12 minutes.

chapter nine

Creamy Delights

Puddings, Frozen Goodies, and Candies

Conversation and Ice Cream

BY JULIA TAYLOR EBEL, JAMESTOWN, NORTH CAROLINA

When I was growing up, my family's idea of fun was churning a freezer of homemade ice cream on a Sunday afternoon. As I stood by watching, my mother would prepare the ice-cream mixture, pouring milk, sugar, and eggs into a mixer bowl. I always got to squeeze the lemon (to bring out the fruit flavors, Mom said). Years later, my memory still holds the taste of Mom's flavorings: pineapple-coconut, raspberry, fresh peach. In my mind, no other ice cream could compare with her creations.

When cranking time came, everyone went out to the patio. My father would place the prepared canister of prepared mixture into the wooden bucket of the ice-cream maker and attach the crank on top. Straddling the wooden freezer bucket, he would scoop up a few Daddy-sized handfuls of crushed ice, drop them into the bucket, and begin to crank while I added ice. I remember how cold my hands felt. After a while, my brother or I would take over. We never missed our turn to crank.

Now, in my own family, I, like my mother, prepare the mixture. My husband sets up the freezer and starts the cranking. We have an understood rule: If you want ice cream, you help crank. With four willing participants, the job of cranking gets done—and no one complains.

I find no surprise in the fact that my sons love ice cream and ice-cream making as much as I do.

Just as in the ice-cream-making days of my childhood, we talk as we crank. Happily engaged in an activity we all enjoy, we are relaxed and

Creating family memories around the ice-cream maker

jovial, and conversation is natural. With each round of the crank, family bonds are more firmly secured. Simplicity, peace, and connection take precedence over the convenience of store-bought ice cream or of homemade ice cream made quickly with a noisy machine.

When I was growing up, we often cranked our last freezer of ice cream at the very end of summer vacation. It was a way to mark the year and to share the changes we'd experienced and those ahead. "Are you excited about school?" "Wow! You'll be in middle school this year!" "This year you can drive yourself to school." "Are you almost packed?" "Could you play a song or two on your guitar? I'll miss your music when you're away."

Through the years, my family circle has lost a generation, but this year our circle grew. As we crank our end-of-summer ice cream, I look forward to sharing conversation with my new daughter-in-law.

Families need time together to build and nurture relationships. Sometimes, the moments shared are grand and exciting: the long awaited trip, the exciting adventure, the joyous celebration. Sometimes, they are as simple as sharing one another's company over a bowl of hand-cranked ice cream.

Some may wonder why we choose muscle over modern convenience, opting to mix and crank and crank and crank. For one thing, the longer turning time and the fresh ingredients make for a creamier, more tasty ice cream. The best ice cream is worth the wait, and I'll gladly share in the cranking. But today, more than ever, I understand the real reason I crank ice cream. I crank to share moments. I crank to celebrate memories. And I crank to create new ones.

Julia's Homemade Ice Cream

SUBMITTED BY JULIA TAYLOR EBEL, JAMESTOWN, NORTH CAROLINA

My family is convinced that there is no better ice cream than the homemade, hand-cranked frozen kind.

Servings: 5 quarts

4 eggs
1 pint half-and-half
1 can (14 ounces) condensed milk
2 to 2½ cups sugar
1 to 2 Tbs. vanilla extract

Squirt of lemon (about ¼ tsp.)
Fruit (2½ to 3 cups), or juice or flavoring, to taste (optional)
Whole milk (as indicated by level on ice-cream maker)

1. Mix all ingredients except the milk. Pour the mixture into a 5-quart freezer container.

2. Add milk to the level specified for your ice-cream freezer (about ¾ full).

3. Churn in the ice-cream freezer/maker until the mixture feels very firm and resists movement. For firmer ice cream, allow the churned mixture to stand for 15 to 30 minutes before serving.

Note: Experiment with flavorings—peaches, strawberries, dark cherries, blueberries, nuts, chocolate chips, mint, caramel, etc.

Chocolate Pudding

Silky texture is half of what makes this luxurious pudding comforting. The other half is the fact that it's even better than what you remember your mom making.—J.W.

Servings: 4

1/2 cup sugar

1/3 cup plus 1 Tbs. cocoa powder
   (unsweetened)

Pinch of salt

1/3 cup warm water

1 ounce semisweet chocolate, finely
   chopped

2 cups half-and-half, divided

3 Tbs. cornstarch

1 1/2 tsp. vanilla extract

Whipped cream

Extra chocolate for shaving

1. In a heavy saucepan, combine sugar, cocoa powder, and salt. Slowly stir in 1/3 cup warm water to make a smooth paste. Cook slowly over a low flame, stirring constantly, until the mixture boils. Remove from heat. Stir in chopped chocolate until melted.

2. Add 1¾ cups of the half-and-half; stir to combine. Mix the remaining ¼ cup half-and-half with the cornstarch, and then stir this mixture into the pudding. Cook, stirring steadily, over low heat until mixture has thickened fully, about 3 minutes.

3. Remove from heat, and stir in the vanilla. Pour into 4 (6-ounce) custard cups, or into 1 medium-size (16-ounce) serving bowl. Cover with plastic wrap and chill. Serve with a dollop of fresh whipped cream and a sprinkling of shaved chocolate.

My tongue is smiling.

Abigail Trillin

Abuelita's Rice Pudding

SUBMITTED BY YVONNE SMITH, APTOS, CALIFORNIA

My abuelita as a child

It's my favorite dessert—rice pudding. . . . I love it so much that in 1991, in a restaurant in Madrid, I ordered four servings, and then a fifth for dessert. I ate them down without blinking, with the vague hope that that nostalgic dessert from my childhood would help me bear the anguish of seeing my daughter so ill. Neither my soul nor my daughter improved, but rice pudding remains associated in my memory with spiritual comfort.

Isabel Allende

My abuelita (grandmother) would prepare Rice Pudding on special days (birthdays, Easter, Christmas) for her children in Pequeros, Mexico, and later, for her grandchildren in Watsonville, California. She'd always put extra cinnamon sticks in my bowl, just the way I liked it! After my abuelita left this world, my mom continued to soothe me with her version of this recipe. To me, this pudding represents the comfort and strength, the spiciness and consistency, and the sweetness that is my mom.

Servings: 8

2 cups hot water
1 cup white rice
1 can (12 ounces) evaporated milk
2/3 cup hot water
3/4 cup sugar
2 sticks cinnamon
1/4 cup raisins (optional)
1 Tbs. powdered cinnamon (optional)

1. Bring 2 cups of hot water and 1 cup of rice to boil, then lower the heat and simmer until the rice has soaked up the water, about 15 to 20 minutes.

(recipe continued on next page)

2. When the rice is done (tender), add the evaporated milk, 2/3 cup hot water, sugar, cinnamon sticks, and raisins. Bring to a slow boil, stirring constantly, and then remove from heat. Before serving, remove the cinnamon sticks (or leave one in for little girls who like to lick the pudding off the cinnamon stick).

3. Spoon into 4 (4-ounce) bowls or 1 medium (16-ounce) serving bowl. Sprinkle top with powdered cinnamon (optional). Serve warm, or refrigerate and serve cold.

Coming Home
By Sharon Munson, Eugene, Oregon

He comes out of the anesthesia slowly
eyelids flickering on beige walls
not seeing, but becoming aware.
"He's coming out," the nurse says
watching me hover close, kissing his forehead
inhaling an odor that was antiseptic, not him.
He focuses and turns his head
seeing me he smiles.
I murmur the surgery is over and successful.
In answer he whispers, "I love you."
I kiss his cracked and hardened lips
gently laying my head on the cool sheets
and listen as he softly continues,
"I'll have rice pudding."

Gourmet Granny

By Linda S. Clare, Eugene, Oregon

Growing up in the Arizona desert, nearly every winter, I'd catch a dilly of a virus or tonsillitis so severe I could barely swallow. During those dark days, bedded down in my mother's room, I'd plead for Granny's stir custard and lime Jell-O. I came to believe that I'd never get well without it.

My mother would bribe me with the usual fare—chicken soup, Popsicles, even cherry or orange Jell-O—but nothing but my grandmother's custard concoction would do. If I whined enough, my mother would phone Granny to put in my order. By that afternoon, a quart jar of custard and a bowl of wiggly green Jell-O would arrive. Mom would pour the custard over the Jell-O, and I'd be on my way to health and regular meals.

Granny was from Kentucky and an era when people called bathrooms "commodes" and recipes "receipts." Her "people," as she called them, had come from the hill country and were neither educated nor refined. But could they ever cook! I thought stir custard was just another hillbilly "receipt" of hers until I saw a gourmet chef making crème anglaise one day on television. I had watched my grandmother cook up batches of stir custard, making it just like the chef was making it. Every step, from boiling and straining the milk, to whisking the eggs and sugar, matched Granny's.

The chef announced that the crème anglaise was ready, holding up a spoon as proof. My grandmother, after stirring her custard for what seemed like forever, had tested her creation the same way—by checking to see whether it coated the back of a wooden spoon. I don't know whether that TV gourmet chef knows it, but crème anglaise is the best cure for a winter cold . . . but only if it is served with green Jell-O.

(recipe appears on next page)

Hillbilly Crème Anglaise

SUBMITTED BY LINDA S. CLARE, EUGENE, OREGON

Gourmet puddin' a la Granny—it's just what the doctor ordered!
Don't forget the lime Jello-O!

Servings: 8

2 cups milk

1 tsp. vanilla extract or 1 vanilla bean,
   split and scraped

6 egg yolks

¼ cup sugar

1. Combine the milk and vanilla in a saucepan, and bring to a boil. Remove the pan from the heat, cover, and set aside for 30 minutes.

2. Strain the milk into another saucepan using cheesecloth or a strainer (to remove skin that forms when milk is boiled). In a separate bowl, whisk together the egg yolks and sugar until the mixture is light colored and thick.

3. Reheat the milk over medium-low heat (do not overheat), and then gradually add it to the egg mixture, stirring constantly. Return the entire mixture to the saucepan and cook over low heat, stirring constantly with a wooden spoon, until the mixture thickens slightly and coats the back of the spoon. (Do not allow it to boil, or the mixture will curdle.) Remove the pan from the heat and transfer the mixture to a bowl or glass jar to cool to room temperature.

4. Refrigerate and serve over Jell-O or sponge cake.

····§····

The ornaments of a home are the friends that visit it.

Proverb

Quick Chocolate Mousse

SUBMITTED BY ANN REISFELD BOUTTÉ, HOUSTON, TEXAS

My Diabetic Granny
By Joan Bond,
Eugene, Oregon

chunks of pecan ice cream
crunchy banana fritters
mounds of
lemon meringue
soft creamy éclairs
steaming raisin rice
   pudding
your hands toil and touch
bowls turn with
elbow ease
crisp cinnamon
moist peppermint
musky nutmeg
your table is laden
Granny
but you hardly sample
this forbidden feast
such discipline is sweet

My favorite recipes are quick and easy to prepare, yet so scrumptious they easily pass for gourmet. Five common ingredients, three simple steps, and there's nothing left to do but smile and say bon appétit!

Servings: 8 (small)
4 squares semisweet chocolate
2 squares German chocolate
¾ cup evaporated milk (heated to boil)
3 Tbs. Triple Sec
3 Tbs. hot strong coffee (liquid)
3 eggs

1. Put all ingredients in blender and mix for 1 minute. Pour into small custard cups.

2. Refrigerate, and serve with a small dollop of whipped cream.

Love and eggs are best when they are fresh.
Russian Proverb

Raspberry-Cinnamon Bread Pudding

SUBMITTED BY JUNE BURNS, APACHE JUNCTION, ARIZONA

A whimsical combination of fruit and spices gives a palate-pleasing new twist to an age-old favorite. (You'll never feed birds your stale bread again!)

Servings: 16

8½ cups day-old bread cubes

6 cups milk

2 Tbs. Chambord or other berry liqueur
  or extract

1½ cups sugar

¾ tsp. cinnamon

1 tsp. ground mace or nutmeg

6 Tbs. melted butter

2¼ tsp. vanilla extract

3 extra-large eggs, beaten

½ cup fresh raspberries

2 Tbs. cold butter, chopped

1. Heat oven to 350°. Combine the bread cubes, milk, and raspberry liqueur; soak until bread absorbs liquid, about 45 minutes. Meanwhile, combine sugar, cinnamon, and mace. Add sugar mixture to the bread mixture. Stir in the melted butter, vanilla, and eggs. Transfer to a buttered 9- × 11- × 2-inch baking dish, and mix in the raspberries. Dot the top with butter.

2. Place baking dish on a sheet pan to catch any drippings (the pudding will rise as it bakes). Bake in center of oven for 1 hour. Turn off oven, and leave pudding in oven for 30 minutes more. Cool to room temperature before cutting into 16 portions.

Nobody can be insulted by raspberries and cream.

Barbara Kafka

Sublime Bread Pudding

with Bourbon Whiskey Sauce

SUBMITTED BY JENN SAINT-JOHN, MILTON, FLORIDA

We were Southerners, college freshmen, in Wisconsin, and we couldn't wait to get home for Christmas. Naturally, the night before we were to leave, a blizzard struck, closing the airport. We were cold, stuck, and homesick. Southerners believe in comfort food. So, we raided dorm fridges for ingredients, and I cooked with a toaster oven and a hot plate. A few hours later, we had the sublime comfort of my bread pudding with bourbon sauce. We felt so much better afterward; we staged a rousing snowball fight. When we all finally made it home for the holiday, we missed the snow and one another.

Servings: 24

1-pound loaf French bread*

1 quart milk

3 eggs, well beaten

2 cups sugar

2 Tbs. vanilla extract

¾ cup golden raisins or coconut

3 Tbs. butter

1 recipe Bourbon Whiskey Sauce

1. Heat oven to 325°. Break bread into chunks, place in large shallow bowl. Add milk, and let soak for about 10 minutes. (I like more texture to my pudding, but if you don't, crush the soaked mixture with your hands until well mixed.) Add eggs, sugar, vanilla, and fruit; stir gently until combined.

2. Melt butter, and spread into a 9- × 13-inch baking dish or pan. Transfer bread mixture into buttered baking dish, and bake 40 to 45 minutes or until firm.

3. Cool to just above room temperature before cutting, and serve topped with warm Bourbon Whiskey Sauce.

Note: If using dried bread, add up to 1 extra cup of milk and 10 extra minutes of soaking time.

Bourbon Whiskey Sauce

SUBMITTED BY JENN SAINT-JOHN, MILTON, FLORIDA

The sauce gives the bread pudding its dazzling finishing touch! Ahhh!

Servings: 24

1 cup butter, softened
2 cups sugar
2 eggs, beaten

½ cup bourbon whiskey
Pinch of salt

1. In the top of a double boiler, or in a steel bowl atop a pot of simmering water, cream together butter and sugar until light. Cook over boiling water 30 minutes, stirring often, until very hot.

2. In a separate bowl, whisk a small amount of the sugar mixture into the beaten eggs; then stir the egg mixture back into remaining butter-and-sugar mixture. Cook an additional 3 minutes, whisking constantly. Cool to room temperature. Stir in whiskey and salt to taste.

3. To serve with bread pudding, warm sauce in microwave or on stovetop (do not boil) and pour over cut portions of pudding.

Food, like a loving touch or a glimpse of divine power, has that ability to comfort.

Normal Kolpas

Jude's Matzoh Pudding

SUBMITTED BY JUDY GILBERT, VALLEY STREAM, NEW YORK

Aunt Judy put this soft, sweet (not sensations usually associated with matzoh) pudding on the table at every Passover feast, until five years ago. That was when her daughter, Jayne, started putting it on our holiday table. Future generations watch out: Jayne's daughter, Emma, loves it too.—J.W.

Servings: 8

4 matzohs, broken up into large pieces
2 medium apples, peeled and thinly
   sliced
¾ cup raisins
½ cup sugar

2 Tbs. oil
3 eggs, beaten
1 tsp. lemon zest
Pinch of salt
¼ tsp. cinnamon

1. Heat oven to 350°. Butter a 1½-quart casserole. Soak matzohs in water until soft, like cooked noodles. Drain off all excess water.

2. Combine softened matzohs with apples, raisins, sugar, oil, eggs, lemon zest, salt, and cinnamon; toss to coat. Transfer to prepared casserole dish. Bake 45 minutes, until bubbly and lightly browned on top. Serve hot or at room temperature.

···· ❦ ····

Our favorite attitude should be gratitude.

Anonymous

Noodle Pudding

SUBMITTED BY ELLEN HOPE TODRAS, EUGENE, OREGON

Luction Kugel (noodle pudding) is the queen of kosher comfort foods. There are hundreds of variations of Noodle Pudding, but my family claims this one as the best. I got it from my eighty-two-year-old mother, who got it from the woman my siblings and I know as Aunt Ellie—my mom's best friend since they were teenagers in the Catskill Mountains of New York.

Servings: 12

12 oz. wide egg noodles, cooked
1 cup sugar
4 eggs, beaten
1 tsp. vanilla extract
2 cups milk

1 package (8 ounces) cream cheese
1 stick butter
½ cup crushed cornflakes
1 Tbs. sugar mixed with 1 tsp.
   cinnamon

1. Preheat oven to 350°. In a mixing bowl, combine the noodles, sugar, eggs, and vanilla. In a small saucepan, heat together (but do *not* boil) the milk, cream cheese, and butter, stirring until smooth.

2. Mix all together and place mixture in a buttered baking dish (9 × 13 inches). Sprinkle crushed cornflakes on top until covered; sprinkle on mixture of cinnamon and sugar.

3. Bake for 45 to 50 minutes until pudding is done. (It will pull away from the edge of the pan.) Let cool slightly before cutting.

Basis for happiness: something to do, something
to love, something to look forward to.

Proverb

Oh Fudge!

BY JILL (J. B.) ALLPHIN, CORVALLIS, OREGON

My dad was a great cook. He could make almost anything from almost nothing. Every once in a while, on a cool evening in the twilight hours before bedtime, while the family sat around watching television, Dad would decide to make fudge. This was thrilling news. Fudge was the unanimous family favorite, and Dad was the only one who ever attempted it. It was also, ironically, the one thing he could never make right.

My brother, sister, and I would rush to the kitchen, where Dad would be assembling the ingredients: the five-pound coffee can of sugar, a tin of cocoa, a bottle of vanilla, a stick of butter, and so on. After the ingredients would come the pans. Invariably, Mom would be called in to help find this or that: a saucepan for cooking, a cake pan for cooling, a set of metal measuring spoons, a measuring cup.

Once the ingredients, the cooking utensils, and the family were assembled, Dad would set to work, opening, pouring, measuring, slopping, and eventually stirring the now delectable mixture over a burner. With ten eyes peeled on the pan, there wasn't a chicken's chance on a freeway that it would ever boil. So, after about a hundred hours (thirty seconds in adult years) my sister would strike up the chorus—

"Is it done yet?" My brother and I would join in, "Is it done yet? Is it done yet?"

"Now you kids get out of here," Dad would say. "I'll let you know when it's done."

Mom would shoo us from the room, and we'd head back to the living room, to the black-and-white console and the couch. Of course, it was impossible to concentrate on television with the intoxicating smell of steaming chocolate streaming from the kitchen. The clink of the spoon against the pan drew us like a pack of Pavlovian pooches to a dinner bell, back to Dad's elbow, where we would spontaneously burst into our favorite chorus—

"Is it done yet? Is it done yet?"

Dad would order us out again, Mom would shoo us away again, we would try T.V. again, the dinner bell would ding again, and the chorus would begin again. After numerous repetitions (probably only two or three), Dad would finally say, "All right, all right! We'll test it. Someone bring me a cup of water."

We would fetch three. Dad would hold the spoon over one, dribbling a thin trickle of shiny chocolate into the cold water.

"Is it done yet? What are you doing? Is it done yet?"

"First we have to see if it will make a ball," Dad would say as he passed the stirring spoon over to Mom. With the rest of us craning for a peek, Dad would use a teaspoon handle to try to make a ball. "Nope, it's not done yet."

Then, Dad would go back to stirring the fudge as it continued to cook. We would take turns sticking our fingers in the cup, hoping that a miracle fudge ball would appear. Sure enough, by swirling it just right, we could see a sort of flat, watery, dissipating fudge ball.

"Daddy, Daddy! We found one!" But he would look at it and say that wasn't what it looked like. So, we would go back to, "Is it done yet?"

After a thousand (probably three or four) cup-of-water tests with interminable (minute-long) bouts of stirring between, finally we would find the real fudge ball.

"Daddy, Daddy! Look again. It's in here. See? See?" A perfect fudge ball (which had been dropped into a mud puddle and run over by a lawnmower).

Dad would look. "Well . . ."

"You gotta see it," we would say. "It's right there."

"Sure." He would catch Mom's eye. "I think I do see a fudge ball in there."

Hallelujah! In the midst of ecstatic hopping and twirling, Mom would guard the counter, while Dad poured the boiling syrup into a cake pan to cool.

"Cool?" Life was so unfair. We wandered back and forth between the living room and kitchen for days—

"Is it done yet?"

Dad would check with a spoon. No. Still only steaming syrup. Weeks passed.

"We're hungry! We're starving!" we wailed.

"I'll put it in the refrigerator," Dad would say.

Months passed. We opened and shut the refrigerator a million times.

"Is it done yet? Is it done yet? It's almost our bedtime." (We were that desperate.)

Dad would check it again. No, only hot soup. "I'll put it in the freezer," he would say.

We opened and shut the freezer a bizillion times. We hopped up and down like pogo sticks to see inside. Years passed.

"Is it done yet? Is it done yet?" "We're soooo tired, Daddy. We're falling asleep."

"All right, all right," he would laugh.

Dad would check. It was only warm sludge.

"Don't you kids want to wait until it's done?" Mom would ask.

"No!" Hop, hop, hop. "We want it now! We love it hot!"

"Well, I guess it's as done as it's going to get," Dad would say.

"Yay!" Gyrate. Twirl. Hop, hop, hop.

At that, Mom would hand us each a saucer and a spoon. Dad would swipe a big, brown glop onto each saucer.

"I just can't seem to make fudge right," Dad would wink at Mom. "For some reason, my fudge never seems to harden up."

Then, the five of us would carry our saucers and spoons into the living room and sit on the sofa. We'd spoon a bite of the warm, fudgy, granulated goo into our mouths, and sigh—and let it melt away everything but the moment. ❧

Spirited Spirit-Lifting Chocolate Truffles

SUBMITTED BY LEAH A. ZELDES, PROSPECT HEIGHTS, ILLINOIS

I first made truffles one holiday season when I was feeling low. The heavenly chocolate scent and the therapeutic effect of rolling the little balls took my mind off my troubles. Since then, I traditionally give them as gifts, not only at Christmas but whenever a friend needs a pick-me-up. For gift giving, put them in little fluted foil cups and pack in a pretty container. Or just put them in a sealed container and hide them in the freezer for when you need a boost.

Servings: 40 pieces

1/2 cup heavy whipping cream

12 ounces bittersweet chocolate, finely chopped

4 Tbs. butter, cut in small pieces, at room temperature

1/2 cup seedless jelly or jam of choice, melted (optional)

2 to 3 Tbs. liqueur of choice (such as citrus, raspberry, or coffee liqueur)

1/8 tsp. salt

1/2 cup unsweetened cocoa powder (not Dutch processed, if possible)

1. In a saucepan over low heat, bring the cream just to a simmer; remove from the heat. Stir in the chocolate, continuing to stir until it has melted completely and the mixture is smooth. Let cool slightly. Add the butter, bit by bit, stirring until smooth.

2. Add the melted jam, stirring until smooth; the liqueur; and the salt.

3. Cover and chill for at least 4 hours, or overnight, until firm.

4. Put the cocoa powder in a shallow dish. Form heaping teaspoonfuls of the chocolate mixture into balls. (A mini ice-cream scoop, available at cookware stores, is helpful if you want them to be about the same size.) Roll each ball in cocoa. Chill on a baking sheet lined with wax paper for 1 hour or until firm. Keep refrigerated until just before you serve them.

Cocoa Puffs

SUBMITTED BY LOIS L. LEVINE, SAN CARLOS, CALIFORNIA

Who says recipes have to be complicated to be good? Some of my favorites are also the simplest. And who says a cookie recipe must be loaded with fat and carbohydrates to be tasty? Here is a yummy candylike cookie recipe made with no shortening, no egg yolks, and no flour.

Servings: 4 dozen pieces

3 egg whites

¾ cup sugar

1 tsp. vanilla extract

⅓ cup unsweetened cocoa

1¼ cups sweetened shredded coconut

1 cup chopped walnuts or pecans

1. Heat oven to 325°. In a deep bowl with mixer on highest speed, whip egg whites to thick foam. Continue to beat while adding sugar, 1 tablespoon at a time, until stiff peaks form, about 6 minutes total. Fold in vanilla.

2. Sprinkle cocoa over whites and fold in. Fold in coconut and chopped nuts.

3. Drop mixture by the tablespoon about 1 inch apart onto buttered baking sheets. Bake until firm and dry to the touch, about 15 minutes. Slide spatula under cookies and transfer to racks to cool. Store airtight at room temperature up to 1 week.

···· ❦ ····

It was a delightful visit—perfect, in being too short.

Jane Austen

Pralines

SUBMITTED BY ANN REISFELD BOUTTÉ, HOUSTON, TEXAS

When I was attending college in New England, far from my New Orleans roots, these buttery pecan pralines brought Dixie home to me. Though I loved the vibrant autumn colors of the Northeast, I was glad to return to the warmer climate, slower pace, and softer speech of the South. My son enters college this fall. Whether he chooses a campus north of the Mason-Dixon line, east or west, or across the Big Pond, soon after his arrival he will receive a package brimming with pralines made from a splotched and dog-eared recipe. It will be my confectionary reminder to him that when he leaves home, he takes part of it with him.

Servings: 2 dozen pieces

1½ cups sugar

½ cup milk

1 Tbs. white corn syrup

½ tsp. baking soda

¼ cup butter

½ tsp. vanilla extract

1 cup chopped pecans

1. Combine sugar, milk, syrup, and baking soda in a heavy-bottomed pan. Cook slowly until the mixture reaches 235° on a candy thermometer and forms a soft ball, about 20 minutes. Remove from heat.

2. Add butter, vanilla, and pecans to hot mixture, and beat until smooth and creamy with a wooden spoon.

3. Drop by tablespoons onto waxed paper.

God is at home; it's we who have gone out for a walk.

Meister Eckhart

It Was Eggs-Actly Right

BY KATHLEEN D. BAILEY, RAYMOND, NEW HAMPSHIRE

At Easter, my mother would fill our baskets with every kind of treat. But the one we anticipated the most appeared not in a basket, but on a cut-glass plate at Easter dinner—Mom's to-die-for chocolate-covered Easter eggs with a creamy fondant filling. Sometimes the filling incorporated peanut butter or sweetened mashed potatoes or coconut. She often tinted the filling, and she made dozens of eggs. Sometimes we'd let the store-bought candy go stale, as we nibbled Mom's eggs until we felt queasy.

In February of her seventy-second year, my mother became very weak. She entered the hospital, first for pneumonia, then for a gall-bladder operation. For a time, her medication made her confused and weepy. She lost twenty pounds. She looked like a little old lady, and I started preparing to lose her. But Mom pulled through, and she came home to begin a slow recuperation.

As the New England spring dried off, I shopped for dresses and packaged candy for my daughters' baskets. It would be more than enough, I told myself. I had no right to expect Mom's eggs.

Drained but smiling, she met us at the door for an Easter dinner prepared by my dad. After admiring my children's outfits, she led us to a sideboard. There they were—dozens of eggs, maybe a hundred, their dark or milk chocolate coatings gleaming.

"I made too many," she said, as she always did. "Of course you'll take some home."

Though Thanksgiving was still holidays away, my heart overflowed with gratitude as I bit into one of the creamy fillings.

(recipe appears on next page)

Mom's Easter Eggs

SUBMITTED BY KATHLEEN D. BAILEY, RAYMOND, NEW HAMPSHIRE

*Kids of all ages will be delighted to find these in their
Easter baskets—or as a special treat any time.*

Servings: 3 dozen

1 cup mashed potatoes, cooled
½ pound butter or margarine
4 pounds confectioners' sugar
2 Tbs. vanilla extract

1 package (12 ounces) chocolate chips
1 Tbs. paraffin (for canning and
  cooking)

1. Blend mashed potatoes, butter, sugar, and vanilla. As a variation, add: nut-meats, coconut, ½ cup peanut butter, or chopped maraschino cherries, to filling.

2. Put filling mixture on table and knead until smooth and satiny. Roll into long roll. Cut off pieces and mold into an egg shape with a large tablespoon. Place each egg on a platter or in a container, covered with waxed paper. Chill for 1 hour.

3. While eggs are chilling, put 1 package chocolate chips and 1 tablespoon paraffin in the top of a double boiler. Warm until thoroughly melted, stirring slowly.

4. Dip chilled eggs into warm chocolate, drain, and let harden on waxed paper. Refrigerate till serving.

As with most fine things, chocolate has its season. There is a simple memory aid that you can use to determine whether it is the correct time to order chocolate dishes: any month whose name contains the letter A, E, or U is the proper time for chocolate.

Sandra Keith Boynton

Mud Pies

SUBMITTED BY KATIE O'SULLIVAN, HOUSTON, TEXAS

"Skeeter" Perez and I were best friends when we were three years old and made mud pies in the gardens outside our homes in Shanghai, China, before World War II. Our fathers, both U.S. Navy doctors and close friends, were stationed there. After both families returned to the United States, my buddy and I parted ways. I didn't see Skeeter again until many years later, when he made admiral at a base near our home. We had a marvelous reunion.

Servings: 8 (one 9-inch pie)

8 ounces chocolate wafers

¼ cup melted butter or margarine

1 quart coffee ice cream, softened

1½ cups chocolate fudge sauce

½ cup whipped cream

¼ cup chopped nuts (walnuts, pecans, hazelnuts, peanuts)

1. Crush wafers in bowl. Add butter and mix well.

2. Press wafer mixture into a 9-inch pie pan, and then cover with softened ice cream.

3. Cover with foil and place in freezer until ice cream is firm.

4. Remove from freezer and top with fudge sauce. Return to freezer for 10 hours. Before serving, top with whipped cream and chopped nuts.

Oh the Mud Pies You'll Make!
By Katie O'Sullivan
–For Skeeter–

We made one last mud pie together,
moist and dark.
We sprinkled it with sand,
for sugar.
We ate it,
every bite,
rubbed our tummies
and said it was good.
You were in the paper,
Admiral of the fleet,
sea-hawking off the China coast.
Do you remember
the day you choked
and "Amah" pulled the worm
from your throat?
They said,
"You'll not go far
eating mud pies."

Chocolate Gravy

SUBMITTED BY VICKIE PHELPS, LONGVIEW, TEXAS

I left home immediately after high school and moved several hundred miles away from my mother's wonderful cooking, but I never forgot her Chocolate Gravy. No one I knew had heard of it until I met my husband. Soon after we married, Sonny mentioned that his mother used to fix Chocolate Gravy. I was delighted to find someone else who loved this dish. We especially like it for breakfast, served over hot biscuits. Sharing it together never fails to bring back childhood memories.

Servings: 2–4

1 stick butter
6 Tbs. flour
3 to 4 Tbs. cocoa
1¼ cups sugar

1 tsp. salt
1½ to 2 cups milk
1 tsp. vanilla extract

1. In a large skillet, melt butter. Add flour, cocoa, sugar, and salt. Mix well.

2. Add milk and cook over medium heat, stirring occasionally, allowing gravy to thicken. Adjust milk amount, as needed, to bring gravy to desired consistency. Add vanilla.

3. Pour warm over biscuits, scones, shortbread cookies, or ice cream.

Strength is the capacity to break a chocolate bar into four pieces with your bare hands—and then eat just one of the pieces.

Judith Viorst

Crème Caramel

The complex flavor of this ultrasmooth French classic belies its simplicity.
When unmolded, this crème creates its own caramel sauce.—J.W.

Servings: 8

1½ cups sugar, divided
½ cup water
3 cups heavy cream

6 egg yolks
1 tsp. vanilla extract

1. Heat oven to 350°. In a small, heavy-bottomed skillet, combine ¾ cup sugar with ½ cup water. Bring to a boil, over medium-high heat, and cook until sugar caramelizes to a deep orange-brown. Watch the sugar closely when it begins to color, swirling the pan to keep it evenly colored. Pour immediately from the pan into the bottoms of 8 (6-ounce) custard cups or ramekins.

2. Bring cream and remaining ¾ cup sugar just to the boiling point, stirring to dissolve the sugar. Place egg yolks in a bowl, and pour the scalded cream mixture over them, whisking vigorously and constantly. Remove from heat and stir in the vanilla extract. Ladle this cream mixture into the caramel-lined custard cups. Set the cups into a deep roasting pan or casserole dish, and place on the center rack of the oven. Carefully pour hot tap water into the roasting pan, filling just past the cream-and-egg mixture in the cups.

3. Bake for exactly 50 minutes. Remove from oven to cool to room temperature, then refrigerate at least 8 hours or overnight.

4. Unmold the Crème Caramels by loosening the edges of the custard with a small knife, then inverting the cups onto a plate.

···· ❦ ····

I've been on a diet for two weeks and all that I've lost is two weeks.

Totie Fields

chapter ten

Wetting the Whistle

Milkshakes and Hot and Cold Beverages

Family Cooks

By Susan Persons Uecker, Houston, Texas

"What are you doing cutting off all that good meat? My dogs never had scraps that good!" said Gerta, Laura's mother-in-law, as Laura trimmed the sirloin for their meal.

Laura and John had invited their families for dinner in their first home. Laura was cooking beef stroganoff. This was before heart-healthy cooking, when fixing a nice cut of beef was expected for special guests.

The table was set with the china and crystal wedding gifts. Laura had things pretty well under control until her mother-in-law wandered into the kitchen and made the comment about the dog scraps. Laura bit her tongue and tried not to get upset. She and John had been married only a short time, and she wanted very badly to be accepted by Gerta, a frugal farm wife.

Gerta washed and reused plastic bags and tinfoil long before recycling was popular. She considered such habits a benchmark of what made a good wife. Continuing to linger in the kitchen, she inspected Laura's cupboards, looking for the bread ties she instinctively knew Laura tended to throw away instead of keep. Soon, to Laura's relief, Gerta left the room.

Laura's mother, Doreen, entered almost at once and exclaimed, "What are you doing? Why are you leaving so much fat on that meat! You need to trim it more."

Laura shook her head and forced back tears. She had wanted this meal to be perfect.

Later, when they all sat down to the meal, Laura's brother said, "If being married means eating like this, I need to get hitched." Laura almost jumped up to hug him.

Many years later at Christmastime, Gerta and Doreen sat at the kitchen table as Laura prepared the meal. They talked about family recipes and favorite foods. Gerta and Doreen no longer cooked, and so they both loved to eat at Laura's house. Laura figured enough water had passed under the bridge to bring up their advice of long ago. She realized how foolish she had been to be so hurt by their remarks, but also how seriously new brides took things.

Gerta remembered the occasion well and considered it only a foreshadowing of Laura's extravagant nature for which she reluctantly forgave her. Gerta grudgingly admitted that Laura and John's marriage of thirty years seemed to be working out so far. Laura smiled to herself and realized that Gerta's comment was as close to a compliment as she could expect from her. Gerta would be amazed to realize how unkind it sounded. She was, Laura knew by now, cautious by nature.

Doreen, on the other hand, didn't recall the incident at all, but still felt one needed to trim the sirloin very closely in preparing beef stroganoff. Laura revealed to her mother and mother-in-law her fears that day of not being accepted. Both Gerta and Doreen seemed surprised by her revelation, but soon were caught up in their own stories as new brides.

Gerta had moved to her husband's farm, as was the tradition in that German, Texas, hill country community, near her own not-so-kind mother-in-law. As the houses were next door to each other and doors were never locked, Gerta's kitchen was always open to inspection. Later, Gerta cared for this woman in her declining years while at the same time taking care of three growing children, her husband, and the multiple tasks of a farm wife. She had never warmed up to her mother-in-law.

Doreen, as a World War II bride, had been uprooted from San Francisco to a rural Texas town. Her city ways were not the country ways, and she and her new in-laws were wary of each other. After her mother-in-law's death, Doreen took over cooking for her father-in-law. She told how he would simply walk out the door if his noon meal were not prepared on time or to his liking.

Later, after Gerta and Doreen had enjoyed Laura's meal with the rest of the family, they all gathered to open their Christmas gifts. John and Laura's son, Jeff, and his girlfriend, Karen, were among the family members gathered that day. Jeff pointed out that his mother had misspelled Karen's name on the gift tag. Laura said emphatically, "No, I haven't. I know how to spell Karen's name."

Jeff and Karen glanced at each other and grinned.

The truth dawning, Laura said, "You got married!"

Jeff and Karen grinned and nodded.

Laura looked at Jeff and Karen, a flood of feelings and thoughts crowding her mind. She was disappointed not to have been there for the ceremony. She worried about their future, wondered if they were ready. Then, she remembered the young bride she once was and realized how important this moment, and her response, was.

"This calls for a celebration," Laura said. "Let's get the bottle of champagne out and make a toast."

A look of relief and gratitude filled the young couple's faces. Doreen and Gerta nodded their approval. And Laura savored the warm hug of her new daughter-in-law. 🙠

···· 🔊 ····

There has always been a food processor in the kitchen. But once upon the time, she was usually called the missus, or Mom.

Sue Berkman

Chocolate Ice Cream Shake

*The great American folk artist Norman Rockwell often painted scenes
depicting the simple pleasures of life, such as young people in
malt shops, slurping on thick shakes like this one.—J.W.*

Servings: 1

3 scoops chocolate ice cream
2 cups milk

1. Combine ice cream and milk in a blender. Purée until smooth, stopping to
stir with a wooden spoon if necessary.

2. Serve in a tall glass. Top with a swirl of whipped cream and a cherry, if desired.

Old-Fashioned Root Beer Float

*While any soda pop tastes delicious as a float (think black cherry
soda, or a cola), root beer's distinctive foamy head adds tons
of visual appeal to this malt-shop favorite.—J.W.*

Servings: 1

1 maraschino cherry
8 ounces root beer
1 hefty scoop chocolate or vanilla ice cream
Dollop of whipped cream

1. Place the cherry in the bottom of a tall (16-ounce) milkshake or cooler glass.

2. Add root beer. Place the scoop of ice cream afloat on the root beer.

3. Top with whipped cream. Serve with a fat straw and a long sundae spoon.

Chocolate Milkshake

Even when you have no ice cream in the house,
a frosty shake is only a blender-whirr away.—J.W.

Servings: 2

1 tray ice cubes
½ cup sugar
3 Tbs. unsweetened cocoa powder

1 tsp. vanilla extract
1 cup milk

Combine all ingredients in a blender. Purée until very, very smooth, adding extra milk if necessary, stopping blender to stir with a wooden spoon. This shake should be utterly free of crunchy bits of ice, so keep going until it's like velvet. Serve in a tall glass.

Banana Smoothie

Nutritionists explain why bananas give us a feeling of well-being, noting that both their potassium and high starch content satiate and stimulate pleasure centers in the brain. I think it has to do with their luscious texture, especially in a smoothie like this one.—J.W.

Servings: 1

1 banana
2 Tbs. sugar
¼ tsp. vanilla

7 ice cubes
1 cup milk

1. Place peeled banana, sugar, vanilla, and ice cubes into a blender. Add three-quarters of the milk.

2. Blend at high speed, stopping and stirring if the ice cubes get stuck, and adding the remaining milk, if necessary to help it purée. Run until it is very smooth.

3. Serve in tall glass, with a fat straw.

Limeaid Slush

SUBMITTED BY AMY MAIDA WADSWORTH, SALT LAKE CITY, UTAH

My husband is a musician, and when he was in high school, he formed a barbershop quartet with three of his classmates. These men have beautifully blended not only their voices, but also their lives, for more than seventeen years. They still get together to sing the old songs, plus a few new ones, and they perform together whenever they can. All four are happily married, and between them, they now have fifteen children, plus one on the way, and a foster child. Last summer, we all got together in our new home, and I made this slush. Hope you and your friends enjoy this as much as our friends and we have.

Servings: 8

1 quart water

4 cups sugar

1 can (10 ounces) frozen limeaid concentrate

2 liters lemon-lime soda

Amy Maida Wadsworth and her husband, Jason

1. Bring water to boil. Dissolve sugar in the water. Mix with the limeaid concentrate until the concentrate is melted and mixed well. Put in the freezer overnight.

2. When ready to serve, use an ice-cream scoop and put one scoop in an 8-ounce glass. Fill the cup with cold soda. Stir to make it slushy. Serve with thick straws.

Greenie Magic

BY SUSAN BILLINGS MITCHELL, TAYLORSVILLE, UTAH

Grandma Hazel arrived at our home with her big, green suitcase. We had moved away from our hometown when I was very small, so my memories of Grandma were few and dim. What she did during that visit is etched forever in my memory.

It started the first night, about bedtime, when I followed her into the guestroom. She plopped the suitcase onto the bed and removed a polka-dotted cardboard box. I could hardly wait to see what was inside. Nothing. Then, with my own eyes, I saw Grandma lift the hair right off her head and stuff it into that box!

Next, Grandma pulled a small, plastic, horseshoe-shaped container from her bag. Again, when she opened it, nothing was inside. I thought to myself, "What in the world could she do with that?" I soon found out. Grandma pulled out her teeth and, you guessed it, plopped them into that container—so she "could brush them better," she explained. I couldn't imagine how she did that. Now, Grandma looked funny and talked funny.

Then, she pulled out a brown paper sack containing two large bottles of pop. That's right, the stuff you drink. She had that in her suitcase too.

"Let's put these in your fridge," she said. "After breakfast tomorrow, you and I will use this to make magic." Magic? She knew magic, too? I had a difficult time falling asleep that night. Breakfast took forever, too.

At last, it was time. Her magic ingredient was green punch, and she really did do magic with it. Why, she concocted the best treat I'd ever tasted—"greenies."

Many years later, when I lived far away in a very warm climate, I wrote to Grandma that some greenies sure would be nice. My aunt, upon reading the letter, thought I was asking for "greenbacks" (money). No . . . my wish was for magic that money can't buy.

(recipe appears on next page)

Great-Granny's Greenies

SUBMITTED BY SUSAN BILLINGS MITCHELL, TAYLORSVILLE, UTAH

I have yet to learn how to take out my teeth and remove my hair (thank goodness), but I regularly practice the magic of greenies for my family. I have the recipe—and those magical visits with Grandma—memorized. Whenever I make up a batch of greenies, I feel the nearness of my sweet, funny grandma.

Servings: 6–8
1 cup sugar
1 cup pineapple juice
1 package of powdered lemon-lime punch (or 6-ounce frozen limeaid concentrate)
2 cups warm water

1. Pour sugar, pineapple juice, and punch mix into a bowl. Add the water and stir until the sugar and punch are dissolved.

2. Pour into an ice-cube tray and freeze.

3. Serve floating in a glass with lemon-lime soda pop, or in a dish, or wrapped in a napkin. Greenies are fun in a punch bowl, too.

When people enter the kitchen, they often drag their childhood in with them.

Laurie Colwin

Tropical Smoothie

You may not be able to sail away to Aruba, but you can take a flight of fancy with this frosty cooler.—J.W.

Servings: 2

1 tray ice cubes

1 cup pineapple chunks

1 sliced banana

1 cup sweet coconut cream or coconut milk

1 tsp. vanilla extract

½ cup orange juice

Combine all ingredients in a blender. Purée until smooth. Stop and stir with a wooden spoon, and add a little extra juice if necessary.

Marmalade

SUBMITTED BY TARA J. CHAPMAN, WINDSOR, ONTARIO, CANADA

We whipped up this concoction during a heat wave a few summers ago and found it deeply satisfying. We serve this refreshing drink to visiting family and friends during the summer months or just when we need a reminder of summer.

Servings: 5 (8-ounce) glasses

4 lemons

2 limes

3 cups cold water

1 Tbs. grated fresh gingerroot

1 cup sugar

1 tray ice cubes

5 maraschino cherries

1. Slice lemons and limes very thinly. Place citrus slices into cold water. Add ginger and sugar, and mix vigorously until sugar is dissolved.

2. Add ice cubes and stir. Serve with a cherry in each glass.

Almost Orange Julius

SUBMITTED BY LINDA CLARE, EUGENE, OREGON

My kids love to make this drink for their friends on hot summer days.

Servings: 3

1 small can (6 ounces) frozen concentrated orange juice

1½ cups milk

½ cup water

1 tsp. vanilla extract

⅓ cup sugar

2 cups (about 1 full tray) ice cubes

1. Combine all ingredients in a blender except for the ice cubes, mix well.

2. Add ice cubes one at a time while blender is running, until smooth. Pour into glasses and enjoy.

Java Smoothie

For a cool quencher with the pick-me-up power of the mighty coffee bean, try this deluxe iced coffee blender drink. Not only will it brighten your day, but it'll go a long way toward supplying that eight glasses of water nutritionists are always saying we need every day.—J.W.

Servings: 1

1 cup chilled coffee

Almond extract

1 Tbs. sugar

6–7 ice cubes

¼ cup cream or half-and-half

Combine all ingredients in a blender. Purée at high speed until very smooth, stopping and stirring with a wooden spoon if necessary. Serve in a tall glass.

The Lemon Bread Pan

By Greg Beatty, Bellingham, Washington

"Is there anything you regret about the breakup?" Kathleen asked.

"No!"

Kathleen looked at me, clearly surprised by how emphatic I was. I tried again.

"I was so tired by the time we split up. We had tried hard to stay together. We talked; we fought; we went to counselors. By the end, we were just exhausted. We'd tried everything. There wasn't anything left to regret."

I was quiet for a moment, and then said, "Well, there is one thing. It's going to sound kind of silly. When we separated, I left all of my cookware. Sarah had her daughter to cook for, and I guess I still thought we'd get back together."

"And you regret . . . ?"

"Well, like I said, it's going to sound silly, but my little brother had given me a bread pan for a gift one year. It came with this great recipe for lemon bread. I made that bread for parties and holidays. I always thought of it as my special lemon bread pan."

I shrugged. "I know . . . it sounds stupid, but I miss that pan."

That conversation occurred early in my relationship with Kathleen. In fact, I had forgotten about it until much later. It was Christmas, the first major holiday I'd spent with Kathleen and her kids, who were hardly kids; they were all in high school, college, or working. We were opening gifts, and it was generally a happy time. Kathleen liked her giraffe, Corey liked his shirt, and Josh, Amber, and Adrianne liked their CDs, the gifts I'd brought for them.

I'd opened my gift from Kathleen and wasn't expecting much, if anything, from her kids, who were still getting used to me. Then Kathleen handed me a large package, and she, Josh, and Amber all sat up.

"For me?"

Kathleen nodded, and I opened the box. Inside was a terra cotta bread pan. Shocked, I lifted it for a better look.

Kathleen said, "Josh asked what he and Amber should get you, and I was stuck. Then I remembered the bread pan."

I turned the pan in my hands. It wasn't the same as my old one, but it was of good quality, with heavy stone to absorb food oils and cure itself, so the bread would bake smoothly and evenly.

I started to thank them, but Amber said, "There's more." In the bottom of the box was something flat and white. I pulled it out. It was a spiral-bound book. On the front was a picture of a lemon and handwritten yellow letters that read, "A Lemon Bread Cookbook." I flipped through it, and found page after page of recipes.

The pan had left me speechless. Now, with the cookbook, I was like a deer in the headlights. Stunned, I listened as Josh explained that his mom had told him that I missed my recipe, but she didn't know anything specific about the recipe, only that it was for "lemon bread." So, Josh had downloaded almost four hundred recipes from the Internet and culled them to remove the 300 duplicates. He said he hoped that my recipe was among the ninety-six different recipes he'd transferred to the spiral cookbook.

Still too choked up to talk, I managed to say that it was fine, great. Amber took over, telling me of Josh's repeated trips to Kinko's, how he had wanted to make it an even 100 recipes, but ran out of time.

This time, my voice was firmer, clearer. "It's fine. This is amazing! Fantastic!"

Later, I took Kathleen aside to tell her how wonderful her kids were, but, of course, she already knew that.

I'd offer you a lemon bread recipe to close this story, but I don't have one. I have ninety-six of them. I also have a lemon bread pan. And wonderful people to share them with. 🙠

····· 🔊 ·····

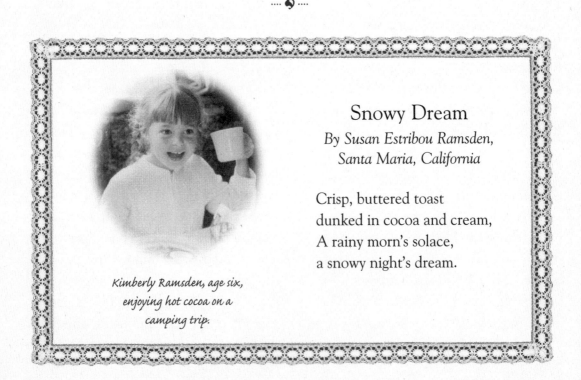

Snowy Dream

By Susan Estribou Ramsden,
Santa Maria, California

Crisp, buttered toast
dunked in cocoa and cream,
A rainy morn's solace,
a snowy night's dream.

Kimberly Ramsden, age six,
enjoying hot cocoa on a
camping trip.

Brooklyn Egg Cream

No. There's no egg in an egg cream. The name comes from the white foam that floats on top, which looks like whipped egg whites. The sign of a true Brooklynite is to see him/her consume one of these in a single gulp.—J.W.

Servings: 1

¼ cup whole milk

1 cup seltzer

2 Tbs. chocolate syrup (preferably, Fox's U-Bet brand)

1. In a tall (21 ounce) glass, stir together the milk and chocolate syrup.

2. Stir in the seltzer. Drink in one gulp.

Fruit Sparkle

Submitted by Dixie R. Clifford, Orem, Utah

My original drink recipe for Fruit Sparkle was featured in a 1952 article in Farm Journal, *after I'd attended a National 4H Club Congress in Chicago as a national winner in the food preparation category.*

Servings: 6–8

6 oranges

1 cup water

2 lemons

3 ripe bananas, mashed

¾ cup sugar

1. Squeeze all of the juices from the oranges and lemons. Combine the fruit juices with the sugar and water, blending to dissolve the sugar.

2. Add the mashed bananas, and mix thoroughly.

3. Pour into an ice-cube tray or a pan suitable for freezing. Freeze overnight.

4. When ready to serve, place frozen fruit mixture in individual glasses and cover with lemon-lime soda.

Sparkling Orange Slurpee

SUBMITTED BY KRISTINE ANDERSEN HOWARD, SAN JOSE, CALIFORNIA

I grew up in sunny California, where our public school system saw no need for cafeterias. Instead, we ate our lunches outside on benches under the noonday sun. In the fall and spring, the temperatures reached well into the nineties. I invented this simple drink when I was in high school, and brought it with me to school in a thermos. You have to make it the night before, but it sure was cool and refreshing on those hot days.

Servings: 1
1 8-ounce bottle sparkling mineral water
8 ounces orange juice
Grenadine to taste (usually 1 to 2 Tbs. per serving)

1. Pour the mineral water, orange juice, and grenadine into a plastic beverage container (one with a lid), preferably with a wide mouth. (Straws don't work with this one.) Make sure to leave at least 1 inch between the top of the liquid and the upper rim of the container, to allow room for expansion as the beverage freezes. Do not cover the container.

2. Place container in the freezer overnight (6 to 8 hours).

3. At least 1 hour before serving, remove from the freezer and allow to thaw partially at room temperature. (Do not heat or blend.) When ready to serve, put the lid on the container, and shake well. Transfer the slurpee to a chilled mug or simply enjoy straight out of the plastic beverage container. As a bonus: You can take the frozen, covered container with you wherever you are going—to school, the beach, on a picnic, or a bike ride.

Anna's Sangria

SUBMITTED BY FELICIA FERLIN, SAN FRANCISCO, CALIFORNIA

In my youth, my exposure to different types of food was pretty limited. My mother was far more interested in taking us on "field trips" to see the world, or at least the regional wildlife, than she was in cooking or baking. So, when I went off to college in New England, I started experimenting with different types of food and was fortunate to have roommates from different countries and ethnic backgrounds. One stifling hot summer evening, my roommate, Anna, brewed up an aromatic concoction, which we drank out on the rooftop porch. Now, I live in San Francisco, where we rarely have hot days, let alone hot evenings. But when the wind blows warm from the East, I find myself craving a tall, cool glass of sangria.

Servings: 12–16

1 orange

1 lemon

1 lime

¼ cup sugar

1 bottle full-bodied Beaujolais or
    Burgundy wine

½ piece fresh seasonal fruit (peach,
    apple, etc.), cut into thin slices

¼ cup orange juice

¼ cup Cointreau or Grand Marnier
    liqueur (optional)

1 10-ounce bottle sparkling water

1. Cut citrus fruits into fourths.

2. Squeeze juices from the citrus fruits into a pitcher.

3. Add citrus fruits' rinds and sugar.

4. Stir with a wooden spoon, pressing the rinds against the bottom of the pitcher.

5. Add wine, seasonal fruit, orange juice, and liqueur (if desired).

6. If you have time, refrigerate covered for 4 to 6 hours.

7. Add sparkling water.

8. Pour into tall, ice-filled glasses. If you like, garnish with a slice of orange.

Chocolate in Paris

By Eve Gordon and Harold Gross, Issasquah, Washington

We each have had two great loves in our lives: each other and chocolate. To celebrate the first, we spent our honeymoon in Paris. A friend, knowing of the second, recommended we go to Angelina's on the Rue de Rivoli for their transcendent *chocolat chaud* (hot chocolate).

On the final day of our trip, we went to Angelina's and ordered hot chocolate for two and a lemon tart. The server returned a short time later with two china cups, a large china teapot of melted chocolate, a dish of whipped cream, and the tart. The whipped cream, to our surprise, was to mix into the chocolate. While not what we'd expected, as we tend to prefer hot cocoa, the combination was an amazing treat, exceedingly rich and smooth. It was almost immediately apparent, however, that we should have ordered a single serving and skipped the tart altogether. As good chocolate should never be wasted, we rose to the task and eventually finished off the whole pot—and then spent the rest of the evening giddy with chocolate.

To keep that last spring day in Paris alive in our memories, we decided to start a tradition. We bought two china cups and created our own recipe for *chocolat chaud*. We haven't had the opportunity to return to Paris, but we often bring Paris to us, especially on cold, wet nights in front of a toasty fire.

(recipe appears on next page)

....

Chocolate is no ordinary food. It is not something you can take or leave, something you like only moderately. You don't like chocolate. You don't even love chocolate. Chocolate is something you have an affair with.

Geneen Roth

Decadent Hot Cocoa

SUBMITTED BY EVE GORDON & HAROLD GROSS, ISSAQUAH, WASHINGTON

To remind us of the sweetness of our honeymoon in Paris, we make this rich hot cocoa. Though we've blended these rich ingredients together, rather than stirring whipped cream into a cup of melted chocolate, ours is nearly as decadent as Angelina's chocolat chaud—and not as sweet and strong. As we have grown older and farther from our honeymoon, we have even adapted a low-fat version that still captures the ambiance of that afternoon in Paris.

Servings: 2

1 super heaping teaspoon of Dutch process cocoa

1 scant teaspoon of Turbinado sugar (unrefined, available in gourmet stores) or regular sugar

¼ cup cold heavy cream

1–2 teaspoons of real vanilla or very fine cognac

1¾ cup cold whole milk (approximately)

1. Mix cocoa and sugar together in a 4-cup heat-resistant glass measuring cup. Stir in heavy cream a little bit at a time until you have a mixture the consistency of mud. Then, add either vanilla or cognac, stirring to combine. Add whole milk ¼ cup at a time, stirring after each addition, until you've got 2 liquid cups.

2. Microwave the mixture for 1 minute on high. (In the absence of a microwave, heat the mixture in a saucepan over medium heat until piping hot.) Remove from microwave and stir. Return the mixture to the microwave oven and continue heating on medium-low and stirring at 30-second intervals, until cocoa reaches desired temperature.

3. Pour into cups and serve.

Cambric Tea

SUBMITTED BY MELISSA PASANEN,
BURLINGTON, VERMONT

I grew up in England, which does not elicit much envy from food connoisseurs. The traditionally stodgy food of my childhood has been justly lampooned. I never did develop a taste for the pub beverage of choice—stout English ale—having left the country before reaching legal drinking age. I am grateful, however, for fond memories and for my enduring taste for weak, sweet, milky tea. The part of me that will always love England and English food remains forever thirteen, sipping cambric tea.

Servings: 1

1 cup of hot milk
1 tablespoon hot brewed tea, preferably Earl Grey
1 tablespoon sugar

1. Combine all ingredients in a small mug, ideally with little bunnies painted on it. Stir well and sip carefully.

2. Serve with fresh scones, fancy cookies, tea cakes, or finger sandwiches.

Strange how a teapot
Can represent at the same time
The comforts of solitude
And the pleasures of company.

Zen Haiku (translated by Gary Crounse)

Tea Time
By Sharon Munson,
Eugene, Oregon

Tea time
every evening
at nine.
I listen from afar
to sounds
from the kitchen.
Cowboy boots on
    linoleum.
Running water.
Mournful whistles
from an ancient kettle.
Cupboard doors
creaking.
The tinkling of china.
Silverware sliding
along countertops.
Sugar cubes stirred
slowly with care.
Milk poured
from a spout.
I wait.
He appears
before me,
cup and saucer
in hand.
I am served
in my robe.
Queen Elizabeth
without her crown.

Chai

Any spiced Indian tea drink containing milk or cream and sugar is called chai. Its richness distinguishes it from other teas, and makes it more comforting, even luxurious.—J.W.

Servings: 12

6 cups water
2 Tbs. black tea, such as Darjeeling or Oolong
1 cinnamon stick
1 cardamom pod, broken open
3 whole cloves
4 whole peppercorns
1 Tbs. sugar
1 cup cream or whole milk

1. Bring 6 cups pure water to a rapid boil. Remove from heat.

2. Add tea leaves, cinnamon stick, cardamom, cloves, and peppercorns. Cover and steep 5 minutes.

3. Strain, and stir in sugar and cream. Serve hot or iced.

This seems to be the basic need of the human heart in nearly every great crisis—a great hot cup of coffee.

Alexander King

Irish Coffee

Although not from Ireland (San Francisco, actually),
this voluptuous warm-up has always brought me luck.—J.W.

Servings: 2
3 ounces Irish whiskey
12 ounces strong coffee
2 tsp. sugar
Sweetened whipped cream to taste
Crème de menthe

1. Combine the whiskey, coffee, and sugar, and mix until the sugar is dissolved.

2. Pour into 2 glass mugs, and top with dollops of whipped cream and a drizzle of crème de menthe.

···· § ····

Only Irish coffee provides in a single glass all four
essential food groups: alcohol, caffeine, sugar, and fat.

Alex Levine

Spiked Iced Tea

PAULA JOHANSON, LEGAL, ALBERTA, CANADA

*I most enjoy this drink while swinging in my
hammock after a full day of working in my garden.*

Servings: to desired quantity
2 parts lemonade
2 parts iced tea
1 part wine (red or white) or
*   champagne*
Ice cubes
Thin slices of citrus fruit (any kind)

1. Mix lemonade, cold tea, and wine in a chilled pitcher.

2. Place ice cubes in pitcher, and pour tea mixture over ice.
Add citrus fruit slices.

3. Serve in a tall glass or in an unbreakable mug that can be
taken out to the hammock.

We seek the comfort of another. Someone to share and share
the life we choose. Someone to help us through the never-
ending attempt to understand ourselves. And in the end,
someone to comfort us along the way.

Marlin Finch Lupus

Hot Mulled Apple Cider

*Winter nights take on a festive air when the house is
perfumed with cinnamon and clove-scented apple cider.—J.W.*

Servings: 6–8

1 quart apple cider
3 cinnamon sticks
10 whole cloves
10 whole allspice berries
Pinch salt

Combine all ingredients in a saucepan. Cover,
and heat slowly, but do not boil, for 15–20
minutes. Keep warm until you serve it.

Note: Spices from mulled cider may be used
for several batches, if they're strained and set
to dry, or used again right away.

Hot Mulled Wine

Mulled wine, which warms
holiday revelers in the
chilly Austrian winter, can
be made with the same
ingredients as this hot
cider, by simply substituting
wine for the apple cider.

I play my sonatas on the stove.
*Nella Rubinstein (wife of pianist and
composer, Anton Rubinstein)*

My Cups of Comfort

By Teresa Rosado, Yonkers, New York

Being rocked to sleep by my mom as a child,
Eating her great home cooking,
Cuddling with a soft teddy bear
little cups of comfort.
Enjoying chocolate fudge cake,
Smelling fresh cut flowers,
Experiencing my first love
little cups of comfort.
Snuggling up with my honey,
next to a roaring fire,
Sipping hot cocoa while reading my favorite book,
A Cup of Comfort.

Index

Weights and Measures

a pinch or dash = less than $1/8$ teaspoon

3 teaspoons = 1 tablespoon

4 tablespoons = $1/4$ cup

$1/3$ cup = 5 tablespoons + 1 teaspoon

$1/2$ cup = 8 tablespoons

$2/3$ cup = 10 tablespoons + 2 teaspoons

$1/2$ pint = 1 cup

1 pint = 2 cups

1 quart = 4 cups

4 quarts = 1 gallon

8 ounces = 1 cup liquid

8 ounces = $1/2$ pound

16 ounces = 2 pints or $1/2$ quart liquid

16 ounces = 1 pound

32 ounces = 1 quart

64 ounces = $1/2$ gallon

1 liter = 1.06 quarts

1 quart = .95 liter

About the Authors

Colleen Sell, the editor of the bestselling *A Cup of Comfort* series, lives on a forested retreat in the Pacific Northwest, where she cooks up comforting foods for family and friends, and spins tales of truth and fancy.

Jay Weinstein, a professional chef and food writer, is a food commentator for National Public Radio. He is the author of *The Everything®️ Vegetarian Cookbook.* He lives in New York City.

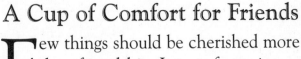

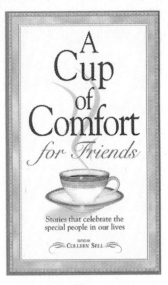

ISBN: 1-58062-622-X
Trade Paperback, $9.95

A Cup of Comfort for Friends

Few things should be cherished more than friendship. It transforms joyous occasions into priceless memories that last forever—and provides much-needed comfort and support during difficult times.

These true stories take you through all the wondrous experiences everyone can relate to—from powerful moments where a friend's appearance adds a sense of renewal to acts of selfless generosity.

✦ Two very different girls form a lifelong friendship on the way down a ski slope.

✦ A new bride finds a true friend in her husband's ex-wife.

✦ A pair of longtime friends witness their grown children falling in love and planning to marry.

Savor the warmth of *A Cup of Comfort for Friends* with the people who are nearest and dearest to you.

For more information, or to order, call 800-872-5627 or visit *www.adamsmedia.com*

CUP OF COMFORT SERIES

A Cup of Comfort for Women

Celebrate the boundless spirit of womanhood with A *Cup of Comfort for Women*, the third book in the bestselling A *Cup of Comfort* series.

The more than fifty uplifting stories in this collection present everyday women living, loving, and accomplishing—often against overwhelming odds. Lift your heart and enliven your spirit with real women's remarkable stories.

ISBN: 1-58062-748-X
Trade Paperback, $9.95

✦ A mother and grown daughter travel to Italy together—and find each other.

✦ A forty-year-old learns to pay attention to herself and the woman she's become—and finds the results exhilarating.

✦ A fourteen-year-old sends her babysitting money to tide her grandmother over until her Army widow's benefits begin.

Enjoy the warmth of A *Cup of Comfort for Women* with your daughter, your mother, your sister, your grandmother, and all of the women in your life.

Available wherever books are sold. Adams Media Corporation, 57 Littlefield Street, Avon, MA 02322.

THE BOOK THAT STARTED THE SERIES

A Cup of Comfort

Stories that warm your heart, lift your spirit, and enrich your life

COLLEEN SELL

ISBN: 1-58062-524-X
Trade Paperback, $9.95

The stories in this inspiring collection are pick-me-ups that will soothe and refresh your spirit.

Written by people just like you, these uplifting, true stories take you through some of life's most special moments. You will feel a renewed sense of fulfillment at the joy present in everyday life.

✦ A teacher unknowingly gives two five-year-olds their first birthday party.

✦ A young couple is able to buy their dream house because of the generosity of strangers.

✦ A teenager learns the value of hard work when he spends the summer working for his grandfather.

✦ A despairing single mother rediscovers the blessings in her life because of a special surprise from her six-year-old.

Lie back and relax with a nice, warm *Cup of Comfort*!

Come visit us at *www.cupofcomfort.com*!